T0361268

Social Media Risk and the Law

Social media has many advantages for professional communication – but it also carries considerable risks, including legal pitfalls. This book equips students and communication professionals with the knowledge and skills to help minimise the risks that can arise when they post or host on social media.

It offers them strategies for taking advantage of the opportunities of social media while also navigating the ethical, legal and organisational risks that can lead to audience outrage, brand damage, expensive litigation and communication crises. The book uses stakeholder theory and risk analysis tools to anticipate, identify, address and balance these opportunities and risks. It takes a global approach to risk and social media law, drawing on fascinating case studies from key international jurisdictions to explain and illustrate the basic principles.

Whether you are a corporate communicator, social media manager, journalist, marketer, blogger or student, you will find this book an essential addition to your professional library as the first reference point when social media and legal risks arise.

Susan Grantham is an Adjunct Fellow with the Centre for Social and Cultural Research at Griffith University. Her research focusses on the use of social media in public relations, investigating reputation management, crisis communication and legal and ethical consequences with a focus on these evolving professions within government and pseudo-government environments. She has more than 15 years' professional experience working for and with government in strategic communications, crisis management and social media engagement.

Mark Pearson is Professor of Journalism and Social Media at Griffith University and is a journalism and media law educator, blogger and author. He has written or edited 11 books, including six editions of Australia's leading journalism law text, *The Journalist's Guide to Media Law* (with Mark Polden, 2019), *Blogging and Tweeting Without Getting Sued* (2012) and *Mindful Journalism and News Ethics in the Digital Era* (with Shelton A. Gunaratne and Sugath Senarath, 2015).

'This is a highly practical, well-written book with up-to-date law and case studies that I will recommend that my Social Media and the Law students read.'

Dr Marilyn Bromberg, *Director Higher Degrees (Coursework)*
The University of Western Australia Law School

Social Media Risk and the Law

A Guide for Global Communicators

Susan Grantham and Mark Pearson

Routledge
Taylor & Francis Group

LONDON AND NEW YORK

First published 2022
by Routledge
2 Park Square, Milton Park, Abingdon, Oxon OX14 4RN

and by Routledge
605 Third Avenue, New York, NY 10158

Routledge is an imprint of the Taylor & Francis Group, an informa business

British Library Cataloguing-in-Publication Data
A catalogue record for this book is available from the British Library

Library of Congress Cataloging-in-Publication Data
Names: Grantham, Susan, 1983– author. | Pearson, Mark, 1957– author.
Title: Social media risk and the law : a guide for global communicators / Susan Grantham, Mark Pearson.
Description: Milton Park, Abingdon, Oxon [UK] ; New York, NY : Routledge, 2021. | Includes bibliographical references and index.
Identifiers: LCCN 2021013578 (print) | LCCN 2021013579 (ebook)
Subjects: LCSH: Social media—Law and legislation. | Online social networks—Law and legislation. | Privacy, Right of. | Data protection—Law and legislation. | Risk management—Law and legislation.
Classification: LCC K564.C6 G737 2021 (print) | LCC K564.C6 (ebook) | DDC 343.09/944—dc23
LC record available at https://lccn.loc.gov/2021013578
LC ebook record available at https://lccn.loc.gov/2021013579

ISBN: 978-1-032-01800-3 (hbk)
ISBN: 978-1-032-01799-0 (pbk)
ISBN: 978-1-003-18011-1 (ebk)

DOI: 10.4324/9781003180111

Typeset in Bembo
by Apex CoVantage, LLC

For Eamon, Jasper, Silas and my writing buddy, Wolfe.
Susan Grantham

For our newest grandchild Henry. May you be safe, well and content.
Mark Pearson

Contents

3 Risk management theories and practice in social media   22

PART 2
Social media attributes contributing to opportunity and risk   33

4 The role of the audience: embracing the opportunities
social media presents   35

11   Business, corporate and consumer law and social media

12   Intellectual property law and plagiarism

Figures

Tables

Images

Cases

Preface

Social media has earned its place as a key means of communication in organisations globally. It has numerous advantages but also carries risks, not least of which are the potential legal hazards. Professional communicators, students and anyone who uses social media need to know the key risks and to equip themselves with strategies for minimising those risks, particularly with regard to the key laws affecting their posting and hosting both privately and on behalf of their organisations.

This book offers a framework for that vital aspect of social media literacy. It aims to equip professional communicators and tertiary students with a basic grasp of the opportunities that social media presents along with the ethical, legal and organisational risks inherent in social media use, and to offer a theoretical lens through which they can anticipate, identify, address and balance these opportunities and risks.

Given the global nature of social media and the fact that audience outrage and legal problems can cross borders in an instant, the book takes an international approach to the issues. This means it draws upon examples, laws and cases from a range of key jurisdictions and attempts to cover the basic legal principles of key areas of social media law rather than offering a comprehensive account of the laws and regulations of particular countries. Some references to resources internationally and in various nations appear in the appendix, but professionals and students seeking further detail should complement this work by getting access to media law and business law texts focussing on their own jurisdictions.

The book is not aimed at a particular professional group – the journalist, the public relations practitioner, the marketer or the manager. Instead, it embraces all professional communication roles in acknowledgement of the industry shift towards the multidimensional communication professional who might encounter social media in a host of occupational contexts.

We work from a stakeholder theory and risk analysis model to offer techniques for anticipating, identifying, balancing and addressing risks against opportunity as they arise in their social media communications and management. We then apply this lens and these techniques to key areas of social media law – including defamation, privacy and confidentiality, justice, employment law, consumer and corporate law and intellectual property. Along the way we use international case studies of social media mastery and mishaps to illustrate the main ethical, legal and organisational risks facing professional communicators in this dynamic digital space. In so doing we aim to add global social media risk management and some basic legal understanding to the career repertoire of every communication professional.

Each of the 12 substantive chapters includes a brief glossary and chapter summary, case studies, an application of stakeholder theory to the topic, a suggested risk analysis strategy, practice tips, discussion questions and project topics.

The book is divided into five parts, containing overall 12 substantive chapters. Part 1 introduces and contextualises social media risk management and the law, with Chapter 1 defining the boundaries of the theory and practice covered, Chapter 2 introducing and explaining the importance of stakeholder theory and Chapter 3 exploring risk management theories. This lays the groundwork for Part 2, where social media attributes are examined for their contribution to opportunities and risks – firstly with regard to the role of the audience (Chapter 4) and then the global perspective looking at how different cultures, systems and jurisdictions contribute to social media and legal risk analysis (Chapter 5). Part 3 introduces brand and reputation opportunity and risk from a communication and legal perspective. In a pioneering approach, Chapter 6 links corporate reputation with the legal action for defamation in the social media context with fascinating insights and examples. This feeds into the role of social media in crisis communication and reporting (Chapter 7). Part 4 explores a range of risks at the intersection of human rights, law and ethics in the realm of social media, with Chapter 8 examining privacy and confidentiality in social media from legal and ethical perspectives. Chapter 9 offers communicators skills for navigating the sensitive areas of the justice system where social media commentary can assist the openness and transparency of the court and criminal system while at the same time damaging reputations, invading privacy and impeding the right of an accused to a fair trial. The book concludes with Part 5, containing three chapters vital to minimising social media risks in the corporate arena. Chapter 10 considers employment law where personal social media posting sometimes comes into conflict with organisational social media policies, leading to both fair and unfair dismissals of staff. Chapter 11 takes up the important business laws impacting on social media use, including exposure to contract and negligence suits and industry regulatory infringements as well as the crucial area of trade practices and the ways social media posts can mislead and deceive consumers with legal consequences. The final chapter (Chapter 12) introduces basic principles around intellectual property, most notably copyright and trademark law and the law of 'passing off', where readers learn to identify potential pitfalls in copying, pasting, linking and sharing the original work of others.

Our fundamental aim is not to make every professional communicator and student a walking encyclopedia in the detailed aspects of all topics in social media risk and law, but rather to equip them with enough basic skills and knowledge to sound the alarm bells when an issue arises, to pause and reflect using some key techniques and to seek the advice of supervisors and legal experts to prevent a matter from escalating into costly litigation or damage to brands and reputations.

Acknowledgements

We are grateful to many who have helped with the conception, content and execution of this book. Thanks to our students and colleagues at Griffith University and beyond whose insights, examples and discussions in our courses and professional gatherings have added depth and colour to the material. We also thank for their encouragement and financial support the Griffith Centre for Social and Cultural Research, Griffith University's School of Humanities, Languages and Social Sciences and Griffith's Arts Education and Law Group.

Thanks also to the international reviewers whose confidence in the book encouraged us, and whose various suggestions have improved it.

To the publishing team at Routledge, thank you for your professionalism and guidance through the process – publisher Katie Peace, editors Lucy Batrouney, Yongling Lam and Lucy McClune, copy editor Cindy Crumrine, editorial assistant Sarah Pickles, Apex CoVantage project manager Autumn Spalding, and the Routledge sales and marketing team.

Finally, we send our fondest thanks to our families who have tolerated our respective absences labouring at our desks over the past considerable period to bring this to you. We send you our love.

Part 1

Social media law and risk management

Introduction and context

1 Introduction – defining the boundaries of the theory and practice of social media risk

Glossary

Excellence theory: A landmark organisational theory premised on effective communication with stakeholders, acknowledging equity and a socially responsible approach to public relations as a key and discrete managerial function.

Risk: The chance of adverse ethical, legal and/or organisational reactions based on the combination of probability and impact.

Risk management: The process of identifying and controlling risk, and the implementation of strategies to mitigate organisational risk.

Social identity: Defining someone through their many social interests and values.

Social media risk: The potential ethical, legal and organisational dangers in social media communication.

Stakeholder theory: An important theory of public communication and management that acknowledges the range of participants who might benefit – or be impacted by – the decisions and actions of an organisation, including its social media activities. It stems from business and management scholarship and allows us to identify and map the key stakeholders affected by organisational decisions and announcements.

Abstract

Social media is now a key communication tool used by professional communication practitioners to engage audiences directly. It offers many rewards, but it is just as important to know about its risks. The uptake of social media by professional communicators was initially slow, but it is now an essential part of organisational communication, both internally and externally. This chapter explores the history of traditional communication methods and the impact traditional theory has on the current approach to social media. It further considers the ways social media has become central to organisational communication before explaining how the dynamics of this multi-channel, real-time and global communication method has created significant risks that need to be anticipated, identified and addressed.

DOI: 10.4324/9781003180111-2

In this chapter

- Introduction
- The changing landscape
- Case study 1.1 – Indian Ocean tsunami
- Case study 1.2 – Christchurch terror attack
- Case study 1.3 – Footballer's post case: *Folau v. Rugby Australia*
- Understanding risk: ethical, legal and organisational
- Theoretical underpinnings
- Discussion questions and project topics
- Practice tips
- Cases cited
- References

Introduction

Justine Sacco, corporate communications chief of a major Internet company, posted this flippant tweet just before her flight departed from London to Cape Town:

> *Going to Africa. Hope I don't get AIDS. Just kidding. I'm white!*

By the time her 11-hour flight landed, the tweet had gone viral under the hashtag #HasJustineLandedYet and had been reported in 24/7 online media. Within a few hours she had been sacked from her highly paid position for her 'hateful statements' despite claiming this was not the intention of her post.

That was back in 2013, and you might think corporate communicators would not be as naïve in their use of social media today. Sadly, in each year that has passed since then, there have been countless examples of personnel causing reputational and legal damage to their organisations through their social media posts. This book is aimed at helping you better understand the theory and practice of social media risk management and the law so you learn to pause and reflect before you post something that might damage your organisation and your career.

By 2021 there were reported to be more than 4.2 billion active social media users globally (Smart Insights 2020; Hootsuite 2021). Social media has changed the way individuals communicate with large corporations, governments, media and each other. It allows users to share information and participate in online discussions as part of a networked society (Castells 2011; Eriksson 2016). Organisational use of social media can tend to overlook the fact that people, their intentions and social desires are at the heart of engagement. Although social media has sped up the rate at which information can circulate, the human agency involved in deciding whether or not to engage tends to be underestimated.

Social media has created unique ways to document events, and offers individuals new ways to communicate with organisations, including the media. Citizens can produce factual video or photographic evidence of events either live or very soon after their occurrence, creating a cost-effective approach to news collection, production and distribution. This is also an extremely useful tool in other forms of professional and strategic communication, where user generated content (UGC) can be used to enhance engagement with an audience. It is also a source for crowdsourcing ideas and obtaining specific information from the audience. Social media allows this to occur because it creates a voice for the community to communicate in unprecedented ways and engage with organisations about topics that are important to them. While this is a powerful tool, it comes with risks that need to be anticipated, identified and minimised.

The changing landscape

First, we need to lay the platform for our understanding of social media by considering traditional organisational communication methods. Two-way communication between organisations and their stakeholders has been considered an important approach since the 1980s when Grunig and Hunt (1984) developed four models of public relations. Two of their four models required two-way communication, encouraging an organisation to engage directly with its relevant public and develop an appropriate communication method. Following the development of this important communication theory, the Excellence Team conducted what is still the largest longitudinal public relations research study of best practices. It produced the Excellence Theory, which highlighted the importance of two-way communication. This theory has influenced public relations literature and professional practice (Grunig & Grunig 1996; 2008; Grunig, Grunig & Dozier 2002; Grunig, Grunig & Toth 2007) and has created an expectation for professional communicators to incorporate engagement with the public into their communication practice. Despite the decades that have passed since the development of the original Excellence Theory, there is strong alignment to the use of social media that now involves organisations engaging in direct communication with their publics.

Why do we start here? Traditionally this two-way communication approach would entail focus groups, surveys and market research among other techniques to ensure the communication outputs of an organisation are suited to its intended purpose. Instead, social media use has established direct engagement with the target audience or stakeholder, providing an opportunity for circular discussion – with the potential for gauging whether communication outputs are appropriate for the designated purpose. Success in social media requires engagement. However, engagement through multi-channel communication on social media has allowed the community to develop voices that can be heard by many. It has created an environment for so-called 'echo chambers' to form, where people with similar views can come together and strengthen opinions. It has also created a platform for 'dark social', which is the space where information can be shared without trackable analytics, providing power and freedom to its users but making it impossible to trace the origin of certain messages. Social media is a positive change to the way organisations can communicate important messages, but it does open up the possibility of serious risk.

One of the most serious concerns with social media risk is the speed at which it has become a key communication tool used by professionals and organisations. Let's take a quick look at the timeline of social media, focusing on its professional applications:

1979 – UseNet. Early stages of a networked society through a virtual newsletter. It is now one of the oldest online communication examples still in use.

1988 – Internet Relay Chats (IRC). Designed by a Finnish IT professional, it was the first chat network. It was designed to allow group communication on discussion boards by transferring data between servers.

1994 – First blog – Live.net. Created by Justin Hall, it is considered the first blog site that started as a web-based diary. In 2021 it is estimated that one-third of all websites worldwide are blogs.

1997 – SixDegrees. The first example of social media, SixDegrees was popular between 1997 and 2001. At its height it had 3.5 million members.

2003 – LinkedIn. In its first year the site had 1 million professionals sign up to use it. By 2021, the number of monthly users had risen to 722 million, with more than 55 million companies having LinkedIn pages.

2003 – WordPress. Set up as a content management system available to everyone, WordPress now hosts more than one-third of websites on the Internet and is a ubiquitous host for blogs.

2004 – Facebook. Approximately 1 million users were recorded in its first year. By 2021 the site recorded 2.74 billion active monthly users and 90 million small business users.

2005 – YouTube. In its first year, YouTube had huge success including an uploaded video that received more than 1 million views. Most recent statistics show that YouTube has 2.3 billion active monthly users uploading, sharing and viewing content.

2006 – Twitter. There are now more than 353 million users on Twitter with 500 million tweets being sent each day, including world-changing tweets by then US president Donald Trump in the 2017–2021 period.

2007 – The hashtag. Now a powerful distribution strategy, the hashtag is what brings the social media community together on topics of interest and allows topics to 'trend' across platforms. It has been the core of significant social movements including #metoo and #blacklivesmatter.

2009 – Large companies and governments started using social media to communicate directly with audiences in an easy and cost-effective way.

2010 – Instagram. One of the first mainstream social media platforms that focussed on images, 25,000 people signed up to use Instagram on its first day and it reached 1 million users within three months. By 2021 it recorded more than 1 billion users.

2011 – Snapchat. In 2021 this platform had close to 400 million active monthly users and in excess of 1 billion 'snaps' (time-limited multimedia posts) per day.

2016 – TikTok. Originally released as Douyin, it was launched as TikTok in 2017 as a video-sharing platform that allows users to share 15-second videos accompanied by a soundtrack. By 2021 there were 689 million monthly users of this platform.

2016/2017 – Livefeed video and 'stories' added to mainstream social media platforms. This revolutionised the way organisations communicated with audiences and allowed for events, such as press conferences, to be livestreamed for all to witness. In 2021, both Facebook and Instagram recorded more than 500 million accounts using 'stories' each day.

While there are many other technological developments that contributed to the use of social media as a professional communication tool, the previous events show how quickly things have unfolded and why social media is still an emerging professional tool. To set the scene, we will look at some key events that prompted significant changes in the way professional communicators engaged with their audiences using technology and social media sharing platforms.

Case study 1.1 – Indian Ocean tsunami

The 2004 Indian Ocean tsunami claimed more than 227,000 lives and was the first crisis where a large number of sensational first-person accounts appeared in citizens' blogs and webpages, giving detailed accounts of personal experiences. With Facebook still in its infancy, and Twitter not yet on the scene, these individual posts were seen as unique and extraordinary contributions to mainstream media coverage and precursors of many more to come in the social media era. It created a new way to manage natural disasters and involved the government relying on public engagement to understand the specifics of the incident as it unfolded and how to respond appropriately. This shows us the power of social media for both government and large corporations and reinforces why social media has become the key communication tool used worldwide.

Case study 1.2 – Christchurch terror attack

The 2019 Christchurch terror incident was the first time a social media live video was used to stream such an horrific act to the world. As well as prompting governments to pass laws prohibiting the hosting of such live-streamed atrocities, it has changed the landscape for organisations when planning and managing risk and reinforces that each member of the public holds the potential to be a social actor and to be heard. Although risk has been of concern in social media professional use for some time, this incident manifested these concerns via an unexpected use of social media. It highlighted the need for organisations to consider and mitigate risk that comes with audience engagements. While this is a unique example, it sets the scene of the social media age and citizens' freedom to use social media in almost any way they choose. This example also allows us to consider the way in which the New Zealand government and Prime Minister Jacinda Ardern engaged with the public to channel and steer conversations around religious tolerance.

Case study 1.3 – Footballer's posts case: *Folau v. Rugby Australia*

A further case example that brings together ethical, legal and organisational risk involved the footballer Israel Folau. In 2019 the international Rugby Union star found himself in a legal battle with Rugby Australia after he was dismissed for a breach of its code of conduct. The breach was a result of an investigation into comments Folau made on social media regarding homosexuality and his religious beliefs. It was reported that Folau had been warned previously for making comments on social media, particularly those that implied discrimination. This case highlighted the ethical dimensions of religious tolerance and appropriate speech. It also had legal elements concerning rights, contracts and alleged unfair dismissal. Finally, there was an organisational dimension to do with crisis and brand management. Rugby Australia's code of conduct had a clause stating players must use social media appropriately. The code stated:

> *Treat everyone equally fairly and with dignity regardless of gender or gender identity, sexual orientation, ethnicity, cultural or religious background, age or disability.*

It was this section of the code of conduct that prompted Rugby Australia to terminate Folau's $4 million contract. However, the same code of conduct also allowed Folau to challenge the termination when he appealed against the sacking in the courts as an 'unfair dismissal'. The matter was eventually settled for an undisclosed sum. Rugby Australia suffered reputational damage, although it can be argued that reputational damage could have been significantly worse if it had not taken action. The case offers lessons in the management of social media risk. If we consider what might have happened if the case had involved a relatively unknown employee rather than a celebrity sports star, would the outcome have been different? Of course, reputational damage could be reduced if the matter did not play out in the public eye, but as we saw in the example of Justine Sacco at the start of this chapter, you don't need to be a household name to have a social media post go viral, particularly when it can be interpreted as inappropriate by the general public (*Footballer's posts case* 2019).

Understanding risk: ethical, legal and organisational

These case examples show ways technology has changed the general use of social media platforms. While it is a powerful tool when communicating with an audience, the risks are high and must be understood to ensure appropriate ethical, legal and organisational use of social media.

Public understanding of social media risk has been slow to develop, with many organisations and individuals shamed publicly or pursued legally over their social media comments. Either can have profound organisational consequences including potential damage to the brand.

For the purposes of this book, we define the three key risks in the following way:

1   *Ethical risks.* There are two main types of ethical transgressions – a. actions that might be considered immoral by common societal standards (for example lying, cheating or exposing someone to harm); or b. actions that are in breach of a professional ethical code or code of conduct (such as a public relations code of practice or a journalism code of ethics).
2   *Legal risks.* These are actions that could have criminal or civil consequences – either a breach of the criminal law where you might face a fine or jail term or by infringing someone's civil or individual rights where people or organisations could sue you for damages or obtain a court order against you.
3   *Organisational risks.* While ethical or legal transgressions can present risks to an organisation, there can also be many other consequences of social media posts – including damage to brand reputation and revenue, industrial action by employees, boycotts by customers and lobby groups, regulatory action by government agencies and many more.

Some of the key areas of risk that are discussed throughout this book include:

- *Reputation management* – Citizens can now engage on topics that matter to them and 'echo chambers' and 'unanticipated publics' are created among like-minded commenters, contributing to the creation of trending topics which carry the potential to destroy an organisation's reputation within minutes. An organisation needs to monitor the trends and look for ways to enhance reputation.
- *Defamation* – The courts can be used to seek compensation for reputational damage. Defamation is becoming one of the main legal issues associated with social media use. Although it is traditionally an issue for professional publishers, social media now means that everyone is a publisher, and there has been an increase in defamation suits as a result.

- *Covering court matters* – Society has an expectation that judicial matters are dealt with appropriately, and social media audiences engage in detailed discussion about cases that carry public interest. Most members of society do not fully understand the risks in discussing matters before a court. There have been examples of prejudicial commentary causing criminal cases to be dismissed, and social media commenters being fined or jailed.
- *Employment law* – Managing internal stakeholders is also a significant risk, and internal policies and codes of conduct must be considered to ensure risks are mitigated. Employees can be fired for their misuse of social media, but they can also win fair work appeals if social media policies were unfair or training was inadequate.
- *Privacy* – There are elements of privacy that all users of social media should understand. Privacy has both legal and ethical dimensions as a fundamental human right. Legislation exists that protects personal data. In some places people can also sue when their privacy has been invaded or their confidentiality has been breached. Understanding the balance between privacy and free expression is essential to effective social media use.

Theoretical underpinnings

This book considers these kinds of risks through the lens of two key theories – stakeholder theory and risk management theory – discussed in depth in Chapters 2 and 3. We provide a basic understanding of the use of these theories here to establish our approach to social media risk.

The first – stakeholder theory – can be used to understand the social actors of an organisation (stakeholders) and the importance they hold for organisational outcomes. Stakeholder theory is an essential tool for an organisation. It is argued that lists of different types of stakeholders (for example, customers, staff, investors and shareholders) are meaningless if the organisation does not acknowledge the interconnections that can be made between stakeholder groups. Stakeholders can draw on other social identities and form further social groups, reinforcing the 'echo chambers' concept discussed earlier, where those with similar views can come together and strengthen those views. To fully understand stakeholders, the organisation must find the connection between stakeholder groups and appreciate that people who sit within one stakeholder group may also have other views, sometimes at odds with their expected positions. This textbook considers the work of R. Edward Freeman (1984, 2005) as the basis of stakeholder theory, particularly with regard to the connection between stakeholders and corporate social responsibility. It further explores social identity theory (Schneider & Sachs 2017; Crane & Ruebottom 2011) as the fundamental framework to determine the risks posed by stakeholders and their many associations and identities.

The second main theory considered is risk management theory. Risk management is considered from the perspective of risk assessment and social amplification and is defined as being the chance of adverse reactions based on the combination of probability and impact. Using a risk assessment matrix, you can map the potential impacts of risk for an organisation based on the probability of it occurring versus the impact it will have. However, further consideration is given to understanding discrepancies between the hazard (or harm that may be caused) versus the outrage some stakeholders may have as a result of the risk occurring (sometimes via social media). Chapter 3 explores the work of Peter Sandman (1993) who found the correlation between hazard and outrage to be vastly different, meaning if you took a list of risks and ranked them from highest to lowest hazard, and highest to lowest outrage, they would appear as two very different lists. To explore this further we discuss the Social Amplification of Risk

Framework (SARF), which was developed in the 1980s to help understand why some minor risks sometimes caused significant impact while other more harmful risks did not (Kasperson et al. 1988).

Discussion questions and project topics

1   Go back to the start of the chapter and review the first few paragraphs about corporate communications chief Justine Sacco and the fallout from her pre-flight tweet. Make a list of the three main ethical, legal and organisational errors she made in that situation and explain how you might avoid or minimise them if you were in that position.

2   Let's have our first brainstorm in stakeholder theory by using the university as an organisational case study. List three primary stakeholders in a university. Then add seven more 'secondary stakeholders' – types of groups or individuals who might be impacted by a social media post on behalf of the university.

3   Even a simple social media post can have ethical, legal or organisational risks and consequences. Workshop this one. You are a communications intern at a major toy retailer. You've been asked to build a social media campaign around a new pink tiger doll aimed at 8–11-year-old girls. You want to run a competition across several platforms with this message: 'Here's our new tiger doll – but she needs a name! Post a photo of yourself with your favourite doll with your suggested name for our new tiger doll to the hashtag #TigerDolly'. Identify the key stakeholders involved here and the ethical, legal and organisational risks and consequences. Then suggest a safer approach.

Practice tips

•   Whenever working in the social media space as a professional communicator, it is essential to carve out opportunities to anticipate, identify and address the ethical, legal and organisational risks of social media use. Every time you are about to use social media, you need to pause to think about the risks for all the stakeholders involved. Once you identify them you might need to adjust your planned course of action to minimise risk or perhaps take legal advice on the safest course of action.

•   Part of that anticipating and identifying process requires a detailed understanding of the stakeholders who might be affected by a social media communication. It is worth developing a basic table of stakeholders in your organisational context extending beyond the basic list of shareholders, employees and customers. Go further to include related industry groups, sponsorships, affiliated entities, communities, action groups, causes and others you can imagine. Once this is done, the implications of a single social media post might appear much more nuanced and widespread.

•   State your organisation's approval process for dealing with legal, ethical and organisational consequences of social media posts. What is the chain of command for approving a particular social media strategy, campaign or comment? Who decides whether to engage lawyers if someone threatens to sue or prosecute over a social media post? What is the organisation's social media policy, and who is responsible for its ongoing revision and associated training? These are key matters that need to be clarified well before a social media crisis arises.

Cases cited

Footballer's post case. 2019. *Isileli 'Israel' Folau v Rugby Australia Limited & Anor* [2019] MLG2486/2019. <www.federalcircuitcourt.gov.au/wps/wcm/connect/fccweb/about/media/pic/folau>

References

Castells, M. 2011. *The rise of the network society.* Germany: Wiley.

Crane, A. & T. Ruebottom. 2011. "Stakeholder theory and social identity: Rethinking stakeholder identification." *J Bus Ethics, 102,* 77–87. https://doi.org/10.1007/s10551-011-1191-4

Eriksson, M. 2016. "Managing collective trauma on social media: The role of Twitter after the 2011 Norway attacks." *Media, Culture & Society, 38*(3), 365–380. https://doi.org/10.1177/0163443715608259

Freeman, R.E. 1984. *Strategic management: A stakeholder approach.* Marshfield, MA: Pitman Publishing Inc.

Freeman, R.E. 2005. "The development of stakeholder theory: An idiosyncratic approach." In K. Smith & M.A. Hitt (eds.), *Great minds in management: The process of theory development.* New York: Oxford University Press.

Grunig, J.E. & L.A. Grunig. 1996. *Implications of symmetry for a theory of ethics and social responsibility in public relations.* Meeting of the International Communication Association, Chicago, USA, May.

Grunig, J.E. & L.A. Grunig. 2008. "Excellence theory in public relations: Past, present, and future." In A. Zerfass, B. van Ruler & K. Sriramesh (eds.), *Public relations research.* Wiesbaden: VS Verlag für Sozialwissenschaften. pp. 327–347.

Grunig, J.E., L.A. Grunig & E.L. Toth. 2007. *The future of excellence in public relations and communication management: Challenges for the next generation.* Mahwah, NJ: Lawrence Erlbaum.

Grunig, J.E. & T. Hunt. 1984. *Managing public relations.* Fort Worth: Harcourt Brace Jovanovich College Publishers.

Grunig, L.A., J.E. Grunig & D.M. Dozier. 2002. *Excellent public relations and effective organizations.* Mahwah, NJ: Lawrence Erlbaum.

Hootsuite. 2021. "The global state of digital communications." *Hootsuite.* Accessed 7 March 2021. www.hootsuite.com/pages/digital-trends-2021

Kasperson, R.E., O. Renn, P. Slovic, H.S. Brown, J. Emel, R. Goble, J.X. Kasperson & S. Ratick. 1988. "The social amplification of risk: A conceptual framework." *Risk Analysis, 8*(2), 177–187. doi:10.1111/j.1539-6924.1988.tb01168.x

Sandman, P.M. 1993. *Responding to community outrage: Strategies for effective risk communication.* Fairfax, VA: American Industrial Hygiene Association.

Schneider, T. & S. Sachs. 2017. "The impact of stakeholder identities on value creation in issue-based stakeholder networks." *Journal of Business Ethics, 144*(1), 41–57. doi:10.1007/s10551-015-2845-4

Smart Insights. 2020. "Global social media research summary 2020." *Smart Insights.* Accessed 9 October 2020. www.smartinsights.com/social-media-marketing/social-media-strategy/new-global-social-media-research/

2 Theory into practice

Why is stakeholder theory important?

Glossary

Corporate social responsibility: An ethical concept that encourages organisations to integrate social concerns into their operations to generate interaction with stakeholders.

Echo chamber: The phenomenon where people connect with others who have similar views on social media, often entrenching those opinions.

Shareholders: Those who have a financial interest in a company through the ownership of shares.

Social identity: Defining someone through their many social interests and values.

Stakeholders: Groups of people who can be impacted by an organisation's decisions and announcements due to the stake they have in the situation.

Stakeholder theory: An important theory of public communication and management that acknowledges the range of participants who might benefit – or be impacted by – the decisions and actions of an organisation, including its social media activities. It stems from business and management scholarship and allows us to identify and map the key stakeholders affected by organisational decisions and announcements.

Unanticipated public: A group of latent publics that can form in a social media environment.

Abstract

Stakeholders are an important part of social media engagement. The multi-channel and interactive nature of social media allows messages to reach a variety of stakeholders and audiences. Understanding how to recognise, establish and map stakeholders provides professional communicators with a framework through which they can look at social media laws and risks, and the ways they might apply in an organisation's use of social media. Social media use can impact a range of stakeholders that are involved with an organisation, and sometimes this is an unexpected group. Underestimating the voice of active social media users can increase risk. However, the process of identifying stakeholders who could be affected by an organisation's activities helps communicators better understand the value it might add to their endeavours and to the brand. Ultimately social media engagement is about adding value to an organisation (including reputation, legitimacy and financial value) and minimising risk.

DOI: 10.4324/9781003180111-3

In this chapter

- What is a stakeholder?
- Case study 2.1 – Heart Foundation of Australia's 'Heartless words' campaign
- Understanding stakeholder theory
- Social identity theory
- How to identify stakeholders
- Case study 2.2 – #AskJameis
- Discussion questions and project topics
- Practice tips
- References

What is a stakeholder?

A stakeholder is an individual, group or organisation that has a vested interest – or stake – in the activities of an organisation. Stakeholders can be internal or external to an organisation. It is a term that can be mistaken for 'shareholder' but usually includes some groups who have a non-financial interest in the organisation. Examples of stakeholders can include those within the organisation, such as staff, customers and the board of directors; others like shareholders who have a direct relationship, such as suppliers and investors; and others whose affairs might overlap with an organisation, such as industry groups, unions and community organisations. Each stakeholder group may have a different interest in the organisation or activity. Sometimes a stakeholder's interest may create conflict with an organisation's policies. That is, while a business decision may be supported by one stakeholder group, it may be opposed by another. This is where stakeholder theory plays an important role in allowing you to understand your stakeholders and how they interact with your messages. It must be acknowledged that stakeholders have a level of power and influence, and therefore it becomes increasingly important to manage the relationships with them. Stakeholder management is about managing the gap between an organisation's actions and the expectations of the stakeholders – and social media can play a crucial role. If we were to consider this definition of stakeholder for a large multinational mining company, we might consider the stakeholders listed in Figure 2.1.

While Figure 2.1 shows the complexity that comes with mapping stakeholders, we can also start to get a sense of the levels of power that stakeholders might have. For instance, if you worked for this organisation and were about to release a social media post announcing the appointment of a new CEO, then the board of directors carries a much higher power over that decision and its messaging than the environmental scientists who do contracted work for them. However, if the social media post related to a technical report prepared by the scientists, then they might hold more power over the message and its communication than the company's board. This example provides some insights into the role a stakeholder might play, and the fact that such a role can vary depending on the activity.

Some literature does suggest that the terms 'publics', 'audiences' and 'stakeholders' have been merged in the communication field (Wakefield & Knighton 2019). Chapter 4 discusses the concept of the audience, being those with whom an organisation aims to interact through social media engagement. Social media engagement will sometimes gain the attention of a public, being a larger group of people with a common interest. The idea of the public in social media can be linked right back to the work of Dewey (1927),

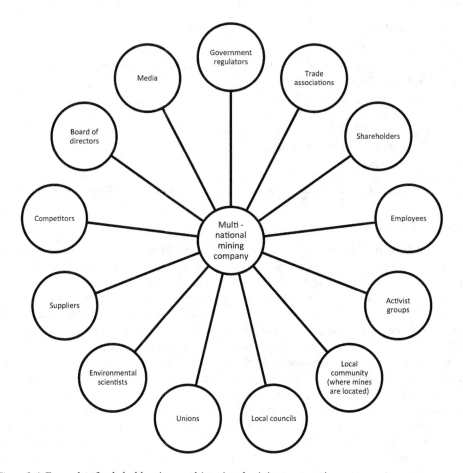

Figure 2.1 Example of stakeholders in a multi-national mining corporation

who proposed that the public was a relationship between people who shared a common interest or need. His work focussed on the idea that consequence, a negative result of a particular situation, is a contributing factor to bringing publics together. However, a stakeholder is someone with a stake in the situation at hand. Some of this confusion may stem from the fact that activists are often key stakeholders in crisis situations because they hold a stake in the outcome of such significant disasters. For instance, if the mining company experienced an oil spill, then an environmental activist group might be considered a stakeholder because what they advocate – protection of the environment – is at stake. This stakeholder group can mobilise and create social media 'noise' about what it is they stand for and call upon the support of others who have an underlying interest in environmental issues, ultimately generating power. This is where a stakeholder group can become an unanticipated public.

The concept of the unanticipated public was developed by Wakefield and Knighton (2019) in their research about the differences between audiences, publics and stakeholders. The concept draws on leading public relations theories, particularly Grunig's Situational Theory of Publics (1989), which highlights four different types of publics:

active, aware, latent and non-public. An active public is more likely to have strong opinions about a situation and therefore be more likely to act. An aware public may recognise a situation but be unlikely to take an active role. A latent public includes those who are aware of the situation but do not recognise it as a problem. Finally, a non-public consists of those who are unaffected. Wakefield and Knighton (2019) use this theory to introduce the term 'unanticipated public' to describe a group of latent publics that can form in a social media environment. Social media allows such groups to form. These groups have clearly defined identities and connections, and the nature of their existence carries the potential for them to drive unintentional activism and become echo chambers, allowing trends to develop (Colleoni, Rozza & Arvidsson 2014; Urman 2019).

'Echo chamber' is a term often used to describe the ability for people to connect with others on social media who have similar views – essentially communicating within a 'bubble' where those views can solidify and become entrenched. A more detailed definition is provided in Chapter 4, but an echo chamber originates from the concept of 'homophily' which is the inclination of people with likenesses to gravitate to each other (Lazarsfeld & Merton 1954; Hanusch & Nölleke 2019). Social media has created a public sphere where those with similar opinions can connect despite geographic distance, creating a stronger voice. Although there has been some debate regarding the legitimacy of echo chambers (Dubois & Blank 2018; Bruns 2019), it must be acknowledged that when themes develop in online communication, non-engaged members of the community may listen and act. An unanticipated public can form and have both positive and negative effects, and many social media examples show what can happen when stakeholder groups form publics and come together to voice concern or seek change. When people have opinions and a vested interest, consequences also matter, and when the online voice is strengthened through echo chambers and unanticipated publics, the drive for change can be significant. Later in this chapter we will explore the way individuals can shift between stakeholder groups. This helps to understand how these unanticipated publics can carry power. However, the example that follows shows how the online voice can be strengthened by an unanticipated public (a key stakeholder) and change the outcome for the organisation.

Case study 2.1 – Heart Foundation of Australia's 'Heartless words' campaign

In mid-2019 the Heart Foundation of Australia released its 'Heartless words' campaign on both social media and television platforms. Within two days the campaign had been pulled from all media following significant public backlash due to the 'insensitive' nature of the videos. The videos depicted patients with heart disease admitting to their loved ones that they did not love them enough to look after their own health. While at the end of the video there is a reference to a heart check, which suggests the campaign was aimed at those who did not get regular medical check-ups, it received negative feedback because of the unacknowledged prevalence of genetic disorders in people suffering heart disease. For an organisation such as the Heart Foundation of Australia, a key stakeholder group consists of those who experience heart disease. The Heart Foundation's initial response was to back its campaign, and it engaged in social media commentary highlighting the need for an uncomfortable approach because the impact was to urge people to have their heart health checked as a preventative measure and to reach those who did not consider heart health a priority. But they did not consider those who were most impacted by the campaign, and the organisation was accused of exploiting emotions such as the shame and guilt of those with heart disease – causing subsequent outrage amongst a range of different stakeholders. Despite making amendments to the videos to appease public calls for action, the campaign was ultimately cancelled.

Let's look at the case study through the lens of stakeholder theory. Those with the highest stake in the campaign are those who have heart disease and are being depicted in the video. Health care professionals may also be considered a high-power stakeholder as they witness the impact of heart disease every day and can either support the message or negate it. Another stakeholder we might consider in this campaign includes those who make regular donations to the foundation. These are often people personally impacted by heart disease, perhaps through a parent or partner. By identifying these few stakeholder groups, we gain insights into the impact the campaign may have had on them emotionally. It can be assumed, based on current costs of creative development, that significant funds were expended and ultimately wasted in the production and rollout of this campaign. This highlights the importance of identifying and understanding the key stakeholders in all communication activities prior to development.

Understanding stakeholder theory

Stakeholder theory has its origins in the literature of business and management studies. A key scholar in the development of stakeholder theory is R. Edward Freeman. In his early work, Freeman (1984) set out a strategic management approach to enhancing business by understanding the key stakeholders and how these groups stood to affect the direction of the organisation. Although there are a number of definitions of stakeholder theory, it fits within the realm of business and management because the purpose of business is to create value for stakeholders in order to succeed. Therefore, an organisation must keep the interests of key stakeholders aligned, including customers, suppliers, employees and shareholders. It is important to note that although there are a number of definitions that have a strong capitalist influence, thinking of the implications for all stakeholders is an increasingly important approach. One of the key elements of stakeholder theory is the ethical and moral dimension, and this is reflected in some of Freeman's later work (2005), where he begins to embed the concept in business ethics literature and links stakeholder theory with corporate social responsibility (CSR). CSR encourages organisations to integrate social concerns into their operations. Consumers expect organisations to conduct their business in a socially responsible and ethical way, and often actively choose to support those who do so. This has a flow-on to stakeholder theory because understanding stakeholders allows us to do the right thing by all rather than just focussing on the financial benefits to customers, shareholders or executives.

The ethical and moral aspects stress the focus of stakeholder theory should be about how an organisation sits in an ethical way within the broader society and reinforces the role of CSR in this process. You could apply this concept quite easily to a government department or other organisation and see that stakeholder theory emphasises that maximising the value from an organisational decision is more important than maximising the wealth that might emanate from it. In the realm of crisis communication, stakeholder theory suggests that how organisations behave will largely influence how stakeholders react to a situation. Stakeholders are more likely to support an organisation that they trust, again providing a link to ethics and CSR.

Of course, stakeholder theory cannot exclude the interests of internal stakeholders when considering implications for external stakeholders and society more broadly. As a theory it is designed to give us a way of thinking about, and understanding, both the ownership of large organisations and how decisions should be made within them. It is important to consider which internal stakeholders should be involved in decision making and how these determinations can add value to the organisation and the overarching perception that its external stakeholders hold. Again, this comes back to ethical decision making and trust. If a decision considers the best interests of stakeholders, it might generate positive perception and trust, which might in turn contribute to the health (and wealth) of the organisation.

Social identity theory

One of the key aspects of stakeholder theory is identifying who a particular organisation's stakeholders might be. This is often seen in a simple transactional way – with stakeholders defined as anyone impacted by a decision. However, social identity theory adds a complex dimension to the way we consider stakeholders. Stemming from social psychology research, social identity theory considers the relationship between people's roles as stakeholders and other social identities that may apply to them. It suggests that stakeholders should no longer be defined by their relationships with the organisation, but instead as actors who can affect an issue. They should also no longer be categorised by their generic economic function but must also be defined by their social identities and shared interests that might influence their roles within stakeholder groups (Schneider & Sachs 2017).

This is described by Crane and Ruebottom (2011) as the 'social glue' or 'social cohesion' that occurs within stakeholder theory. Social identity theory asks us to consider reasons why stakeholder groups might mobilise or gain traction when pressing their claims over their stake in a situation. Stakeholders are not always those who have experienced a simple transaction with an organisation but are often connected in other ways, such as via their social identities. This part of stakeholder theory considers the bonds that connect people from other transactional stakeholder groups – for example, a sponsor of a major corporation might gain extensive media exposure by having its logo on the shirt of a world champion team. However, it might withdraw its sponsorship if the sports organisation fails to act upon racist social media posts by its players or fans because this runs counter to its inclusive messaging as an organisation. This highlights the potential for a stakeholder to switch between stakeholder identities – in this instance from financial sponsor to social critic. A staff member might sit within the stakeholder group of employees but also have a strong social connection to an activist group whose views might come into conflict with the corporation. Therefore, their salient stakeholder identity may shift.

By considering our stakeholders in this more complex approach we start to understand the level of risk that can occur and begin to appreciate the need for appropriate policies and organisational codes of conduct that may assist in managing the potential issues – particularly in the context of social media. Of course, the shifting of stakeholder identities will not always be a negative concern. In some situations, understanding the salient identities of key stakeholders (particularly internal stakeholder groups) may be of benefit in establishing engagement with other stakeholder groups. For example, if a number of staff have school-age children (and thus a stake in local education and sporting groups), they might assist with social media campaigns promoting scholarships and awards as part of a company's CSR initiatives.

How to identify stakeholders

Although our initial discussion about stakeholders and stakeholder theory highlights the risks that can come with social media use, we must also acknowledge the benefits and opportunities that can come from understanding our stakeholders. This beneficial concept will be discussed more in Chapter 4 in relation to the role of the audience, but in establishing stakeholder theory a broad approach must be taken to understanding who might be impacted by the organisation's actions – particularly its social media messaging. Initial stakeholder identification should be done in a generalised way. There will, of course, be times when stakeholder identification can be quite specific. For instance, if you worked for a large global mining corporation and a social media post was planned to announce a new mining lease, you could easily predict certain activist groups would be high on your stakeholder list. However, if you consider social identity theory as part of this scenario, there may be people within other stakeholder groups, such as employees, who have a particular view on the announcement and may exist across stakeholder groups. For example, the social identity allegiances of an employee might be quite complex. The mining venture might well bring staff more job security, but equally it might impact their identities as stakeholders in the local community where the livelihoods of their families and friends are dependent on eco-tourism, which could be jeopardised by the new mine. When identifying stakeholders, you need to imagine not only those who will be immediately affected but those who could be impacted further down the line. This can help you predict the type of response your organisation might receive and how much power a group might have in influencing leverage on an idea, particularly in social media.

Stakeholder mapping can assist in this process. The concept behind stakeholder mapping is that an organisation should respond to stakeholders who have a higher level of power but also a higher stake in the activities of the entity. It is essential that we identify this group of stakeholders with both high power and high stake and work closely with them through regular communication and by taking notice of what such groups are saying. Conversely, if stakeholder groups have little power and only a small stake in the activities of the organisation, they might not be a stakeholder group that you need to follow as closely. But remember, this is a complex environment, and although a stakeholder group may have little power, they should be mapped regardless, and acknowledgement given. It is important to identify the existence of these low-power and low-stake groups and monitor them routinely because their outrage can escalate via social media echo chambers and unanticipated publics. Nevertheless, the management of stakeholders through stakeholder mapping suggests you should spend more time working closely with the most powerful stakeholders who have the greatest interest in the organisation's operations, decisions and communications.

Let's return to our fictitious scenario involving a large multinational mining company that is about to announce a new mining contract. Figure 2.2 begins to map the potential stakeholders for this scenario based on power and stake. When considering Figure 2.2, please remember that this scenario is related to the announcement of a new mine, and we assume that all appropriate regulatory processes and approvals have been obtained and the announcement is to provide details to stakeholders only.

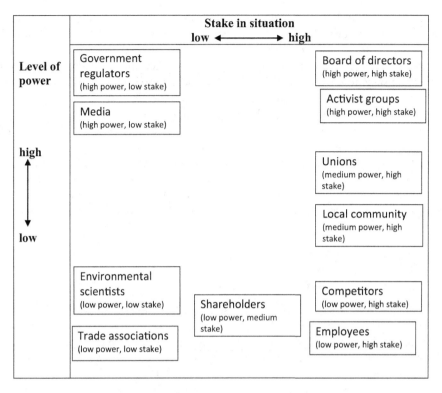

Figure 2.2 Stakeholder map example of a large multinational mining company announcing a new contract.

Case study 2.2 – #AskJameis

An example that highlights the importance of identifying potential stakeholders occurred in August 2014 when the Florida State University Football team used its Twitter account to ask its followers to submit questions for their superstar quarterback, Jameis Winston, using the hashtag #AskJameis. The post stated:

> *#Noles Fans: Do you have a question for our starting QB Jameis Winston? Tweet us using #AskJameis.*

Within moments they began to receive questions, but few were about football. The quarterback at the centre of this social media experiment had been allegedly involved in a number of incidents including an alleged sexual assault (over which he was investigated but not charged) and theft of food items from a local grocery store. Many of the questions posed under this hashtag related to these alleged crimes while others were found to be of a general sarcastic nature (Sanderson et al. 2016). Within a few hours things had become nasty. While there are obvious risks that could have been managed to prevent this from escalating into the crisis it became, we can align this example to stakeholder theory to better understand the role stakeholders play in our social media engagement and risks that can arise. If the stakeholders had been identified and social identity theory considered, the risks associated with this social media campaign would have been obvious. For instance, the athlete himself would be a key internal stakeholder and considerations would be made regarding the stakeholders that would be attracted to his involvement in the campaign. By using social identity theory, we would start to see that the social identities of some of the university's football fans would begin to shift and move them from the stakeholder group of 'fan' to the stakeholder group of 'activist'. This stakeholder group – 'activist' – would carry high power and have a high stake in the situation. They were thus a group that needed to be considered, engaged with and closely monitored.

The examples presented in this chapter highlight the role stakeholder theory can play in social media engagement. It is essential to not only understand the stakeholders who will be affected by our posts but also their social identities and the impact they can have on the outcomes. The next chapter talks more about risk management theory, and Chapter 4 discusses understanding the audience. However, stakeholder theory is the foundational framework we need to understand in order to inform our social media use and to assess its potential risks.

Discussion questions and project topics

1   Consider your place of work or study and think of someone you are familiar with but do not work directly with. Then consider social identity theory and list five examples of the 'social glue' that connects you across multiple stakeholder groups.
2   You work for a large supermarket chain and are about to post on social media about a new vegan range of food products about to hit the shelves. Use the stakeholder mapping process to map all of the stakeholders and how they fit within this scenario. What level of stake and power do they hold? What is the impact of social identity theory? Could unanticipated publics form? If so, what might be their focus?
3   Map the stakeholders involved in the #AskJameis case example. Consider social identity theory and start to cross-map the connections between stakeholder groups.

Practice tips

•   An organisation should have an overarching stakeholder list. This is often mapped in order of prioritisation with contact details and other relevant information to ensure the members of stakeholder groups can be contacted via a range of media forms when required.
•   Each significant campaign or social media engagement should be considered against the impact it could have on the relevant stakeholders with consideration also given to the role of unexpected publics and social identity theory.

References

Bruns, A. 2019. *Are filter bubbles real?* Cambridge: Polity.
Colleoni, E., A. Rozza & A. Arvidsson. 2014. "Echo chamber or public sphere? Predicting political orientation and measuring political homophily in twitter using big data." *Journal of Communication, 64,* 317–332. doi:10.1111/jcom.12084

Crane, A. & T. Ruebottom. 2011. "Stakeholder theory and social identity: Rethinking stakeholder identification." *J Bus Ethics, 102,* 77–87. https://doi-org.libraryproxy.griffith.edu.au/10.1007/s10551-011-1191-4

Dewey, J. 1927. *The public and its problems.* Athens: Swallow Press.

Dubois, E. & G. Blank. 2018. "The echo chamber is overstated: The moderating effect of political interest and diverse media." *Information, Communication & Society, 21*(5), 729–745. https://10.1080/1369118X.2018.1428656

Freeman, R.E. 1984. *Strategic management: A stakeholder approach.* Marshfield, MA: Pitman Publishing Inc.

Freeman, R.E. 2005. "The development of stakeholder theory: An idiosyncratic approach." In K. Smith & M.A. Hitt (eds.), *Great minds in management: The process of theory development.* New York: Oxford University Press.

Grunig, J.E. 1989. "Sierra club study shows who become activists." *Public Relations Review, 15,* 8–24.

Hanusch, F. & D. Nölleke. 2019. "Journalistic homophily on social media." *Digital Journalism, 7*(1), 22–44. doi:10.1080/21670811.2018.1436977

Lazarsfeld, P. & R.K. Merton. 1954. "Friendship as a social process: A substantive and methodological analysis." In M. Berger, T. Abel & H. Charles (eds.), *Freedom and control in modern society.* New York: Van Nostrand.

Sanderson, J., K. Barnes, C. Williamson & E.T. Kian. 2016. "'How could anyone have predicted that #AskJameis would go horribly wrong?' public relations, social media, and hashtag hijacking." *Public Relations Review, 42*(1), 31–37.

Schneider, T. & S. Sachs. 2017. "The impact of stakeholder identities on value creation in issue-based stakeholder networks." *Journal of Business Ethics, 144*(1), 41–57. doi:10.1007/s10551-015-2845-4

Urman, A. 2019. "Context matters: Political polarization on Twitter from a comparative perspective." *Media, Culture & Society.* https://doi.org/10.1177/0163443719876541

Wakefield, R. & D. Knighton. 2019. "Distinguishing among publics, audiences, and stakeholders in the social media era of unanticipated publics." *Public Relations Review, 45*(5), 101821. doi:10.1016/j.pubrev.2019.101821

3 Risk management theories and practice in social media

Glossary

Legal risk escalation: The organisational policies for identifying and escalating legal advice and actions, with key tasks and responsibilities assigned to identified personnel in the reporting line.

Outrage: The level of fear or anger an audience feels about a hazard, often expressed via social media. Outrage factors are emotional factors that contribute to the perception of risk.

Risk: The chance of adverse ethical, legal and organisational reactions based on the combination of probability and impact.

Risk management: The process of identifying and controlling risk and the implementation of strategies to mitigate organisational risk.

Risk perception: The subjective judgement made about a potential risk.

Social media risk: The potential ethical, legal and organisational dangers inherent in social media communication.

Abstract

Society presents risk in all facets of life. It is ever-present for us personally every time we travel in a car, participate in sports or go on a vacation. It is also experienced professionally within employment in the form of workplace health and safety hazards – and every time we communicate via the written or spoken word. As communication is predominantly online and published in emails, social media or other online applications, we must understand the risks that exist and how to minimise and manage them if they arise. This chapter explores risk management approaches and theories to help understand the professional aspects of risk management when using social media. It focusses on the fact that the public responds more to outrage than to hazard, and therefore when using social media we must understand what could cause outrage in order to understand what is considered a risk.

DOI: 10.4324/9781003180111-4

In this chapter

- Defining risk
- Historical development of risk management
- Perception of risk and outrage factors
- Risk assessment
- Social amplification of risk and the role of social media
- Case study 3.1 – The Crock-Pot case
- Legal risk and escalation policies
- Risk management theory
- When theories meet: risk management in a stakeholder theory context
- Discussion questions and project topics
- Practice tips
- References

Defining risk

Although risk has different definitions across disciplines, all point to risk being the chance of adverse reactions based on the combination of probability and impact (Jaques 2014; Sandman 1993). The financial implications of risk are evident in the form of the multi-trillion-dollar international insurance industry where we pay premiums to help minimise impacts of unforeseen events upon our lives, our businesses, our health and our possessions.

The insurance industry typically deals in quantifiable risks which are calculated via sophisticated actuarial algorithms designed to predict the risk of a particular hazard or event based upon previous events and claims in similar scenarios. Thus, if your house sits within the established 100-year flood level, you might pay a higher annual insurance premium than someone who lives on a mountaintop because of the higher risk of flood damage, and your premiums are likely to rise as water levels increase due to climate change.

However, in the field of professional communication, some risks are considerably less tangible and much harder to predict because they centre upon human interpretation and emotion in the context of rapidly changing technologies. Such risks are typically uninsurable because there are no algorithms to predict precisely the public's likely outrage at a communication via social media. While some products such as professional indemnity insurance can cover a practitioner for breaches of professional duty and exposure to various laws including defamation and negligence and their associated legal costs, insurances cannot cover the unpredictable public reaction to a Facebook, Twitter or Instagram post.

Therefore, to understand risk in a professional communication context properly, you need to take account of the fact that some social media behaviour can be devastating to an organisation but might not fit into the neat and tidy categories such as those covered by insurance policies. It must first be acknowledged that there is a discrepancy that occurs between the hazard of the action versus the potential public outrage it might trigger. Peter Sandman (1993), a respected risk scholar, conducted extensive research into this phenomenon and discovered that across disciplines that carry risk, the correlation between hazard and outrage is only 0.2. This means that if you took a list of risks and ranked them from highest to lowest hazard, then took the same list and ranked it from highest to lowest outrage, you would have two very different lists. This is of importance because our perception of risk and the actual hazard of risk, both carrying threats of causing adverse reactions, are often quite different.

Some argue that a hazard is a real risk or objective risk because of the link between hazard and injury. It is then further argued that outrage is a perceived risk or a subjective risk. However, as will be discussed in this book, often the outrage felt is what creates the problem so you can never underestimate the role that public outrage – or even possible outrage – can have on a situation. Later in this chapter the social amplification of risk framework is discussed, which helps to clarify the impact that societal reactions can have on a risk. However, when considering the definition of risk, regardless of the discrepancy between hazard and outrage, it must be acknowledged that social outrage is real and needs to be taken seriously rather than assuming that where the hazard appears to be low, the risk is also low. Let's return to the case mentioned at the start of this book, that of Justine Sacco, corporate communications chief of a major Internet company, who posted a flippant tweet just before her flight departed from London to Cape Town. This case can be analysed based on the Sandman definition of risk to realise that the identifiable and quantifiable hazards related to her tweet were low, but the potential, and subsequent, outrage at the content and context of her tweet was high and resulted in the tweet going viral.

Therefore, if you can understand how to identify communication risks based on this equation of risk = hazard + outrage (Sandman 1993), you can then proceed to apply risk management tools.

Historical development of risk management

Risk management is still a relatively new concept, having been first researched in the middle of the last century when scholar Snider (1956) recognised that there were no books on the topic. His research highlighted the requirement for risk management in the insurance industry. Other early scholarship considered 'pure risk', which is a matter that can be insured against (Dionne 2019). In the 1970s risk management took a financial approach and by the 1980s and 1990s most risk management frameworks focussed on the mitigation of corporate risk, still with a strong link to financial implications. For instance, a number of frameworks motivate organisations to manage risks because of the financial implications the risk might have (Smith & Stulz 1985; Nance, Smith & Smithson 1993; Mian 1996; Géczy, Minton & Schrand 1997). These models suggest that organisations implement risk management strategies to prevent financial distress, but they do not consider how to reduce volatility. Risk management departments were established in banks, financial institutions and other large corporations. However, this focus on financial implications provides a narrow perception of risk. In some disciplines, such as psychology, risk relates to situations where the 'actor' has a choice that could result in either positive or negative outcomes. This concept of risk is more relevant to online communications, where an interaction on social media could be considered a gamble, sometimes with unpredictable consequences.

In the 1980s and 1990s a number of scholars explored the role of communication in risk. Some of this research forms the basis of our understanding of risk communication and managing risk through communication. Sandman's work, for instance, considered the role that effective communication could play in managing risks and potential crisis events. While his scholarship mainly discussed the way communication could be used to manage these events, his theories do assist in understanding what might constitute a risk when communicating. As explored previously, his equation on risk allows us to recognise the potential impact of risk and is a useful concept to assess and manage risks arising when communicating online.

In the 1980s there was also some significant research conducted by a group of scholars from Clarke University in Iowa, United States, who wanted to better understand the phenomenon of why certain risks that were considered low in hazard were in fact amplified by society. This significant research resulted in the Social Amplification of Risk Framework (SARF) that will be discussed in detail later in this chapter.

Perception of risk and outrage factors

To understand the role that risk management plays in the professional use of social media, you must first understand the concept of risk perception. The perception of risk has played a vital role in what was initially the slow uptake of social media at an organisational level. Many senior executives thought the risks associated with social media use were too great within the context of their existing businesses. Many of these risks related to losing control of the organisation's message; time loss related to staff needing to manage and moderate social media accounts rather than undertaking tasks related to their position; financial implications that being involved in a social media crisis could bring; a litany of legal risks; and reputational impact that could follow. Many did not want to engage in an online, published, space where everyone could see potentially negative interactions. There is a link here to Sandman's research regarding hazard and outrage. The perception of outrage toward using social media professionally was outweighed by the perceived hazards inherent in social media engagement.

Of course, as time has progressed, the perception of the hazards that social media presents have changed. This overwhelming focus on negativity prevented organisations from engaging in social media despite the fact that their customers, targeted audiences and other stakeholders were already there. This attitude towards social media engagement has remained strong for one leading organisation. Apple – one of the world's top 20 companies at the time of writing – has taken an interesting approach to social media by not engaging at all with its customers but instead has used social media predominantly for technical support and promotional purposes. It has been speculated that this is because of the existence of negativity online about Apple as a product and an organisation. It is believed that Apple has avoided engaging in social media to avoid the negative encounters this could create. While Apple does distribute sponsored posts on social media, few of these actually appear in its organic content. Only its Instagram account has organic content, and it is used only to promote #ShotoniPhone images and videos. For example, if you search for Apple on Twitter you will find its official account @Apple has not issued any tweets. While this is an intriguing approach to managing social media risk, and appears to work for Apple, it is not a sustainable approach for most. Instead, organisations must understand these perceived risks and assess the impact they may have upon them in their unique situation to be in a position to manage the risk.

Outrage factors are the emotional factors that contribute to the perception of risk. Sandman (1993) suggested citizens used a moral-emotional approach to assessing risk. They 'think with their hearts', drawing from their ethical and moral beliefs. There are more than 30 'outrage factors' identified by scholars across risk management disciplines (Sandman 2012). The key outrage factors contributing to risk management in online communication are discussed in the following (Sandman 1988, 1993, 2012; Jaques 2014).

Voluntariness: Decision-making is important when assessing risk. People are more accepting of risks they have exposed themselves to voluntarily but are outraged by situations they are forced into.

Trust: Trust in an organisation or an individual has positive effects on the perception of risk. Trusted brands have come back from disastrous circumstances because of the trust of their audiences. Throughout this book we will discuss the balancing act between opportunity and risk, which is important to developing trust.

Control: This outrage factor links to the example given earlier regarding organisations' delayed responses to engaging with social media. When an organisation has control of a situation, it is less concerned about identified risks because it has control and can steer the narrative if necessary. However, when the control is taken over by someone else, the perception of risk is higher.

Familiarity: Risks that are familiar are more accepted than those unfamiliar. This outrage factor is somewhat similar to the first factor – voluntariness – because when someone is more familiar with a situation or circumstance, they are more likely to be involved voluntarily and accepting of any risks.

Effect on the vulnerable: Risks that affect children or vulnerable populations are less likely to be accepted than those risks that affect adult or privileged populations.

These outrage factors highlight the role of tolerance in decision-making, influencing how the audience may react and respond to risks. When engaging in online communication (or any form of publication), it is essential to consider the acceptability or tolerability of your audience to whatever you are about to publish.

Risk assessment

A popular approach to assessing risk is by using the impact/probability risk matrix. Used widely across many industries, it is designed for potential risks to be mapped on a four-quadrant matrix based on the impact of the risk against the probability of the risk (Figure 3.1).

It is believed that the risk matrix is derived from the contribution 17th-century mathematician Blaise Pascal made to theories on probability and decision making (Winch 2009). Pascal developed a wager on the existence of God, stating that God either exists or does not. He said that while we will find out in the end, we do not know right now, so it is instead important to consider the way we respond to these seemingly even odds. This concept makes us think about the impact and probability of an event occurring. In the instance of the 'God wager', you can consider both the impact and probability of what could happen in either scenario. If you do not believe in God, but God turns out to exist, then you may be doomed to an infinity in Hell. Whereas, if you do believe in God and it turns out God actually exists, then you will spend an eternity in Heaven. Clearly, in Pascal's line of reasoning, there seems to be much more at stake in this decision if we are non-believers. It highlights starkly the theory of probability versus the impact these decisions could have upon us. It is a powerful tool that shows us that, even in the abstract and unknown, our decisions stand to impact the outcome.

When using the impact/probability risk matrix, you can map *known unknowns* and *known knowns*. This means the risk matrix can be used to map what is anticipated to occur and what has been witnessed to occur. It is important to note this as later in the chapter a case example is discussed where the risk was an *unknown unknown* (see Case study 3.1). This approach to mapping risk has been widely assessed. Some scholars agree with its appropriateness while others contest its use. However, it is widely accepted that risk is the probability of something occurring against the impact this would have on the

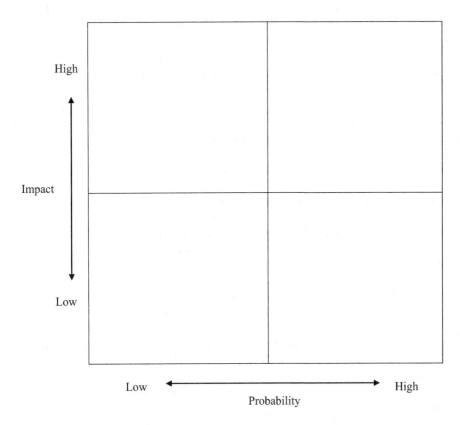

Figure 3.1 Impact/probability risk matrix

organisation or individual. This reinforces the usefulness of the risk matrix as a tool, particularly in the early stages of understanding what risks might occur in a particular circumstance (Jaques 2014). Ultimately, risk is a gamble – with many unknowns – but mapping these to the best of your abilities can assist in identifying and managing risks to benefit your organisation and your own career.

Social amplification of risk framework and the role of social media

The social amplification of risk framework (SARF) was developed in the 1980s by a group of scholars who were interested in understanding why some relatively minor risks were amplified – sometimes causing more significant impact than more serious and harmful risks (Kasperson et al. 1988). This research showed that a key influencing factor to social amplification was the flow of information. It is hypothesised that many risks will remain irrelevant unless there is observation of the risky communication and subsequent sharing of what has been observed. The framework, developed in the original 1988 research, highlights the complexity of the social amplification and attenuation of risk.

There are a number of influencing factors starting with the sources of information (experience or communication) and moving directly into the information channels (personal, social or professional) which are stronger and more varied with social media. Of special note though, particularly regarding the role that social media plays, are the 'ripple effects'. This part of the framework details the way in which opinions about a particular event or publication can be spread to a wider audience using social media platforms, which can then affect the perception and opinions of that wider audience about the event or publication. The framework concludes with the potential impacts on the organisation including financial loss, litigation, loss of confidence and regulatory action (Kasperson et al. 1988).

Because not all risks are experienced personally, society considers a range of factors to process the information, including the statements of those who claim to know or those who are experiencing the risk, along with personal beliefs. At the time of the original research in 1988, the main source of information sharing was the traditional news media, and it played a role in not only communicating the information but framing it for public consumption, affecting the way in which people perceived the news and responded to it (Kasperson et al. 1988). It did recognise that informal communication channels also had a strong influence on the amplification of risk. These of course have now been further strengthened with online communication and social media platforms.

The prevalence of video and image technology and the ability to share this information quickly and easily allows for virality – something 'going viral'. Social media has created an environment that is often unexpected and unpredictable. Because of this unpredictability it is a source of potentially risky communications that can easily be distributed and expanded aggressively through social media interactions. While the identification of risk plays an important role in understanding potential exposure for both individuals and organisations, the unpredictability of social media can make this difficult. It is not always possible to predict the type of risk that could occur on social media but understanding and acknowledging that risk exists can put an organisation in a positive position to manage that risk.

Case study 3.1 – The Crock-Pot case

In an example of social amplification, the kitchen appliances company Sunbeam was sent into crisis response in January 2018 after the scriptwriters of the top-rated fictional television series 'This Is Us' decided to kill off a key character – Jack Pearson – by engulfing him in a house fire sparked by an unbranded faulty old slow cooker he had left overnight to brew chili beans. Social media users went into a frenzy with thousands blaming Sunbeam's 'Crock-Pot' brand – the most famous slow cooker product – for the death of this beloved fictional family patriarch. Within two days the brand's stock dropped 24% (Foss 2019). The audience commented publicly on social media about their new fear of the product, attributing blame to the brand. This was a convincing example of social amplification at work. Sunbeam displayed well versed crisis communication practices by entering the conversation and showing remorse for the situation. The Crock-Pot brand accommodated the grief being felt by the audience over the loss of the character while attempting to restore the brand's reputation. Sunbeam could never have anticipated this risk might ever arise. It is unlikely it was mapped on the organisation's risk matrix if they had one. They might well have anticipated situations where real-life accidents and lawsuits resulted from product malfunctions, but not the possibility of their brand being denigrated via a fictional television drama series without the product even being named. However, it resulted in time, money and energy being spent in the days following the episode to address a situation over which it had no control (Foss 2019). This extreme and unlikely example highlights the potential damaging effects of outrage as a factor in social media risk. It points to the need to recognise risk and manage it effectively to mitigate ongoing damage. An organisation might not have plans to address every possible situation, but it can at least cover the most plausible scenarios and have options available when unpredictable events eventuate.

Legal risk and escalation policies

Risk management theory applies particularly well to the potential for legal risks of social media communication. Media organisations have long had in place organisational 'escalation policies' or 'upward referral policies' for dealing with threats of legal action over their news content. Such policies centre on identifying and escalating legal advice and actions, with key tasks and responsibilities assigned to identified personnel in the reporting line.

While some threats of legal action might be predictable – such as a news site's damaging exposé about a politician's corruption – many legal threats come from left field about stories the organisation might never have anticipated. This aligns with the social amplification of risk framework. Either way, the escalation policy indicates exactly who should be the decision maker in the organisational chain about how to respond to the plaintiff or their lawyer, what retractions or apologies should be made and how they might be worded and whether the matter should be settled out of court or litigated. Junior staffers admitting fault or writing their own corrections or apologies can be a recipe for legal disaster and can deny the organisation defences that might otherwise have been available to them.

In the modern era, it is not just news organisations that need their personnel trained in such legal escalation procedures. Now that all organisations are publishers via the Internet and social media, sound risk management requires training in the basics of social media law to minimise the likelihood of the most basic errors, and also training in the risk management procedures so that lawyers are engaged at the most appropriate time to limit further damage.

The legal example also sits well with the 'impact/probability risk matrix'. Effective social media law training for staff can *lower the probability* of legal action over an organisation's communications, while a well-drafted legal escalation policy (effectively communicated to staff) might *reduce the impact* of a legal threat if and when it arises.

Risk management theory

Taking speedy and responsive or even proactive measures on early warnings is at the core of risk management theory. As will be seen throughout this book, risks must be balanced against opportunity when it comes to social media use. However, understanding and assessing the risks is the first step towards mitigating them.

While there are many risk management frameworks that organisations and individuals can consider in their risk management process, a simple approach to managing risk successfully involves taking four key steps. These are:

1 *Identify the risk* – In this part of the framework you must consider all types of risks that could occur in the circumstance. This includes everything ranging from legal risk to reputational risk.
2 *Analyse the risk* – You can use the risk matrix to analyse the risk according to the likelihood and impact that it could have.

3   *Evaluate the risk* – After confirming the likelihood and impact, consider what outrage factors might apply. Use the social amplification of risk framework to evaluate the potential effect on the organisation and stakeholders – and whether this is a risk you are willing to take.

4   *Make a decision* – Use the preceding tools to consider the impact of the communication you are about to publish, take advice if necessary and make a decision based on whether the risk is one you are willing to take.

Although this appears a relatively simple approach, it must be considered along with the concepts discussed in the earlier parts of this chapter – and the particularities of the various social media laws we consider later. When evaluating the risk, you should consider the social amplification of risk framework as an influencing factor upon your decision making about the risk. If there is potential for social amplification, you must weigh up the risk against the opportunity that publishing your material may present. If a social media legal defence contains certain elements, you must consider those as part of the evaluation process.

When theories meet: risk management in a stakeholder theory context

The focus upon outrage in risk management theory provides a strong link to elements of stakeholder theory as discussed in Chapter 2. Because stakeholder theory aligns with corporate social responsibility (CSR) and therefore ethical decision making, you can see the role that outrage plays in effective risk management. Understanding the relevant stakeholders who could be affected by the situation under analysis, along with the social identities that may exist within those stakeholder groups, provides an organisation with the ability to determine potential outrage.

The first step to understanding the intensity of outrage is to acknowledge the stakeholder group affected. Of particular note when considering outrage is the development of an unanticipated public and the way groups of publics can come together and create social media noise that may amplify any outrage being felt.

When determining the outrage intensity, social identity theory should be at the front of your mind. You must ask yourself why stakeholder groups might mobilise or gain traction when pressing their claims over the stake they have in a situation. Stakeholders are often connected in other ways, such as via their social identities and the bonds that connect people with other transactional stakeholder groups. By considering your stakeholders in this more complex approach, you start to understand the level of risk that can occur and begin to appreciate the need for appropriate policies and organisational codes of conduct that may assist in managing potential issues. Remember, the fluidity of stakeholder identities does not have to be negative. Some members of key stakeholder groups, particularly internal stakeholder groups, may be of benefit in establishing a connection or engagement with other stakeholders.

Discussion questions and project topics

1   Look again at the 'Crock-Pot' case example. List the types of risk that Sunbeam was faced with during this event where the reputation of their leading slow cooker brand was being tarnished on social media. Write a paragraph for each that describes your mitigation strategies.

2 Using the risk matrix, consider the organisation that you currently work for, or have a desire to work for, and map the potential online communication risks that could confront this organisation based on probability versus impact.
3 An organisation whose executive group is all male wants to publish a series of social media posts about International Women's Day activities within the organisation. Follow the four steps of risk analysis to determine the best approach.
4 Consider the outcome of discussion question 3, and map the relevant stake-holders involved in this scenario. Once mapped, consider social identity theory and the impact this might have on the overall outrage factor involved.

Practice tips

• Whenever working in the social media space as a professional communicator, it is essential to carve out opportunities to anticipate, identify and address the ethical, legal and organisational risks of social media use. Every time you are about to use social media, you need to pause to think about the risks for all the stakeholders involved. Once you identify them, you might need to adjust your planned course of action to minimise risk or perhaps take advice from supervisors or lawyers on the safest course of action.
• When posting on social media, consider the intensity of outrage that might be connected to each social media post and map it on a risk matrix to determine the level of risk.

References

Dionne, G. 2019. *Corporate risk management: Theories and applications*. Hoboken, NJ: John Wiley & Sons.
Foss, K.A. 2019. "Death of the slow-cooker or #CROCK-POTISINNOCENT? this is us, parasocial grief, and the crock-pot crisis." *Journal of Communication Inquiry*, *44*(1), 69–89.
Géczy, C., B.A. Minton & C. Schrand. 1997. "Why firms use currency derivatives." *Journal of Finance*, *52*, 1323–1354.
Jaques, T. 2014. *Issue and crisis management: Exploring issues, crises, risk and reputation*. South Melbourne, Victoria: Oxford University Press.
Kasperson, R.E., O. Renn, P. Slovic, H.S. Brown, J. Emel, R. Goble, J.X. Kasperson & S. Ratick. 1988. "The social amplification of risk: A conceptual framework." *Risk Analysis*, *8*(2), 177–187. doi:10.1111/j.1539-6924.1988.tb01168.x
Mian, S.L. 1996. "Evidence on corporate hedging policy." *Journal of Financial and Quantitative Analysis*, *31*, 419–439.
Nance, D., C.W. Smith & C. Smithson. 1993. "On the determinants of corporate hedging." *Journal of Finance*, *48*, 267–284.
Sandman, P.M. 1988. "Risk communication: Facing public outrage." *Management Communication Quarterly*, *2*(2), 235–238. https://doi.org/10.1177/0893318988002002006
Sandman, P.M. 1993. *Responding to community outrage: Strategies for effective risk communication*. Fairfax, VA: American Industrial Hygiene Association.
Sandman, P.M. 2012. *Responding to community outrage: Strategies for effective risk communication*. Fairfax, VA: US Industrial Health Association. First published 1993. http://psandman.com/media/Respondingto CommunityOutrage.pdf

Smith, C.W. & R.M. Stulz. 1985. "The determinants of firms' 'hedging policies'." *Journal of Financial and Quantitative Analysis, 20*, 391–405.

Snider, H.W. 1956. "Reaching professional status: A program for risk management." *Corporate Risk Management: Current Problems and Perspectives: Insurance Series, 112*, 30–35. American Management Association.

Winch, G.M. 2009. *Managing construction projects*. Hoboken, NJ: John Wiley & Sons.

Part 2

Social media attributes contributing to opportunity and risk

4 The role of the audience

Embracing the opportunities social media presents

Glossary

Audience: A group of people with whom you aim to communicate who may benefit from your message or announcement.

Echo chamber: The phenomenon where people connect with others who have similar views on social media, often entrenching those opinions. Also called a 'bubble'.

Public: A wider group of people who may come across your message and have a range of opinions.

Stakeholders: Groups of people who can be impacted by an organisation's decisions and announcements due to the stake they have in the situation.

Unanticipated public: A group of latent publics that can form in a social media environment.

Abstract

This chapter discusses why it is important to engage with an audience via social media. Audiences can engage with the professional communicator directly and can thereby influence the discussion. This interaction establishes how engagement with an identified and desired audience can generate positive impact. For instance, policing organisations worldwide have used social media successfully to enhance public perception by engaging in fun online activities. This chapter discusses the importance of understanding the audience and where they engage. It uses international examples to show how this can be achieved. However, the established voice of the audience can create echo chambers and unanticipated publics and could carry risk. Significant risk exists in some places just by having a social media account that an audience can comment upon. It discusses the need for interaction but explains the ways comments might be managed to ensure risk is reduced.

DOI: 10.4324/9781003180111-6

In this chapter

- Defining the audience
- Finding the right platform
- Strategy
- Ways to engage your audience
- Influencers, celebrity and endorsement
- Case study 4.1 – 'Your Army Needs You' campaign
- Case study 4.2 – Queensland Police Service social media use
- Case study 4.3 – Starbucks #whatsyourname campaign
- Stakeholder theory and the audience
- Discussion questions and project topics
- Practice tips
- Cases cited
- References

Defining the audience

Although the task of defining an audience might appear simple, as was explained in Chapter 2 there has been a merging of the terms 'audience', 'public' and 'stakeholder', and they are sometimes used interchangeably. This chapter looks at 'audience', being the group of people with whom you aim to communicate. Successful social media use starts with knowing who the message is for. Stakeholders and publics continue to play an important function, but before considering their role, you need to identify the intended audience.

Let's first consider the 'public sphere' – which is where people engage. The idea of the public sphere was first developed in the 1960s. This concept focussed on the traditional media being an enabler as it was a platform where information could be shared. Early developments in technology and globalisation meant that this sphere no longer had physical boundaries but became an illusionary sphere because the public had a false perception of participation. This was because most early online communication technology was one-sided. The messages being delivered did not encourage participation. For example, only selected letters to the editors of newspapers were published. Modern technology, however, has created an actual public sphere where engagement is encouraged – and not only between those who know each other. Anyone can engage online, and organisations can target and access the desired audience in a somewhat simpler way.

A 'network society', a term developed in the early 1980s, is used to identify a society where there are no communication boundaries (Castells 2011). As with the public sphere, we now live and work in an environment where communications can travel between parties instantaneously and globally. We need to acknowledge that when these lines of distance and time are blurred, the ideas of hierarchy or status in society can also diminish. Technology – particularly social media – has allowed people more direct channels of communication. A citizen might send a message directly to the account of a celebrity or world leader with little to no human filtering. The theory of social capital is also relevant here. Bourdieu's (1993) initial contribution to the theory looked at the way people obtained and kept their status in society – a hierarchy based on classes. In the professional communication field, the social capital applied is that of reputation and legitimacy for the work being produced. This creates an element of trust between the organisation and the audience. Some argue that after the development of digital technologies, this concept started to fall apart. However, social capital is a relevant concept when understanding reputation and the ways social media can assist in maintaining trust and reputation with the audience. But first you must identify your audience.

The audience is the specific group of people receiving your communication. It likely consists of those who will benefit from your message or announcement. It differs from a public because a public is a group of people who may encounter your message and have a range of opinions about it. Further, it is different from a stakeholder because stakeholders are those who have a stake in the situation. Remember to always consider social identity theory, as it helps to recognise that there could be blurred lines between these groups. You need to take the time to identify both your audience and possible unanticipated publics, being groups who form together in a social media environment. You run the risk of accidentally insulting or antagonising them if you don't use the right language or approach in your social media posts (Wakefield & Knighton 2019).

The nature of social media carries the potential for certain channels to become echo chambers, allowing unexpected trends to develop on topics (Colleoni, Rozza & Arvidsson 2014; Urman 2019; Hanusch & Nölleke 2019). 'Echo chambers' describe the ability for people to connect with other social media users who have similar views and communicate within a 'bubble', where those views can become entrenched. There has been some debate regarding echo chambers (Dubois & Blank 2018; Bruns 2019), particularly around the capacity for social media users to be exposed to non-like-minded viewpoints (Masip, Suau & Ruiz-Caballero 2020). When an echo chamber forms, people with similarities are drawn together and connect despite geographic distance. This creates a stronger voice on the topic and provides increased exposure to non-like-minded people whose views might change to mirror the majority in the bubble, thus creating an unanticipated public. An unanticipated public can have both positive and negative effects. Many social media examples show what can happen when stakeholder groups form publics and come together to voice concern or seek change. When people have opinions and a vested interest, consequences also matter. When the online voice is strengthened, the drive for social change can be significant.

Finding the right platform

There are many platforms used for different forms of communication. As a professional communicator, you must understand the ways your audience communicates so that the messages you are trying to distribute can be found and accessed. Further, you also need to know which platform is best for each message. For instance, a message that is aimed internally at staff within an organisation might not be suitable for the company's Facebook page and might instead be more suited to email or an internal platform like Yammer, Teams or a Facebook Workplace group. During a crisis situation you might choose not to use YouTube because of the time it would take to produce an appropriate clip. You might instead use Twitter or Facebook along with an organisation's website to ensure immediacy.

The complexity of the social media landscape makes this idea daunting, but there are techniques to make it easier to keep across the varying social media platforms when deciding what is most appropriate for the audience. An essential part of this involves monitoring social media for the audience's key topics of interest. You can follow trends and hashtags that relate to your audience to ensure you stay on top of what is interesting to them and use those trends and hashtags to deliver your messages. This chapter will talk a little more about hashtags later, but they are an effective way to get more engagement on messages. Monitoring the topics, trends and hashtags will also point you to the platforms most popular with an audience, which you can then use to create your intended campaign. It is as much about discovering what your audience wants to know and how they want to hear it as it is about deciding what they should know.

Strategy

Social media strategy is an important component of successful social media use and risk minimisation. There are many theories about social media strategy (Effing & Spil 2016; Knight & Cook 2013; Boudreaux 2011) but in this textbook, we look at five key elements to a social media strategy. They are:

- *Context* – What is happening beyond your message that might affect how your communication is received? What are the objectives of both your social media use and of your organisation? How will your message support those objectives?
- *Culture* – What is the culture of your organisation? Is it represented in the proposed social media post or campaign? What are the habits and behaviours of your employees and your audience?
- *Process* – How will you manage your social media accounts and/or posts? What processes exist for monitoring your posts and moderating those of others?
- *Metrics* – How will you measure your success? How will you learn from your mistakes?
- *Policies* – What policies exist within the organisation that will support your use of social media?

The first two points can be explored together because they relate to engaging with the audience. Some of the most successful uses of social media involve organisations or individuals being active on the platform and engaging with the audience. They consistently use their social media accounts to share and inform with content that is interesting and relevant to their audiences. They speak the language of their audiences. For instance, large corporations do not use business jargon. They instead use engaging terms that encourage discussion. See Case Study 4.2 – the Queensland Police Service – later in this chapter as an example of this.

A good social media strategy will also outline a process for social media use. This includes nominating who is responsible for the social media management, determining what level or role is responsible for approving social media use, and it will generally have some protocol regarding the creation of official pages. It is important to have a thorough approval process (also called 'upward referral' or 'escalation' policy) that is speedy and allows for immediacy, particularly when responding to comments. This sounds contradictory, but it is achievable and essential because comments of your audience become your responsibility as host of the comment. A number of cases, including some in Australia, have set this precedent. In 2020, three news organisations were found by the New South Wales Court of Appeal to be responsible for the defamatory comments made by social media followers on an article about 23-year-old former youth detention detainee Dylan Voller (*Voller's case* 2020). (An appeal was being heard by the High Court in 2021.) This is not the first time a ruling of this nature has been made. In 2013 the High Court of South Africa ruled that the responsibility of comments sat with the owner or host of a personal Facebook profile.

A man was sued, and held responsible, by his ex-wife for the comments of his friends on his personal page that were deemed defamatory (*Husband's case* 2013).

Metrics are the most important part of a strategy because they can help to identify the audience and measure the organisation's ability to speak to that group. There are a number of ways professional communicators can boost social media success with the intended audience. One of these is a search engine optimisation strategy which is designed to attract more traffic. There are technical approaches to this type of strategy that we will not go into here, but in basic terms this is a strategy that outlines how the layers of code or words that make up the post can be adjusted to attract both human traffic and algorithms. Metadata also forms part of the optimisation strategy. Metadata is what defines the content. It is the computer-coded explanation behind the scenes. It can include keywords, tags, geo-locational data, IP addresses and author details. For an end user, this could take the form of a hashtag. Hashtags are metadata tags that use words or groups of words linked together with a '#' symbol which makes it a hyperlink or a user-generated tag. Social media users follow hashtags. They are what allow conversations on topics to occur between parties who are not otherwise linked. They are a powerful tool facilitating social movements and the drive for change. The power of hashtags has been witnessed through movements such as #blacklivesmatter (#BLM). By ensuring your content has the right metadata and hashtags you will be more likely to attract the intended audience to your information.

Referral traffic is another important element in drawing the right people to your site, page or information. These sophisticated metric tools allow you to understand how your stories are being distributed online but only work where there is a website link that you are wanting the audience to click. Other metrics that can be gathered and used to measure success include: engagement rate, levels of interactivity (likes, comments, shares) for your posts based on your follower count; impressions (how often a post appears in people's timelines); reach (how many people see your post); and follower growth (the number of followers your page has at any given time compared to previous timeframes). Knowing where your audience communicates and their topics of conversation allows you to better understand them and ultimately share information that will be most appealing.

The final aspect to a social media strategy is policy. This will be discussed in more depth in Chapter 10 when we look at employment law and the role of a social media policy and codes of conduct when using social media both professionally and personally.

Ways to engage your audience

A useful approach to engaging your audience is via user-generated content (UGC). UGC is generally raw, unpolished material provided direct to you for use in professional outputs. It is made by the audience, not usually by professionals, but adds an honest touch to social media campaigns. It is an extremely useful strategy as it is one way to remain current with up-to-date information that you would otherwise not be able to obtain. There is so much that happens across the world, and communicators can be in only one place at a time. UGC allows the relevant information to come to you. It can be edited and incorporated into a professional package to help deliver appropriate news within tight timeframes.

UGC is becoming increasingly more important. Technology has brought the world closer together, so this means that professional communicators must be able to inform audiences about events occurring anywhere and any time. UGC is one of the best options for being kept abreast of events that you cannot attend or ways your products are being used or consumed. It should be used because it provides a layer of information, often direct from the centre of a situation, that can provide greater detail to your target audience. There are a number of ways that UGC can be incorporated. It can be provided as raw, unedited footage or information to support an existing story or campaign. It can also be used to live blog a crisis or promote a campaign.

The portable action camera brand, GoPro, has long been seen as the leader in UGC, having commenced using UGC for campaign production in 2015. Its social media channels are filled with content created by its audience. It seeks UGC through specific hashtags and asks the audience to share their experiences when using the cameras. Given this is a brand that is aimed at thrill seekers, the results can be breathtaking. It is also quite unique in that the promotional material presented by GoPro on its social media accounts rarely shows the product, only what it can do through the eyes of its customers.

Another great example of UGC is the 'FedEx in the wild' campaign, which encouraged customers to snap and share photos of FedEx vehicles from anywhere across the world. FedEx then uses these images on Instagram, creating a platform of only UGC. As a result, the company reported a more than 400% increase in follower growth during the first nine months of the campaign and received more than 1,000 images a week to filter through and choose the best for further promotion on Instagram. While not all images make it to the Instagram page, all are promoting the organisation through the use of the hashtag.

Crowdsourcing is another way of engaging the audience but is generally data-driven. In a similar way to UGC, it allows communicators to access information otherwise not available to them. Crowdsourcing could be as simple as asking your followers to complete a survey, asking for traffic updates while commuters are on their way to work or requesting up-to-date information from those in a crisis area during a disaster. However, some commercial companies are using crowdsourcing to develop successful advertisements. The main difference between crowdsourcing and UGC is that with crowdsourcing, the professional communicators remain in control with the opportunity to seek out the information that is needed to deliver the story, message or campaign. If it is data-based information, it can be presented in whatever way they desire to reinforce their message.

While both UGC and crowdsourcing are useful strategies to increase success, benefits must be weighed against risks. With UGC, doctored, dated or stolen content can be submitted as an original contribution by an audience member, which can create its own crisis if reproduced at face value by an organisation. Brand damage and legal damages for breach of copyright can ensue, so any use of UGC or crowdsourcing has to be accompanied by careful screening, verification and attribution protocols.

It is important not to just check the legitimacy of the information but also the *bona fides* of the person providing it to you. Below is a brief checklist of questions you could ask to help start a verification process:

- Who are they? (Can their identity be verified?)
- Why do they have this information?
- Do they have permission to give it to you?
- Why are they giving it to you?
- Who is the source of the information?
- Are you are breaking any laws by accessing it?
- Do you or anyone in your team or organisation have an existing relationship with this person?
- Have you trusted them in the past?

(Knight & Cook 2013)

If you have any concerns about their answers to these questions, you can ask to meet the contributor or speak to them over the phone. You could also check their online identity and confirm it is consistent across platforms. If you have been provided with data-driven information, you could use technology to assist in the verification process by checking the metadata or confirming whether elements of the information match what you already know. It is becoming increasingly important to verify all information to ensure an organisation remains honest and fulfills its corporate social responsibility (CSR).

Influencers, celebrity and endorsement

The rise of influencers on social media platforms has created a new approach to social media success. Big brands and corporations are aligning themselves to influencers and celebrities for endorsements. While celebrity endorsement has long been used in communication campaigns, the use of influencers is relatively new. If your audience has trust in a particular influencer, it may be suitable to approach that person seeking endorsement. It is a popular marketing strategy, and influencer marketing campaigns have generated significant revenue for some companies. It can also be a great boost for public awareness campaigns. In March 2020, Instagram and the World Health Organisation partnered with Instagram influencer Seth Phillips (better known as 'Dude with sign') to promote best health practices related to the worldwide COVID-19 pandemic. Phillips is renowned for protesting against everyday things using cardboard signs that he holds above his head. He has more than 7 million followers on Instagram, and his partnered posts received a high engagement rate.

However, you must be conscious of potential risks associated with the use of such people. There are many successful social media influencers who are doing excellent work and are responsible, but there are also many who have experienced falls from grace. For instance, Belle Gibson set up an online and social media empire called 'Whole Pantry', claiming her lifestyle cured her of cancer. She generated a significant social media following and made millions through the sale of her book and subscriptions to her app, where she shared insights into the methods she used to heal her cancer. However, her fall from grace was dramatic when it was discovered that her story was a lie. She had fabricated her claims of cancer and other personal details like her upbringing and age. In 2017 she was fined $410,000 by the Australian Federal Court for her deception (*Fake cancer case* 2017).

Another example is vegan blogger Yovana Mendoza, also known as 'Rawvana'. Her online identity, her social media following and her corporate sponsorship are based on her raw vegan diet and lifestyle. The problem arose in 2019 when she was dining with another blogger who filmed her eating a plate of fish. Outrage amongst her followers and sponsors ensued, and she released a lengthy video explaining that she was trialling reincorporating eggs and fish into her diet due to health issues she had encountered. Both of these examples show the possibility of deception on social media, and while influencers and other celebrity endorsements can be a powerful tool to engage with our audience, we must be careful to apply both stakeholder theory and the impact of echo chambers and unanticipated publics to our risk analyses.

Case study 4.1 – 'Your Army Needs You' campaign

The British Army's 2019 recruitment campaign – 'Your Army Needs You' – is an excellent example of a successful campaign that understands the audience. The campaign was the third part to a multi-year recruitment drive with this iteration focusing on the army breaking through past stereotypes and acknowledging young people's potential.

With recruitment being at an all-time low, the British Army needed to take a unique approach. Developed by creative agency Karmarama, the 'Your Army Needs You' campaign focussed on the culture of the target audience. According to Karmarama, the target audience was ambitious and purpose-driven and therefore the campaign had to show that they were valued and desired by the British Army (Karmarama N.D.). Using the historic Lord Kitchener army posters from 1914 as inspiration, the campaign combined images of soldiers with stereotypes like 'snowflake' and 'gaming addict' along with a comment that suggested the potential a person who sat within that stereotype might bring to the army. Despite significant online debate and mocking of the tactics used, particularly the use of potentially insulting terms, the campaign was a resounding success. In the first week the campaign earned a PR reach of 4.8 billion. It was further reported that within the first three weeks of the campaign, recruitment applications doubled from the year prior (Oppenheim 2019), and by September the number of new recruits was at its highest since 2009. There was a strong focus on the audience in this campaign, and the audience was clearly identifiable. The key elements of a strategy were clear; of particular note were context and culture. 'Context' was evident through the detailed research conducted to ensure that the message being delivered would be heard. 'Culture' was also evident through the campaign's use of the audience's habits and behaviours to deliver a message targeted at them.

Case study 4.2 – Queensland Police Service social media use

The Queensland Police Service (QPS) started using social media in 2009. Although it had a slow uptake to begin with, it proved an essential communication tool during the summer disaster events of 2010/11. As Tropical Cyclone Yasi crossed the coast creating a natural disaster and floods that affected 90% of Queensland, the QPS used social media to distribute essential information to its community. As a result, they experienced a significant increase in followers and engagement. The QPS Twitter account, @QPSMedia, was acknowledged as the most reliable source of information during the disaster (Bruns et al. 2012). Using the #qldfloods hashtag, the @QPSMedia account was also the most re-tweeted account (Bruns et al. 2012). QPS used Twitter and other social media platforms successfully to speak directly to their audience with important situational advice and information. Although this disaster event gave their social media pages a boost, it has been the ongoing management that has continued the success. Australians' national identity includes a purported 'laidback' nature, and the QPS drew on this in the approach to social media by incorporating humour and puns into their posts. Police are notorious for using jargon that makes sense to police only. Instead, they incorporated well timed cultural references into posts. For instance, when the final season of *Game of Thrones* was aired they connected with the audience by incorporating relevant hashtags into posts such as:

> Please don't call Triple Zero (000) to report deaths at Winterfell, it is not in our jurisdiction and we have no dragons. #GameofThrones

They used quirky humour to help boost mundane announcements and ensure they were noticed:

> Psst! Don't tell the toddler in your life, but the wheels on the truck on Beaudesert Road/Logan Mwy overpass at Parkinson are not going round and round – the truck is broken down. Heavy traffic delays already being experienced – please be patient. #bnetraffic

Social media is used by the QPS to engage in a two-way conversation with the audience and encourage the public to get involved when reporting people of interest or when finding missing persons. However, the QPS has been criticised for allowing critical public comments on their posts about high profile cases. By 2021 they had more than one million followers on Facebook, which equated to 20% of the Queensland population and was almost double that of the largest Queensland newspaper, the *Courier-Mail*, and about the same as the national Facebook following of Australian television network Channel 7.

Case study 4.3 – Starbucks #whatsyourname campaign

In 2020 Starbucks won the Channel 4 Diversity in Advertising award in the United Kingdom and launched its #whatsyourname campaign. The idea for the campaign was developed out of real experiences of transgender people and those transitioning who chose to test their new names at a Starbucks coffee shop. Starbucks is well known for asking customers for a name to be written on the side of the coffee cup for orders. The campaign depicted a young transitioning boy who continued to be called by his birth name of Jemma. It elegantly portrayed the struggles that a young transitioning person experienced and how this could have an effect on their emotional state. However, being given an opportunity to test out his chosen name of James in a safe and non-judgmental environment provided some contentment. This campaign was successful because it resonated with its audience. Using real stories and experiences of customers added a personal connection with those that the campaign aimed to impact. Starbucks also partnered with United Kingdom charity Mermaids, who were the leading support of transgender, non-binary and gender diverse youth. This collaboration further underscored the way in which Starbucks sought to understand the audience. Engaging the main charity for the target audience meant they had access to appropriate guidance regarding casting and the representation of the stories being told. They used real people rather than actors, providing an honest approach to the topic. Starbucks also showed insight into their customer base, not just the immediate target audience, but of the wider community who at that time held equality and diversity high on its expectation of large corporations. Using a shareable hashtag – '#whatsyourname' – allowed for UGC in the format of real stories of people sharing their own journey.

Stakeholder theory and the audience

Stakeholder theory remains an important consideration when determining the audience for your social media use. As outlined in the first section of this chapter, the terms 'audience', 'public' and 'stakeholder' are often used interchangeably, but a stakeholder is someone with a stake or investment (financial, emotional or values-driven) in the situation at hand. It is important for you to recognise the difference between the three groups and ensure you put effort into establishing the stakeholders involved in both your general social media use and targeted social media use. Stakeholder mapping is a useful starting point. Recall from Chapter 2 that the concept behind stakeholder mapping is that an organisation should respond to stakeholders who have a higher level of power but also a higher level of interest in the activities of the entity. While there is a very strong chance that you will see your target audience high on this list, there will likely be other groups who need to be considered, as it only takes one unanticipated public to destroy an otherwise effective campaign. Consider Case Study 2.1 outlined in Chapter 2, highlighting the Heart Foundation's 'Heartless words' campaign. They had a clear audience and had identified specifically who the campaign was targeting. But as outlined in that chapter, what was not considered were the stakeholder groups who could have been affected by the campaign who ultimately created an unanticipated public. It is essential that you identify stakeholders with both high power and high interest and work closely with them through regular communication and monitor what these groups are saying. Social identity theory is also of particular note given the potential for our stakeholders to exist in other groups including unanticipated publics and targeted audiences.

Discussion questions and project topics

1   Choose a social media campaign that resonated with you and consider who the target audience was. In what ways do you fit within this target audience? Why did it resonate with you? How might it have been improved?
2   Consider your organisation's use of social media. Which of the five points of a social media strategy are present? Take note of the processes set out for moderation.
3   Using one of the case studies presented in this chapter, define the audience. Then conduct a full stakeholder map and identify potential social identity crossovers and where unanticipated publics might emerge.

Practice tips

- When seeking UGC in a campaign or social media post, ensure you include some parameters or terms of use around audience participation. Consider content from Chapter 5 regarding the potential legal issues that can arise.
- Always verify information received from your audience using the checklist in this chapter.
- Consider after-hours moderation. Many organisations use clauses in the terms of use that specify the hours the page is unmoderated. The 24/7 nature of social media means moderation should also be conducted 24 hours a day, seven days a week, and consideration should be given to a rostered approach to after-hours moderation. Some legal cases support this approach.

Cases cited

Fake cancer case. 2017. *Director of Consumer Affairs Victoria v Gibson* [2017] FCA 240. <www.austlii.edu. au/cgi-bin/viewdoc/au/cases/cth/FCA/2017/240.html>

Husband's case. 2013. *Isparta v Richter and Another (22452/12)* [2013] ZAGPPHC 243; 2013 (6) SA 529 (GNP). 4 September. <www.saflii.org/za/cases/ZAGPPHC/2013/243.html>

Voller's case. 2020. *Fairfax Media Publications; Nationwide News Pty Ltd; Australian News Channel Pty Ltd v Voller* [2020] NSWCA 102. 1 June. <www.austlii.edu.au/cgi-bin/viewdoc/au/cases/nsw/ NSWCA/2020/102.html>

References

Boudreaux, C. 2011. "Chapter 2: How to develop a social media strategy." In N. Smith, R. Wallan & C. Zhou (eds.), *Social media management handbook: Everything you need to know to get social media working in your business.* Hoboken: Wiley.

Bourdieu, P. 1993. *The field of cultural production: Essays on art and literature.* New York: Columbia University Press.

Bruns, A. 2019. *Are filter bubbles real?* Cambridge: Polity.

Bruns, A., J.E. Burgess, K. Crawford & F. Shaw. 2012. *#qldfloods and @QPSMedia: Crisis communication on Twitter in the 2011 South East Queensland floods.* Brisbane: ARC Centre of Excellence for Creative Industries and Innovation, Queensland University of Technology.

Castells, M. 2011. *The rise of the network society.* Germany: Wiley.

Colleoni, E., A. Rozza & A. Arvidsson. 2014. "Echo chamber or public sphere? Predicting political orientation and measuring political homophily in Twitter using big data." *Journal of Communication,* *64,* 317–332. doi:10.1111/jcom.12084

Dubois, E. & G. Blank. 2018. "The echo chamber is overstated: The moderating effect of political interest and diverse media." *Information, Communication & Society, 21*(5), 729–745. https://10.1080/1 369118X.2018.1428656

Effing, R. & T. Spill. 2016. "The social strategy cone: Towards a framework for evaluating social media strategies." *International Journal of Information Management, 36*(1), 1.

Hanusch, F. & D. Nölleke. 2019. "Journalistic homophily on social media." *Digital Journalism, 7*(1), 22–44. doi:10.1080/21670811.2018.1436977

Karmarama. N.D. *The British Army.* www.karmarama.com/the-british-army/

Knight, M. & C. Cook. 2013. *Social media for journalists: Principles & practice.* London: Sage.

Masip, P., J. Suau & C. Ruiz-Caballero. 2020. "Incidental exposure to non-like-minded news through social Media: Opposing voices in echo-chambers news feeds." *Media and Communication, 8*(4), 53.

Oppenheim, M. 2019. "Army recruitment applications 'almost double after snowflake millennial ad campaign'." *The Independent.* Accessed 27 October 2020. www.independent.co.uk/news/ uk/home-news/british-army-recruitment-snowflake-millennial-advertising-campaign-phone- zombies-a8771176.html

Urman, A. 2019. "Context matters: Political polarization on Twitter from a comparative perspective." *Media, Culture & Society.* https://doi.org/10.1177/0163443719876541

Wakefield, R. & D. Knighton. 2019. "Distinguishing among publics, audiences, and stakeholders in the social media era of unanticipated publics." *Public Relations Review, 45*(5), 101821. doi:10.1016/j. pubrev.2019.101821

5 Managing legal risk in a wired world

General and specific approaches to minimising damage for stakeholders

Glossary

Jurisdiction: The extent to which a particular court or state has legal authority to hear legal actions. This might be limited by physical borders – the place of publication – or determined by the legislative ambit of a court's power.

Legal risk: The level of exposure to legal consequences of a particular act. In social media, this can include the potential responsibility under criminal or civil law for posting or hosting infringing material.

Professional liability insurance: Also known as 'professional indemnity insurance', this insures against a range of potential risks, including legal acts or omissions by organisations or individuals. Legal coverage can include protection against the financial impact of defamation, personal injury and professional negligence claims.

Social media law: The laws applying to the communication of material via social media which could involve criminal or civil liability.

Abstract

Complex legal issues are the work of lawyers, but social media managers need enough basic knowledge to identify and assess legal risks to prevent exposure, minimise damage and decide whether legal advice is needed. This chapter introduces both general and specific social media legal risk assessment procedures for professional communicators. It offers strategies for becoming familiar with some of the key laws of social media and using them to reduce exposure to legal risks. It establishes the boundaries of social media law and explores the legal implications of a globalised and interconnected world where cultures, systems and jurisdictions can have unexpected consequences. Using selected international cases, it shows how a legal risk management approach might have avoided costly litigation and unnecessary brand damage.

DOI: 10.4324/9781003180111-7

In this chapter

- Defining social media law and legal risk
- Communication and social media law in historical context
- Strategies for minimising legal risk: general and specific approaches for analysis
- Key legal areas of risk with social media
- Jurisdiction: legal implications of a globalised and interconnected world
- Case study 5.1 – Legal risk of political speech in the United States versus Australia
- Case study 5.2 – The Volvo photo shoot case
- Stakeholder theory and social media law
- Discussion questions and project topics
- Practice tips
- Cases cited
- References

Defining social media law and legal risk

What is social media law, which legal topics does it encompass and how does it differ from earlier communication and media laws? Experts will have a range of answers to these questions, depending upon how broadly they wish to cast their net and their preferred areas of focus. The parameters of social media law for the purposes of this book are the topics that are most likely to arise in the work of social media hosting and posting within an organisation, and those where risk assessment strategies might be applied most effectively. With that in mind we define social media law as the main communication laws and regulations impacting the work of social media professionals internationally. These laws and regulations encompass a range of risks to be assessed.

Legal risks of social media could involve various criminal or civil penalties or punitive actions by regulatory bodies. At their extreme, social media managers could face jail terms or hefty fines under the criminal law, court orders to pay damages or to refrain from publishing under civil actions or regulatory decisions that could damage their brand with their customers, peers and industry organisations. Specific legal risks arise in association with particular laws, while organisations also need strategies for assessing their ongoing general social media legal risks. Both general and specific approaches are covered in this chapter.

Communication and social media law in historical context

Social media law is a quite recent extension of communication, and media law can be traced back through recorded history. In fact, many would argue laws to do with communication were foundational to most civilisations. In Ancient Greece in 399 BC, when Socrates refused to agree with the Athens city-state's views on deities, he was sentenced to death by means of drinking the poison hemlock in an early Western European example of communication law controlling his speech.

Further back in history – and even through to modern times – many indigenous peoples had strict cultural rules about who could communicate certain topics of conversation and stories. For example, the Anangu people of the central western desert regions of Australia have long had Aboriginal law called Tjukurpa, under which only designated elders have permission to relate via stories, ritual dances, rock art or ritual objects. Rules around age, gender and ceremonial attendance control this information flow, an ancient form of communication law, with cultural consequences for its breach (Parks Australia 2013–2020, 2). In Samoa, tradition dictated that the mere questioning of an elder was taboo (Masterton 1985). In an historical sense, all of these rules and customs related to a kind of 'social' media, well before the term 'social media' existed as we know it today.

Communication laws have always been used by governments and the courts to restrict the many ways people communicate in a society. In the realm of media law, two of the areas of law examined in this book – defamation and contempt – date back hundreds of years in the English legal system, with the former originally tried in the ecclesiastical (church) courts because an attack on someone's reputation was seen to be an assault on their soul. Contempt laws date back to at least Saxon times, when judges used their royal authority to punish any citizens who defied them. Both continue as important risks for social media professionals today in a globalised and interconnected world where cultures, systems and jurisdictions can have unexpected consequences.

Social media emerged from a number of niche networks to mass audiences in the early 21st century via platforms including LinkedIn (2003), Facebook (2004), YouTube (2005), Twitter (2006) and Instagram (2010). (See Chapter 1 for an expanded timeline). Their common features of instant global interactions between millions of users – without the need for gatekeeping intermediaries like hosts or news organisations – meant that traditional media laws suddenly applied in a challenging new context. Everyone who posted became a publisher and was subject to the same laws over their communication as newspaper editors, television producers and book authors had been previously, but most were blissfully ignorant of their rights and responsibilities. That remains so today, as witnessed by the insults, threats and cyberbullying we see in comment threads and hear about on 24/7 news channels, particularly when celebrities or high-profile citizens become the protagonists or the victims in social media attacks or mishaps. However, communication professionals can no longer plead ignorance as an excuse for a social media legal oversight – if they ever could. There are now enough legal cases and tranches of targeted legislation internationally to establish this as a specific area of knowledge essential for minimising risk in a wired world. Social media law has become its own field of knowledge, involving the combination of the existing media laws with the special cases, statutes and regulations addressing the particular technologies and circumstances of mass many-to-many forms of communication. As a communication professional, you need to know enough about it to conduct a basic risk analysis and to decide whether you then need expert help.

Strategies for minimising legal risk: general and specific approaches for analysis

There are many approaches to minimising social media legal risk, depending upon a range of variables. This chapter offers approaches to help assess: a. an organisation's overall social media legal risk ('general social media legal risk') and; b. a particular social media legal risk ('specific social media legal risk').

Assessing your general social media legal risk

It is important to conduct an assessment of your organisation's ongoing exposure to social media legal risk. The elements of this risk assessment should apply to all organisations, though the significance of each element will vary according to the type of organisation and its social media goals and interactions. As a starting point, it is vital to understand that no organisation has zero social media legal risk. That is because any activity by an organisation or its staff on social media can carry a legal risk, and even if an organisation had minimal social media presence (like the example of Apple in Chapter 3) or if they have even banned all personnel from using social media, then legal risks could still arise via the activities of external parties on social media.

These ten questions are the key to establishing an organisation's general social media legal risk:

1 On what social media platforms does the organisation have a social media presence?

Different platforms carry varying levels of legal risk. For example, in some jurisdictions your organisation can be held responsible for the comments of others on its Facebook site, as explained in Chapters 6 and 11. However, the nature of the Twitter platform means you have no control over the comments of others and are therefore not legally responsible for them because you are not 'hosting' their tweets (unless you re-tweet or link to them, of course). Importantly, some organisations have an inactive, static presence on some platforms which can have legal dangers. It is better to commit fully to particular social media channels and own that decision.

2 Where is the organisation based and where does it have a presence?

Social media is published internationally so it is vital to understand the laws of the jurisdiction where your organisation is headquartered as well as those where it has some kind of legal presence. Legal actions can stem from beyond your borders because social media is often deemed to be published from wherever it is downloaded rather than uploaded, but you are most vulnerable when you do business in a certain locality or have agents or employees based there.

3 How effectively and frequently are the social media sites moderated?

Regular and effective moderation of social media channels is central to the minimisation of legal risk. Courts will look to the methods and frequency of moderation to determine liability in actions stemming from material posted to your sites – by both your own personnel and by third parties. The courts will consider whether there was a 'reasonable' level and frequency of moderation when deciding whether you were responsible and, if so, the extent of your liability. (See Chapter 11).

4 What personnel have responsibility for the posting and moderation?

It is vital that your organisation establishes clearly who is responsible for both the posting and sharing of social media posts on behalf of the organisation and moderation of the various corporate sites and platforms. This needs to be stated specifically in personnel work profiles and position descriptions. Further, responsibility needs to be assigned at a secondary, or perhaps tertiary, level for when those individuals are absent or off duty. Legal risk escalates when there are gaps in this process. It is important to distinguish between organisational responsibility and legal responsibility for a publication. A range of individuals involved in the communication process – as well as the leadership and the organisation itself – can carry legal responsibility and face criminal or civil action.

5 What level of social media experience and legal knowledge do those personnel have?

The days may have passed when social media duties were assigned to the youngest and most inexperienced person in the office because they were active social media users in their personal lives. However, it is vital that professional communicators responsible for posting to organisational social media sites, or moderating those sites, have at least a basic level of experience or training in an organisational (rather than merely personal) use of social media and at least a rudimentary level of social media law knowledge, such as that acquired during a university media law course.

6   What level of social media experience and legal knowledge do their supervisors have?

It is also important that those who are supervising social media managers have a basic understanding of social media in an organisational context, as well as some knowledge of the law of the field. They need this to determine whether professional legal advice is needed.

7   What is the level of access to internal or external legal advice within the organisation?

Importantly, the degree of access to professional legal advice is a factor in assessing social media legal risk. Clearly, the basic knowledge of social media professionals and their supervisors will sometimes serve only to sound alarm bells because formal legal advice is needed. Risk escalates if the organisation's budget does not include a line for legal advice or if relationships are not already in place with a law firm with expertise in social media law.

8   Does the organisation's social media policy cover acceptable use of social media by employees?

With personal use of social media a fact of everyday life in the 21st century, there is a legal obligation on organisations to spell out the extent to which employees can make use of social media in their lives, particularly if it reflects in some way upon the workplace. Jurisdictional obligations vary, but employers need to ensure they have up-to-date social media policies that are reasonable in their requirements, well matched to their type of business or enterprise, communicated frequently and effectively to staff, and introduced and updated with adequate training programs. If organisations have fallen short in such matters, some courts have deemed their dismissal of employees for misuse of social media as unfair and have demanded reinstatement or compensation.

9   Does the social media policy include a legal escalation process?

It is vital that all social media professionals understand the organisational protocols and chains of command involved in escalating a legal matter. What if something appears in a corporate social media feed that is discriminatory, defamatory or contemptuous? Who decides whether legal advice is required? Who is authorised to approve referral of a problem to a lawyer? Whose call is it to agree to that advice and take actions that could be costly, including the publication of apologies, retractions, blocking of accounts and offers of settlement? Organisations will differ in their approaches to this, but the most important thing is that a process is documented, and that staff are made aware of it.

10   To what extent do the organisation's insurance policies cover the legal consequences of social media?

Whether you are a sole operator or a social media manager of a large organisation, a key legal risk minimisation option is to take out insurance against the legal costs and damages that can arise from litigation over social media posts and moderation. This might be negotiated directly with insurance brokers or purchased as part of a professional indemnity/liability insurance policy, either directly from a provider or via an industry-based association.

This is not a quantitative list, where a certain number of ticks or percentage scores adds up to your organisation's social media legal risk. The fact is that a single shortcoming in just one of these ten areas could prove extremely costly to an organisation – in the form of court costs, criminal penalties or damages payouts in addition to any brand damage caused along the way.

The analysis is best completed in an open-ended way, where notes can be entered against each question to trigger further investigation and policy development, as illustrated in Table 5.1, which gives an example of analysis of a small fictional Canadian PR agency's social media general legal risk.

Of course, this could be a much longer list, particularly for organisations that are dealing with highly contentious social media discussion and for those that have particular regulatory obligations controlling the material they can post and host, such as those in the financial, health, pharmaceutical, alcohol and gambling industries. Most social media professionals need enough basic knowledge to be able to identify and assess legal risks to prevent exposure, minimise damage and to decide whether legal advice might be needed so they can refer upwards in their reporting chain.

Assessing a specific legal risk

Legal risk assessment comes into stark focus at the professional communicator's desk when legally dubious material is about to be posted or hosted or has already appeared in an organisation's social media channels. An organisation can have more confidence in this process if the general social media risk analysis has been conducted and actioned effectively (as in Table 5.1). The specific social media legal risk analysis relies upon a combination of experience and knowledge of the social media law topics covered in this book and a sound knowledge of the organisation and its stakeholders. The five-step process involves:

1 **Identifying the potential (or existing) legal problem**

   This step immediately justifies the need for social media professionals to know and understand the key areas of the law affecting their work, and for the general legal risk analysis to have been implemented effectively. After all, how might someone identify a potential or existing legal problem if he or she does not understand the basic topics of social media law? Only then might one recognise that a post damages someone's reputation, impacts an upcoming court case, invades someone's privacy, breaches copyright or perhaps features discriminatory material. A rudimentary working knowledge is necessary here, which hopefully you will have gained as you work through this book.

2 **Reviewing the areas of the law involved**

   Once the particular legal hazards have been identified, it is time to swot up on those topic areas to revise and refresh the key elements as they apply to the key jurisdictions

Table 5.1 Sample social media legal risk analysis for small communications agency 'Optimal Solutions PR' (fictional)

Social media general legal risk analysis	Current status	Action required
1. **On what social media platforms does the organisation have a social media presence?**	Facebook, Twitter and Instagram.	Assess priorities and consider need for corporate YouTube account or other relevant accounts for platforms where key audiences are present.
2. **Where is the organisation based and where does it have a presence?**	Headquarters in Toronto, Canada, with representatives in Hong Kong and Mumbai.	Consider impact of Canadian, Chinese and Indian law on all accounts and posts.
3. **How effectively and frequently are the social media sites moderated?**	Facebook and Instagram are used and checked daily, but Twitter is neglected.	Build daily moderation schedule into all three accounts and review need for Twitter feed.
4. **What personnel have responsibility for the posting and moderation?**	All ten staff can post to the accounts at will, but only Rajiv has moderation duties.	Channel all social media post suggestions through Rajiv for checking and approval and have an alternate to Rajiv trained to deputise for him in his absence.
5. **What level of social media experience and legal knowledge do those personnel have?**	Rajiv did a media law course as part of his Comms degree. Two years' previous experience in social at large firm.	He graduated seven years ago so he needs a social media law refresher. We need to select his deputy carefully on these criteria.
6. **What level of social media experience and legal knowledge do their supervisors have?**	Rajiv reports directly to CEO Sharon who has strong socials background but no legal training.	Sharon needs to do a media law short course, or delegate this role to office manager, Halim, who has a law degree.
7. **What is the level of access to internal or external legal advice within the organisation?**	No problems to date (thank goodness), so this needs to be set up.	CEO Sharon to get details from law firms with social media law expertise on costs and procedures.
8. **Does the organisation's social media policy cover acceptable use of social media by employees?**	Yes, policy requires staff to use personal accounts carefully and not bring the firm into disrepute.	Needs to be updated to be more specific in its boundaries, inclusive of new social media channels, communicated to staff and featured in an online training module.
9. **Does the social media policy include a legal escalation process?**	No.	This must be included, stating CEO Sharon must be advised if legal matter arises, and only she can engage the lawyers or act on the matter.
10. **To what extent do the organisation's insurance policies cover the legal consequences of social media?**	There is a corporate professional indemnity policy via PR association, but defamation claims are limited to $100,000.	Investigate higher coverage with alternative providers given the potential for much higher costs and damages.

where you are publishing. This basic research might set your mind at rest that some of the required elements of a legal action have not been met, or perhaps that a common defence clearly applies to the situation.

3   Projecting the possible consequences for stakeholders

Just because something is legal does not mean it should be published. Legal analysis must take into account other elements of stakeholder theory and risk analysis, so you need to work through the possible implications of the material for stakeholders in your organisation, including at least customers, staff, shareholders, management, industry groups, interest groups and community associations, among others (see Chapter 2). Brand reputation is central here too, because legal infringements can be damaging beyond the walls of a courtroom. Your brand can be impacted by media coverage or social media discussion about you having hosted material breaching copyright or damaging the reputation of a popular celebrity. Of course, for the most obvious gaffes a quick deletion of an item can be a wise move, but you would need to screen capture it first (for future reference) before working through the other steps of risk assessment.

4   Seeking advice/referring upward

Once your rudimentary review of the problem, the related law, and any potential impact on stakeholders has been conducted, if you are still in any doubt you need to take advice from experienced colleagues and perhaps refer upward for potential legal advice if there is not a clear way forward.

5   Publishing/amending/deleting/correcting/apologising

Only then, and subject to any advice and instructions from supervisors and lawyers, would you take steps to publish, amend, delete, correct or apologise for a post. While the 24/7 pressures of social media publishing might seem to demand instant action, the time involved in pausing for all of this momentary reflection and review can pay significant dividends – in the form of saved brand reputation, stakeholder confidence and loyalty and in avoiding expensive damages claims and legal costs.

Table 5.2, which follows, applies this five-point legal risk analysis process to a Facebook comment stream on a fictional local government's page after an image was posted after an organisational event.

Key legal areas of risk with social media

By now it should be clear you need a basic understanding of the main areas of social media law to be able to analyse social media risk effectively. We have chosen those topics that communication professionals are most likely to face on a frequent basis in posting to their organisations' social media accounts and when hosting the comments and posts of others. These include defamation (including libel and slander, and associated with brand reputation in Chapter 6), privacy and its intrusion including data protection, breach of confidence and harassment and cyberbullying (Chapter 8), inappropriate commentary about court cases (Chapter 9), employment/human resources law and misuse of social media (Chapter 10), posts triggering consumer, corporate and financial regulatory laws (Chapter 11) and intellectual property laws (Chapter 12). An overview of the basic

Table 5.2 Sample specific legal risk analysis for a comment stream on a fictional local government organisation's Facebook page

Social media specific legal risk analysis	Current status	Action required
1. **Identifying the potential (or existing) legal problem**	Your council Facebook page features a picture of a local car dealer bidding at a charity art auction. Someone has posted to the Comment stream: 'Looks like Charlie Manson!' It looks as if the comment has been sitting there for three hours.	Obscure or cryptic comments need to be investigated, particularly if they seem to be joking at someone's expense. Google tells you that Charles Manson was one of the most famous serial killers in the United States.
2. **Reviewing the areas of the law involved**	You know from your media law studies that this is Defamation 101. It implies, albeit in an apparent joke, that the car dealer resembles a famous serial killer. A quick check of your textbook demonstrates the material clearly lowers his reputation or holds him up to ridicule, it identifies him, and has been published to at least one other person, meeting the basic elements of the action.	In most jurisdictions (except perhaps the United States with its First Amendment protections) there would be no defamation defence available for suggesting someone is, or resembles, a serial killer. In some places, the likely lack of serious harm stemming from the defamation might excuse it, but deletion is shaping up as the most sensible response.
3. **Projecting the possible consequences for stakeholders**	Numerous stakeholder consequences could result, including damage to the reputation of an important citizen, denigrating the standing of the council's social media presence, encouraging other insults, embarrassment for council's elected representatives and senior management, and more.	Serious damage could arise on a range of fronts, so swift action is required.
4. **Seeking advice/ referring upward**	Despite the obvious strategy being deletion (after a screen capture), a quick check with a supervisor is wise given there can always be unintended consequences. If the car dealer calls or writes to complain, legal advice will be needed on how to draft a response, so referral upward again would be necessary.	Your supervisor agrees you should delete, but also suggests you explain in a direct message to the poster why you have done so and post the standard reminder message to the Facebook site's community to keep commentary civil.
5. **Publishing/amending/ deleting/correcting/ apologising**	Screen capture then delete or hide the post. If the car dealer calls or writes to complain, legal advice will be needed on how to draft a response, so referral upward again would be necessary.	Further, the supervisor will refer the matter to the Council's lawyer in case the car dealer decides to threaten legal action.

principles of these laws will be covered in those chapters, along with an explanation of some of the starkest differences between leading countries in their approaches and case examples, but social media professionals will need to supplement this with the particularities of the case law and legislation in their own jurisdictions. It is certainly not a comprehensive list of topic areas so extra research needs to be done in important topics like cyberbullying, national security, and denial of service if your organisation is more likely to encounter them.

Jurisdiction: legal implications of a globalised and interconnected world

The term 'jurisdiction' refers to the extent to which a particular court or state/province/nation has legal authority to hear legal actions. This might be limited by physical borders – the place of publication – or determined by the legislative ambit of a court's power. With civil matters like defamation (libel) a plaintiff will need to have an established reputation somewhere before they can sue over publication there. A key Australian High Court case in 2002 (*Gutnick's case* 2002) established that Internet publications were considered 'published' in any jurisdiction where they were downloaded, as distinct from the place where the material had been created and from which it was disseminated. While many social media posts would be about people or organisations in a certain regional area, many others would be about those (perhaps sports stars or celebrities) in other jurisdictions. With criminal matters like contempt of court, the jurisdiction becomes a crucial ingredient because you or your organisation might be subject to jail or fines if you are prosecuted for a breach via social media, and perhaps arrested the next time you transit through that country on your travels.

In this and ensuing chapters carefully selected international cases are used to show how a legal risk management approach might have avoided costly litigation and unnecessary brand damage.

Case study 5.1 – Legal risk of political speech in the United States versus Australia

Social media laws and their associated risks can vary markedly across different jurisdictions, even between Western democracies. Compare the legal risks and outcomes of damaging political allegations in Australia and the United States in 2015–2016. In one of Australia's first major defamation cases over communications on Twitter, then national Treasurer, Joe Hockey, sued over a series of newspaper articles, newsagent posters and tweets with the headlines 'Treasurer for Sale' and 'Treasurer Hockey for Sale' (*Treasurer case* 2015). The newspaper articles detailed the 'privileged access' Hockey had offered to donors to his conservative political party's fundraising body (the North Sydney Forum), in the form of exclusive attendance at briefing events where he would provide his inside and expert view on his government's financial policies. The Federal Court held that the longer newspaper articles published by the newspaper defendant had given enough context to the headings to avoid the imputation (meaning) that Treasurer Hockey was corrupt (which he was not). However, the court decided that some readers who viewed the tweets might not look beyond the bare heading to read the linked story, and thus might be left with the bare headline words alone, which could imply Hockey was corrupt. This was never the intention of the newspapers, which only set out to imply that donors were paying the fundraising body for special access to the Treasurer. Hockey was awarded $200,000 in damages over the shorter, headline-style communications including printed news posters and the tweets.

Contrast this with the allegations tweeted by then presidential candidate Donald Trump against his 2016 election opponent Hillary Clinton at about the same time. He had already dubbed her 'Crooked Hillary', implying she was corrupt in her handling of thousands of emails in her private account and allegedly deleting many of them. But on 3 July 2016 he took a step too far by tweeting 'Crooked Hillary – Makes History!' with an image featuring the results of a Fox News poll stating 58% of Americans believed she was corrupt, and his own campaign's image of her face with piles of cash behind her, stamped with a six-pointed red star with the words 'Most Corrupt Candidate Ever!' (The star was changed to a circle after public condemnation of religious discrimination because it looked like the Jewish Star of David, another difference from Australian law, which has a Racial Discrimination Act.)

In stark contrast with the Australian case where there was a veiled and unintended imputation of corruption against the Treasurer, United States law offered Clinton no hope of suing Trump over his much more blatant defamatory assertion of her corruption. That is because the Australian and the United States legal systems have developed quite different approaches to defamatory (or libellous) comments about so-called public figures. In the United States, if someone is a public figure (a term including almost anyone with a public office or public profile), then scathing statements can be made about them without risk of defamation unless they can prove that the statements were both false and 'malicious' – with challenging hurdles to prove either. This is because laws infringing free expression have been shaped by the United States First Amendment over many decades. Australia lacks any such written constitutional protection of free speech, so the defendant newspaper company in the Hockey case was left having to prove either that the meaning of corruption did not arise (which it did), that it was true (which it was not), that it was merely their intended opinion (which it was not) or that it was overwhelmingly in the public interest and that they had a duty to convey an imputation of corruption to the public (qualified privilege, which they failed to establish). In short, Clinton would have had a much better case against Trump if she had been able to sue him for defamation in Australia.

The lesson here for social media managers is that jurisdiction plays a crucial role in legal risk analysis. Given social media communications are disseminated internationally, an important part of the risk assessment process is to consider what legal issues arise in other jurisdictions about the individuals and organisations being mentioned in social media posts. Thus it is vital to pause and reflect upon who is the subject of the material and where they are able to sue, and to factor that into the content of the communication and the decision on whether to seek legal advice.

Case study 5.2 – The Volvo photo shoot case

A specialist automotive photographer and his model filed suit for a range of actions against the Volvo motor company in the United States in 2020 over a series of their images that were used by Volvo in an advertising and marketing campaign after the photographer had posted a selection on his Instagram account.

The plaintiffs (photographer Jack Schroeder and model Britni Sumida) claimed representatives from Volvo had twice messaged them asking permission to use the images for free after he had published some samples of the photo shoot featuring the model and the new Volvo S60 car in the Californian desert in bloom with wildflowers. He claimed he had responded, stating he was a professional and they would need to negotiate a fair price and terms for their use, and directed them to his website to showcase to them some more images from the shoot. Schroeder claimed Volvo proceeded to use photos from both his Instagram account and his website as the feature items in its own 'Volvo Car USA' Instagram account for its campaign without his permission and he sued for copyright infringement. Sumida claimed the photo shoot was meant only for her portfolio and that she had been hired to model in ads for a different car group with a term of her contract banning work for competing automotive companies. She sued for unfair competition, false endorsement and misappropriation of her likeness under United States state and federal laws. The plaintiffs claimed Volvo continued to use the images in various forms even after being notified of the breach (*Volvo photo shoot case* 2020).

In their defence motion, Volvo argued that by sharing his photos on Instagram, Schroeder had granted Volvo a direct licence to reshare them, referring to Instagram's terms of service stating that user content could be 're-shared by others' after they have been made public. They argued the actions should be dismissed immediately. A decision in their favour on this argument would be groundbreaking in copyright law (as explained in Chapter 12). The case was still proceeding as this book was in production, but it offers useful lessons for our understanding of social media legal risk analysis.

We don't know the internal machinations and legal escalation processes within Volvo's communications and marketing team in the lead-up to the case and afterwards. It could be that their legal team advised them from the outset to take this bold approach that 'freely viewed equals freely used', though the emails to the photographer seeking permission early on indicate they were at least attempting to get his licence to use the images. A simple search for the names of the parties gives an indication of the potential damage to the prestige car company caused by the legal action and its coverage. Whatever the outcome of the case, Volvo might well conduct a review of the processes that led to the dispute, including the key questions we have covered in our social media legal risk analyses – general and specific – covered in this chapter. These might include examining the level of social media experience and training in media law of the key personnel involved in the decisions to seek the photographer's permission and then proceeding to post the images to Instagram, the point at which legal advice was sought (legal escalation policy), and the involvement of senior management and the legal team in Volvo's written communications with the plaintiffs. Either side could win the case, or perhaps a mediated settlement will be reached. You might conduct your own research to see how the case has proceeded.

Stakeholder theory and social media law

As we illustrated in Table 5.2, you need to consider the implications of a potential legal problem upon a range of stakeholders when assessing legal risks of social media. Stakeholder theory and risk management theory hold many lessons for social media legal risk analysis. This starts with stakeholder mapping and acknowledging social identity theory along with outrage factors including outrage amplification. Let us revisit the scenario from Table 5.2 and map the relevant stakeholders involved in this social media situation. We must keep in mind that by 'power' we mean power to influence the risk. While the government staff managing the page have the power to remove the post, this does not

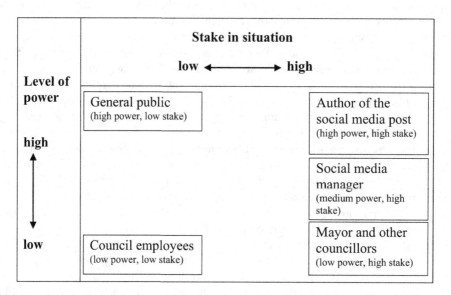

Figure 5.1 Sample stakeholder mapping for a comment stream on a fictional local government organisation's Facebook page

constitute high power, but instead shows medium power as they have some control but not all control over the situation. You will note in Figure 5.1 that the 'general public' carry high power. This is due to the ability for unanticipated publics to form. They will often carry high power and organisations must always factor in potential risks associated with the formation of these groups.

Discussion questions and project topics

1   With time of the essence in social media management, how is it possible to undertake a thorough social media legal analysis while legally dubious material is sitting there on your site? What interim strategies could be adopted?
2   Review the basics of stakeholder theory and explain how several key stakeholder types could be impacted by a blatant breach of copyright on your corporate social media site. Discuss the legal implications in your jurisdiction.
3   Contact someone you know whose organisation has a social media presence. Discuss with them how the general social media legal analysis might apply to their organisation and work with them to fill out the table with the key questions and actions.
4   The managing director of your main competitor firm has been arrested and charged with aggravated sexual assault and will face trial next month. You want to post a news story about the arrest on your Facebook page. Conduct a specific social media legal analysis on this situation. (You might want to look ahead and skim Chapter 9 to summarise some key legal risks.)

Practice tips

- Knowledge is power in assessing social media legal risk. Get a good local media law reference text and keep it close at hand to consult when the legal alarm bells are ringing. Subscribe to media law blogs and mailing lists to keep up to date with the latest cases and laws.
- Know your organisation's social media policy from cover to cover. Get a copy and see how it rates according to our general social media legal risk chart. Then impress your boss by pointing out how it could be improved.
- Create a blank table for the specific social media legal risk assessment featured in this chapter. Copy it and keep it close at hand so you can fill it in when a social media law issue arises.

Cases cited

Gutnick's case. 2002. *Dow Jones & Company Inc. v Gutnick* [2002] HCA 56. 10 December.

Treasurer case. 2015. *Hockey v Fairfax Media Publications Pty Limited* [2015] FCA 652. <www.austlii.edu.au/cgi-bin/sinodisp/au/cases/cth/FCA/2015/652.html>

Volvo photo shoot case. 2020. *Jack Schroeder et al v. Volvo Group North America*, LLC (2:20-cv-05127). California Central District Court, Filed. 6 September 2020. <www.pacermonitor.com/public/case/34619969/Jack_Schroeder_et_al_v_Volvo_Group_North_America_LLC>

References

Masterton, M. 1985. "Samoa, where questioning is taboo." *Australian Journalism Review*, 7(1&2), 114–115.

Parks Australia. 2013–2020. *Tjukurpa Uluru-Kata Tjuta fact sheet*. Accessed 9 October 2020. https://parksaustralia.gov.au/uluru/pub/fs-tjukurpa.pdf

Part 3

Brand and reputational opportunity and risk

6 Brand, reputational management and defamation on social media

Glossary

Brand: The customer's perception of a product or service.

Defamation (also known as 'slander' or 'libel'): The legal action available to those whose reputations have been demonstrably damaged by others. Most commonly pursued as a civil action with the plaintiff seeking damages or an injunction. Sometimes also a criminal charge.

Defamation defences: A range of legal arguments used to defeat an action for defamation, including (depending on the jurisdiction) truth, fair comment, protected report, and qualified privilege (public interest).

Imputation: The defamatory meaning of a communication, coming either from the direct meaning of the words or images or a meaning derived from 'reading between the lines'.

Reputation: The accumulation of the way in which the organisation is perceived by all stakeholders.

Abstract

Citizens can now engage on topics that matter to them, and echo chambers and unanticipated publics are created which carry the potential to destroy a reputation within minutes. The notion of 'brand' is central to modern marketing, corporate communication and public relations. It is created, nurtured and protected – and incorporates a range of elements. One of the most important is an organisation's reputation among its stakeholders and the broader community. Communication professionals need to monitor public perceptions of their organisation's brand and look for ways to enhance reputation. This chapter discusses the implications for reputation on social media platforms from both brand and legal perspectives. It considers why it is important to engage with audiences via social media and highlights some of the significant risks that come with this multi-channel engagement. Damage to a person's or an organisation's reputation can have legal consequences. Defamation (sometimes referred to as slander or libel) is one of the main legal issues associated with social media publishing. Although it is traditionally an issue for professional publishers, social media now means that everyone is a publisher and we have seen an increase in defamation suits as a result. This chapter points to some key cases that established the legal risks associated with reputation damage on social media posts. It also considers some elements of outrage which link to earlier discussions of echo chambers and unanticipated publics and the risks that arise when emotions are involved. It explains how this creates a platform for people to post to social media in the heat of the moment which can impact their lives and careers forever.

DOI: 10.4324/9781003180111-9

In this chapter

- Defining brand, reputation and defamation
- Brand and reputation on social media: pluses and pitfalls
- Strategies for managing brand and reputation on social media
- Defamation as the legal action over reputational damage
- Defamation in an international context: jurisdictional issues
- Elements of a defamation action
- Common defences to defamation
- Strategies for minimising defamation risk
- Case study 6.1 – Are you responsible for defamatory comments by other people on your organisation's Facebook page?
- Case study 6.2 – The Cyprus property case: defamation action might not restore a reputation
- Stakeholder theory and reputational management
- Discussion questions and project topics
- Practice tips
- Cases cited
- References

Defining brand, reputation and defamation

Brand and reputation as marketing terms are often confused and used interchangeably, but they are to be treated quite differently. Put simply, brand relates to relevance, whereas reputation relates to legitimacy. Although the legal tool to protect brand is a 'trademark', brand in a marketing context has a stronger focus on the customer base and sits at the heart of marketing products or services. Reputation, however, is a much broader concept and is the accumulation of actions based on the way an organisation is perceived by all stakeholders. We can see the link to stakeholder theory here, specifically the need to understand your stakeholders and the way in which they perceive your organisation and its ethical and moral decisions. It is possible for a reputation to be tarnished but for a brand to stay strong. For instance, in 2016 technology brand Samsung found itself in the middle of a crisis situation when its newly released Galaxy Note 7 started exploding. By October, the company had recalled more than 2 million devices. Despite this disastrous and expensive situation, the brand survived. It was its customer base – those who love the products – who supported its survival. The reputation of the organisation was affected as evidenced by drops in its share price on the stock market, but years later the brand continues to be a top seller. This example highlights the power of the relationship between an organisation and stakeholders. Certainly, there are circumstances that would see an organisation destroyed by reputational damage, but effective strategies to manage both brand and reputation on social media can shore up the success of an organisation and cushion it from unexpected happenings.

As for defamation – the legal action available to those whose reputations have been damaged – this chapter deals with its basic definitions, elements and defences, after first considering the pros and cons of social media for brand and reputation and suggested strategies for managing them.

Brand and reputation on social media: pluses and pitfalls

There is a connection between social media brands and the concept of 'power'. By power, we mean the relationships between a brand and stakeholders as highlighted in the previous section. A successful social media brand will have a certain amount of power within the relationship it has with its audience. Many organisations use social media to affect their brands in a positive way. For instance, airlines and travel industries often use social media to engage with customers and share travel experiences, particularly photographs and video on platforms like Instagram or TikTok, where the use of hashtags connects consumer posts with organisations. Social media opens the doors to many opportunities to engage with the intended audience and solidify the brand within that consumer group. A strong brand with a commitment to corporate social responsibility will enjoy reputational growth. The way in which a brand engages its audience, as discussed in Chapter 4, can support the shareability of content and ultimately reach a wider audience.

The link between stakeholder theory, corporate social responsibility and brand and reputation management presents many opportunities for success. However, organisations – even those with a strong brand and reputation – are not immune to the audience using social media as a means to sway perception. An example of this was when the United States carrier United Airlines forcibly removed a passenger from one of its aircraft in 2017. This incident was recorded on multiple devices and uploaded to social media sites. The viral nature of these videos saw both the brand and reputation of the airline affected. Of course, there was the influence of an accumulation of incidents that impacted this situation, which further reinforces the need for an organisation to encourage advocacy for its brand but also project positivity to other stakeholders.

Strategies for managing brand and reputation on social media

One of the best approaches to managing brand and reputation on social media is by having a social media strategy with a strong focus on engagement. As you will discover throughout this book, it is necessary to balance opportunity and risk, and if an organisation is able to approach social media with a clear strategy, then it will be appropriately prepared for most risks that may arise. A social media strategy is as important as a business plan and should establish goals for the organisation, along with ways to deal with negative comments that might damage its reputation. Strategy provides an overview to be interpreted depending on the incident being addressed. There is a need for flexibility due to the ever-changing nature of social media, which means there are many variables involved in responding to a social media risk. Inviting user-generated content can be a beneficial approach to showing the relationship an organisation has with its customers, ultimately creating the perception of power. User-generated content and engagement through strategy is discussed and defined in Chapter 4 but what can be drawn from this concept is the connection to the audience.

There is also the legal dimension of managing brand and reputation on social media. The best known area of the law associated with reputational damage is defamation (or libel) law – a legal action available to those whose reputations have been damaged by others. We cover this in detail in this chapter. However, several other areas of the law can be associated with brand and reputational damage. For example, some intellectual property laws discussed in Chapter 12 address brand directly – particularly trademark laws which serve to protect symbols and language associated with an organisation's brand from being misappropriated or misrepresented by others. This could take the form of social media activist movements, fundraising campaigns and memes that use or distort trademarks. Consumer and trade practices laws – covered in Chapter 11 – also operate in this space, particularly those asserting false representations or misleading or deceptive conduct in the course of business, where an organisation's brand and reputation can suffer if the entity is accused of such practices. Even the domain of employment law (Chapter 10) can have brand and reputational consequences – particularly if an employee is using social media to disparage corporate personnel or operations, or if word spreads that an employer has dismissed a worker unfairly because of their social media use.

While we focus on defamation law in this chapter, alternative actions are sometimes used. Breach of privacy and confidentiality might be used against organisations over their intrusive social media posts or perhaps over their infringement of data protection laws (Chapter 8). In some places, companies are unable to sue for defamation and some turn to other laws such as the action for injurious (or malicious) falsehood (or 'trade libel'), which requires a plaintiff to prove there has been a malicious and intentional falsehood published about them which has damaged them financially.

Defamation as the legal action over reputational damage

Defamation is the legal action available to those whose reputations have been demonstrably damaged by others. In some jurisdictions it is called 'libel' – which historically referred to defamation in its permanently published form – or 'slander' which refers to defamation in its spoken form. While defamation remains on the criminal statutes as a crime in many places (sometimes known as 'criminal libel' or 'seditious libel'), it is most commonly pursued as a civil action where a plaintiff seeks monetary damages as recompense for their injured reputation or an injunction (a court order to cease publication). As has been established, defamation is rife on social media – where reputations can be lost in an instant as an allegation goes viral without readers checking the accuracy or substance of a claim.

This happened famously to the late conservative British politician Lord McAlpine of West Green in 2012 when allegations against an anonymous member of parliament of the most serious criminal nature had gone viral on Twitter. Opposing Labour identity Sally Bercow tweeted to her more than 56,000 followers: 'Why is Lord McAlpine trending? *Innocent face*'. After commencing and then dropping defamation action against hundreds of Twitter users and winning six-figure settlements from BBC and ITV, who had repeated the false and baseless allegations against him, Lord McAlpine chose to sue Bercow her for her post. The High Court decided he had been identified in the tweet and that readers were asked to 'read between the lines' the innuendo that he was guilty of the alleged misdeeds, which many would be able to link with other social media posts and coverage. In one of the first cases of Twitter defamation, the Court found in Lord McAlpine's favour and ordered Bercow to pay an undisclosed sum. She published this apology on Twitter: 'I have apologised sincerely to Lord McAlpine in court – I hope others have learned tweeting can inflict real harm on people's lives' (*Lord Twitter case* 2013). Her contrite words speak to the importance of professional communicators knowing the basics of defamation law when using social media and underscore why it is an essential component of social media legal risk management. The judgment (*Lord Twitter case* 2013) is also worth reading in full when you have finished this chapter because it helps us understand some of the basic elements of defamation.

Defamation in an international context: jurisdictional issues

Refraining from speaking ill of another has been a basic teaching of most of the world's great religions, and legal punishment for such slander can be traced back to ancient times. Until the late-16th century in England defamation was tried primarily in the ecclesiastical courts (church courts) because it was then believed that to damage someone's reputation was an attack upon their very soul (Dent 2018). Over ensuing centuries it came to be tried exclusively in the secular courts and throughout the then–British Empire it developed in step with the English law. Those very colonies actively pursued criminal defamation (criminal libel) cases against those who published materials criticising the state, a practice which continues in many countries to this day. While former members of the Commonwealth now share broadly similar defamation laws, most have diverged in the detail over the past century. The United States, once also a British colony, has the most pronounced differences, partly due to its Supreme Court interpretations of First Amendment free press protections through the 20th century. This has impacted the basic definitions of defamation, the elements of the action, and the available defences, particularly when the person defamed (the plaintiff) is a 'public figure'. In short, it makes the United States a very difficult jurisdiction in which to bring a defamation action successfully if the plaintiff has any kind of public profile. More on that follows.

Even the other 50-plus former British colonies have diverged somewhat in recent years, with some preserving intact most of the legislation and case law of the 19th century. The United Kingdom reformed substantially its own defamation law in favour of defendant publishers in 2013, as has Australia with reforms in 2005 and 2020–2021, while in Canada the courts have developed more generous defences for public interest material. Elsewhere in the world, different legal systems have shaped and moulded the extent to which defamation exists in a criminal or civil form, with considerable variation within Europe.

At a United Nations level, Article 17 of the International Covenant on Civil and Political Rights offers all people the right to protection against unlawful attacks on their honour and reputation. And in some countries – most notably Thailand – people can be jailed for defaming members of the royal family under the ancient law of *lèse majesté*. This might sound obscure, archaic and unlikely but the sad fact is that foreigners have been arrested while in transit at Thai airports and jailed for their digital publications considered insulting to royalty – a sobering lesson particularly for those publishing critical or activist commentary on social media.

Such considerable variation in defamation law across jurisdictions sounds a warning for social media professionals. It is impossible to develop a close legal knowledge of all defamation laws internationally, but a core understanding of the basic principles and the most significant differences might help sound the alarm bells when material you are posting or hosting criticises a foreign individual or corporation. Importantly, the Australian High Court decided in *Gutnick's case* in 2002 that defamatory material is considered 'published' wherever it is downloaded from the Internet (as distinct from the location where it was uploaded to the publisher's server). This means that individuals and companies might have standing to sue you in your home country or elsewhere if they have a reputation to defend there.

Elements of a defamation action

Lawyers will often talk about the 'elements of an action', by which they mean the key ingredients that must be established before someone can sue or prosecute another in a particular area of law. Given the criminal version of defamation is rarely prosecuted in leading Western nations (if it even remains on their books), this chapter will focus on the key elements of a civil defamation action in former British Commonwealth nations (such as the United Kingdom, Australia, Canada and New Zealand) and show how these differ from United States law under the First Amendment.

Most nations throughout the former British Empire (Commonwealth) have three key elements required for a civil defamation action, including via social media:

- the material communicated must contain a defamatory imputation (meaning) about the plaintiff – basically one that lowers their reputation in the eyes of others;
- the plaintiff must be reasonably identifiable through the communication (though not necessarily named); and
- the material must be published to at least one other person who knows the plaintiff (otherwise there would be no reputational impact).
- [In the United Kingdom since 2013 (and introduced throughout Australia from 2021) the plaintiff must also establish that the communication has caused them 'serious harm', a reform designed to avoid trivial and vexatious defamation suits.]

Each of these key points has been subject to extensive discussion in cases, and we can touch upon only some highlights here. Judges have already decided upon numerous defamation cases involving social media over the two decades of its extensive use. As has already been established in the *Treasurer case* (2015) in Chapter 5 and the *Lord Twitter case* (2015) mentioned in this chapter, defamatory imputations can be conveyed via either their natural and ordinary meanings or via 'innuendo' – meanings gained by 'reading between the lines'. Such meanings might be conveyed via words, sounds, images, emojis or other symbols – and by combinations of them all.

Examples of imputations that could damage someone's reputation could include a suggestion of criminality, wrongdoing, immorality, lack of integrity, sexual harassment, promiscuity, financial misdeeds, hypocrisy, unsuitability to their occupation and even material that might make others ridicule them such as insults to their physical appearance, intelligence or mental health.

The abbreviated nature of some social media formats adds to the likelihood that some meanings might be conveyed unintentionally – which is no defence. The only intention required in a civil action for defamation is an intention to publish – not an intention to defame. Retweeting or reposting the material of others can leave you or your organisation liable as the new 'publisher'.

Defamation law is usually a combination of legislation and the centuries-old case law (common law). Whether or not the plaintiff is identifiable has been the subject of a litany of cases, where the courts have held it is open to others to sue if they meet the relatively narrow descriptors of the plaintiff. For example, if you just defame someone without further identifiers beyond their name, then others with the same name could sue if they could prove people thought you were referring to them. If you narrow it down with identifiers to just a handful of people, then they could all sue. For example, if you posted to Facebook 'A certain Villagegrove dentist has been molesting his patients' and there were only three dentists in that small town (fictional), then the other two could sue – even if you could prove the allegation against the dentist you were targeting was true. But if you said the same thing about a 'Mumbai dentist' with no further identifiers, then there would be way too many dentists in such a large Indian city for any of them to be able to prove you were referring to them. The courts will always weigh up the identification material to decide whether a person who knew the individual could reasonably think it was referring to them.

As for the requirement that material must be published to at least one other person who knows the plaintiff, the fact is that most social media communications by an organisation are indeed viewed by more than one person. That said, cases exist where courts have held that a social media post reached so few people in a particular jurisdiction, or was deleted so quickly after posting, that the defendant had no case to answer because the plaintiff could not produce anyone who had viewed the material and thought less of them. Of course, if you insulted someone in a direct message (DM) – sent only to them – then no defamation could be established because it would only damage their self-esteem. Yet if you copied in just one other person, or forwarded it to someone else, then they would have a defamation action available because it might then affect their reputation – the way others view them.

United States jurisdictions vary somewhat in their defamation laws, but First Amendment free expression protections create a much higher threshold for the plaintiff in establishing a case. In the United States a plaintiff has to prove – in addition to the three key elements mentioned previously – that the defamatory material was false, that the plaintiff has been 'damaged' by the publication and, if the allegation is of public concern, that it has been published negligently. Finally, if the defamation is of a so-called public figure (almost anyone with some public profile), he or she must also prove that it has been published with 'actual malice', or with complete disregard as to whether the material was true or false. These extra foundational requirements place much of the onus of proof upon the plaintiff, which differs markedly from Commonwealth countries where the onus is on the defendant to prove the truth or public benefit of allegations in their defence. For example, if you had implied in your post that someone had cheated, in the United States the plaintiff would have to prove at the start of the action that he or she had not indeed cheated, whereas in a Commonwealth country like Australia or the United Kingdom the defendant would have to prove the cheating actually happened (on the balance of probabilities) to defend the substantial truth of the imputation. Even though it is much harder to sue successfully for defamation in the United States, there have been some famous victories, even by public figures. For example, rock star Courtney Love had to pay a fashion designer US$430,000 in damages in a defamation settlement after her tweets and blog posts had called the designer a thief, burglar, felon, drug addict, prostitute, embezzler, cocaine dealer and an unfit mother after a dispute over the cost of her designs. Then Love tweeted that a former lawyer had been 'bought off', prompting another defamation claim, but the rock star managed to defend that one because the appeals court held the attorney was a public figure and that Love did not know the statement was false (*Love cases* 2011, 2016).

Countries vary as to whether companies or government agencies can sue for defamation, or whether standing is restricted to private citizens. In some places – including in

Tasmania, Australia – even the dead can sue or be sued for defamation, or at least their estates can do so or be liable on their behalf.

Another major jurisdictional variation is over whether organisations can be sued over material others post to their sites. In the United States, s. 230 of the *Communications Decency Act* offers wide protections against defamation action over the comments of others (protections the Trump administration wanted to take away in 2020), but in other jurisdictions Internet service providers and platform hosts have been held liable for defamatory material posted by third parties, particularly if the material had been brought to their attention and they had failed to remove it within a reasonable time (Pearson 2012).

Common defences to defamation

A range of legal arguments can be used to defeat an action for defamation, including (depending on the jurisdiction) truth, fair comment or honest opinion, protected report and qualified privilege (public interest). Professional communicators cannot be expected to know the technical elements of each defence but should know enough of the basic principles to be able to discuss them with a lawyer when seeking advice.

Truth

While the onus is on United States plaintiffs to prove defamatory material is false at the outset, in most other places the defendant is left trying to prove that the allegation he or she has made is substantially true. This can be harder than we might assume because a court requires hard evidence that complies with its rules on admissibility. Common reasons for rejecting evidence are illegal recordings, photocopied (rather than original) documents, and a shortage of witnesses willing to testify to the truth of the material in court (perhaps confidential sources). Hearsay evidence (trying to justify something on the basis that someone else told you about it) is often rejected too. A further difficulty of using truth as a defence is that a court will likely need you to prove the truth of the meaning coming from a set of facts. You might have evidence to prove each of those facts stated, but not enough to prove the imputation that arises when the reader or viewer 'joins the dots'. For example, you might be able to prove the 'Reverend Brown was recently spotted knocking on a door in the city's brothel district'. You might well have photographs and a witness account, but still be unable to prove the meaning emanating from the publication – that he was seeking the services of a prostitute. That said, a positive of the truth defence is that it is usually part of a civil action, and a defendant only needs to satisfy the evidentiary burden of proof of 'substantial truth' on 'the balance of probabilities' rather than the much tougher criminal standard – 'beyond reasonable doubt' where much more evidence of truth would be required.

Fair comment or honest opinion

Most jurisdictions offer a defence for when you are defaming someone in the course of giving your honest opinion on a genuine matter of public interest or concern. This is often called a 'fair comment' or 'honest opinion' defence. In some jurisdictions such a defence is extended to parody and satire. The requirements for such a defence vary somewhat, but a good example is the Australian statutory defence which requires:

1 The matter was an expression of opinion of the defendant rather than a statement of fact. (This means it only protects material framed as opinion, where you are judging something or someone on a fair qualitative scale. For example, if you said 'John Velgart can't act', it would be a statement of fact, but 'John Velgart's performance was one of the worst I have seen in professional theatre' would be a statement of opinion.)
2 The opinion related to a matter of public interest. (Only defamatory opinions on topics in the public domain are protected – the actions of politicians and public figures, books, films for public screening, professional sports performances and so on.)
3 The opinion is based on proper material. (It needs to be clear that the defamatory opinion is based on true and provable facts, and normally they should appear in the publication to show how the opinion was reached unless they are generally well known. Short social media posts can make this level of justification difficult.)

The defence is usually defeated if the plaintiff can show a lack of good faith or malice on the part of the commenter. For example, a scathing online hotel review would lose the defence if the plaintiff could show the reviewer owned or worked for a competing hotel, or if there is other evidence the reviewer did not truly hold that opinion.

Protected reports

Fair and accurate reports of important public proceedings like court or parliament also earn protection from defamation action in most democratic countries. Some have extended a qualified protection to other occasions including official reports, council meetings, tribunal adjudications and even public meetings – so long as the defamatory material relates to a matter of public interest and is not just a statement of gossip about someone's private life. To earn the defence the report must be both substantially accurate and 'fair', including the coverage of both sides of an argument (though perhaps not to the same extent). Two key issues arise for social media reports on such matters. Firstly, some social media formats such as Twitter make it hard to offer 'fair and accurate' coverage because they are so truncated, though some have covered court proceedings effectively using a hashtag and an indication that the coverage is ongoing. (Note the *Treasurer case* [2015] for the need for caution here because the court might rule that not everyone reads the balancing coverage.) Secondly, social media transcends borders and some of these protected report defences are confined to proceedings in a particular jurisdiction, meaning the plaintiff could sue you somewhere else if your report had damaged their reputation there.

Qualified privilege or public interest

Some places excuse defamatory allegations if they have been made in good faith on a legitimate matter of public interest or concern – even if their truth cannot be proven. This defence brings some of the Commonwealth-based jurisdictions a little closer to the United States public figure protections. The defences usually require you to show the authoritative and reliable sources of your information to establish you were not just speculating or circulating unsubstantiated rumours. These defences better suit long-form investigative journalism than shorter social media sharing by ordinary citizens because they usually require extensive fact-checking and consultation with lawyers prior to publication.

Strategies for minimising defamation risk

Defamation actions over social media are highly publicised and reported, but they still remain relatively rare as a proportion of the billions of social media posts disseminated every day. Much defamatory material is not pursued legally for a host of reasons – because defences might apply, the cost of legal actions, the anonymity of some social media users, the fact that the poster might be based in another jurisdiction, that other embarrassing matter might arise during litigation, and that many could not afford to pay court costs or damages. Organisations can find themselves on either side of the social media defamation case – as a plaintiff when someone has posted something defamatory about you or one of your key stakeholders or as a defendant when something posted to one of your social media channels damages the reputation of other people or organisations. Taking legal action to defend your organisation's reputation (or that of your key personnel) might appear an obvious step, but it can carry its own risks of brand and reputational damage and substantial costs via the legal and court processes. Any such action needs to be weighed carefully from financial, strategic and legal perspectives. In some circumstances, non-legal strategies (seeking apologies, negotiating concerns, threatening legal action etc.) are less costly and more effective, but it is important to stress that even these need legal advice before pursuing them because they can have consequences if legal action later becomes necessary. In some jurisdictions (including Australia) larger companies cannot sue for defamation, which limits the options available.

If your organisation is facing a defamation lawsuit – or even a threat – then the stakes are high and early legal advice is essential. Outcomes can be extremely high damages awarded or out-of-court settlements against your organisation (sometimes in the tens of millions in some jurisdictions), or crippling court orders (injunctions) to remove material from your sites or make humbling and brand-damaging apologies to the plaintiffs. The scale of damages and court costs underscores the need for professional liability (indemnity) insurance to an appropriate level, covering defamation. For the most blatant errors, a speedy apology (and perhaps an offer of amends) on the advice of a lawyer is the best course of action, and this even operates as a defence in some jurisdictions if the plaintiff has rejected a reasonable offer. Central to success here is the completion of a specific risk assessment approach to defamation as foreshadowed in Table 5.2 of Chapter 5. A sample specific legal risk analysis for a defamatory comment stream on a fictional local government organisation's Facebook page could address these key questions:

1   Identifying defamation as a legal problem because the post appears to denigrate or ridicule someone.
2   Reviewing the material to ensure it meets the elements of a defamation action – containing defamatory material, identifying someone by name or other factors and being published to at least another person.
3   Projecting the possible consequences for stakeholders – brand and reputational damage, financial loss, social media outrage and so on.
4   Seeking advice/referring upward – to the supervisor with responsibility for making such decisions or seeking expert legal advice.
5   Publishing/amending/deleting/correcting/apologizing – only after screen capture and after taking legal advice because of potential problems with admissions and implications for defences.

Case study 6.1 – Are you responsible for defamatory comments by other people on your organisation's Facebook page?

Organisations used to be confident that they were not responsible for defamatory comments made by other people on their corporate Facebook sites, but that has changed markedly in recent years. In the United States – under the generous protections of s. 230 of the *Communications Decency Act* – Internet service providers, platforms and social media site hosts are basically absolved of all responsibility for what others post on their sites. The law in most other democratic countries has developed at a varying pace on this point. For many Commonwealth nations – as is typical of many areas of law – the principle stems back to an older English case on who should bear responsibility for a defamatory publication, a decision which has been bent, twisted, advanced and distinguished by various higher courts to apply to social media.

That case centred on a defamation action over words that had been posted anonymously to a golf club's notice board about a member, breaching a club rule that required that permission be obtained before placing a notice. The plaintiff sued the proprietors, who claimed they had not written or authorised the notice but admitted they had seen it and had not removed it. The court held they should bear responsibility for the publication from the moment they knew of its contents and failed to take it down (*Golf club case* 1937).

Wind the clock forward almost a century and that case is still being cited in disputes over whether Internet service providers and social media site hosts can be sued over defamatory comments made by others on their platforms and pages. The *Baby Twins case* (2014) from New Zealand is often cited as an international leader on the principle that Facebook hosts should remove the defamatory posts of others within a reasonable time or they would share liability for them. Journalist Ian Wishart had written a true crime account of a high-profile 'whodunnit?' murder investigation into the death of three-month old twins, centring on the roles of the parents and featuring the side of the mother. Speculation was rife on social media, particularly after the acquittal of the father for the murder. Chris Murray, a concerned citizen, established a Facebook page to boycott the book (partly with his employer's support) which hosted numerous defamatory comments by others about Wishart and the twins' mother. The court held that Murray could be held responsible for the defamatory statements of other Facebook commenters on his site once he had become aware of them and had failed to remove them. However, it rejected the claim that he 'ought to know' such defamatory comments would be made and thus should have been pro-active in preventing them being posted at all – that is, he was not liable from the moment he posted the material that provoked the comments. His employer also shared some liability because it endorsed a link to the defamatory Facebook page from its Intranet.

This was taken a step further in Canada in the *Neighbours case* (2016), where a neighbourhood dispute had escalated between a schoolteacher and the family next door. The neighbour posted to Facebook the false allegation that the teacher had cameras and mirrors set up to spy on her family and children, leading to the imputation that he was a paedophile – a damaging slur for anyone, and particularly a teacher. The court held that she was not only responsible for the defamation in her own posts, but that she should have foreseen that her Facebook friends would make similar comments and escalate the false imputations, particularly with her settings on 'Public'. The judge found she should have been aware of the sharing nature of the medium and that such inflammatory comments would be shared, so she was also liable for the defamatory comments by the third parties, 'regardless of whether or when she became aware of them' (para 113).

There was a similar outcome in the *Voller case* (2020) in Australia. There, three major news groups posted stories to their Facebook pages about indigenous activist and former juvenile detainee Dylan Voller which attracted defamatory comments about him. The NSW Court of Appeal upheld the trial judge's finding that the news groups should bear some responsibility for the posting of the defamatory comments by third parties because their establishment of the page effectively 'encouraged and facilitated' comments of this nature. Their prompt removal of the comments did not detract from the fact that they had contributed to their publication. Australia's High Court was hearing an appeal on that decision when this book was in production and states were considering reforms to legislation to clarify the position. Research the outcome.

Clearly, this is a fluid space in social media law. In the meantime, organisations that choose to continue hosting their own social media sites like Facebook might pause before posting provocative material that might predictably attract defamatory comments.

Case study 6.2 – The Cyprus property case: defamation action might not restore a reputation

Facebook allegations over a lawyer and her firm's handling of clients' cases in the aftermath of an international property dispute led to a defamation case in the United Kingdom courts centering upon whether the plaintiffs had been identified and whether they had actually suffered any serious harm to their reputations. The publication took the form of a Facebook post published by Georgios Kounis and a webinar he hosted (attended by just 14 clients). Kounis was a consultant to a rival law firm who was campaigning for the rights of British claimants who had lost money in Cyprus-based property investments. The Facebook post took the form of a press release stating that one investor had been driven to suicide because of the scandal, and mentioned 'a London legal firm who took almost £30,000 in fees, before apparently breaching the terms of their retainer and forcing the Davies' to fund alternative representation' (*Cyprus property case* 2019). The court held the plaintiffs were identifiable through the posts, although they were not named, but that the press release had not caused 'serious harm' to them because the few people who most likely read it and knew it was that lawyer they were referring to already had an adverse view of the lawyer and her firm so no further serious harm had been caused. There was insufficient evidence that the webinar contained defamatory material or that it had impacted in any way on the lawyer's reputation with her clients.

There are key lessons in this case for organisations. One is that the pursuit of a defamation claim can have a financial cost and a reputational cost. In this instance the plaintiff lost her claim, and she and her firm likely suffered further reputational damage via the publicity about the case and the way the litigation was handled. Another is that identification of a plaintiff within a publication on social media can arise even if they are not named. They can be identified by other factors in the material which prompt some readers to understand that it does in fact refer to them. Finally, just because some defamatory material is published on social media does not mean it is not defensible. More jurisdictions are now requiring evidence of serious harm emanating from a post in order to establish a case, and in other places damages will be severely limited if it can be shown that a post was read by very few people or that the plaintiff's reputation was already diminished in the eyes of those who saw it.

Stakeholder theory and reputational management

Although elements of stakeholder theory are discussed earlier in this chapter, we will take a moment to recognise the role of stakeholders in matters of reputation, particularly regarding brand. Social media carries opportunity to engage which can solidify brand. A strong brand often starts with corporate social responsibility. The way in which a brand engages its audience, recognises its stakeholders and makes ethical and moral decisions can impact the brand and overarching reputation of the organisation. Stakeholders play an important role in maintaining reputation and the way in which you are perceived. Ultimately social media is about adding value to an organisation including reputation and legitimacy. Defamation litigation can impact a host of stakeholders through brand damage, financial costs and potential outrage.

Discussion questions and project topics

1   Select a not-for-profit organisation and summarise both its brand and reputation along the lines explained in this chapter.
2   Choose a large corporate communications firm and suggest how it might have exposure via social media to defamation, a. as a social media publisher and platform host; and b. as a target of defamatory material on social media.
3   Write an extended social media defamation risk analysis (500–700 words) for a boutique public relations agency with just three staff in your jurisdiction.
4   Find a recent defamation case involving social media in your jurisdiction. Explain how the reputations of those involved were impacted by the original communication and (potentially) by the court proceedings.

Practice tips

*   Review the material in this chapter and undertake a specific social media defamation risk analysis for your organisation on an annual basis.
*   Examine your social media operations – active platforms, staff moderation roster and duties, legal escalation procedures etc. – and adapt them in light of the defamation elements and defences as they apply to your jurisdiction and those where you operate.
*   Purchase a specific media law/social media law text applying to your jurisdiction and obtain copies of key defamation legislation to review and have on hand to inform your discussions with lawyers when advice is needed.
*   Search for recent defamation decisions in your jurisdiction so you can keep abreast of developments in the law and better understand how it applies to various fact scenarios.

Cases cited

Baby Twins case. 2014. *Murray v Wishart* [2014] 3 NZLR 722; [2014] NZCA 461. <www.nzlii.org/nz/cases/NZCA/2014/461.html>

Cyprus property case. 2019. *Dr Katherine Alexander-Theodotou and others v Georgios Kounis* [2019] EWHC 956 (QB). <www.bailii.org/ew/cases/EWHC/QB/2019/956.html>

Golf club case. 1937. *Byrne v. Deane* [1937] 1 K.B. 818.

Gutnick's case. 2002. *Gutnick v Dow Jones & Co Inc* [2002] HCA 56; (2002) 77 ALJR 255.

Lord Twitter case. 2013. *Lord McAlpine of West Green v Sally Bercow* [2013] EWHC 1342(QB). <www.judiciary.uk/wp-content/uploads/JCO/Documents/Judgments/mcalpine-bercow-judgment-24052013.pdf>

Love cases. 2011, 2016. Matthew Belloni, Courtney love to pay $430,000 in Twitter case. *Reuters*. 3 March. <www.reuters.com/article/us-courtneylove/courtney-love-to-pay-430000-in-twitter-case-idUSTRE7230F820110304>; *Gordon & Holmes v. Love* CA2/4, No. B256367, 2016 WL 374950, (Cal. Ct. App. Feb. 1, 2016). <www.courts.ca.gov/opinions/nonpub/B256367.PDF>

Neighbours case. 2016. *Pritchard v. Van Nes*, 2016 BCSC 686. <www.canlii.org/en/bc/bcsc/doc/2016/2016bcsc686/2016bcsc686.html>

Treasurer case. *2015. Hockey v Fairfax Media Publications Pty Limited* [2015] FCA 652. <www.austlii.edu.au/cgi-bin/sinodisp/au/cases/cth/FCA/2015/652.html>

Voller case. 2020. *Fairfax Media Publications: Nationwide News Pty Ltd: Australian News Channel Pty Ltd v Voller* [2020] NSWCA 102. <www.austlii.edu.au/cgi-bin/viewdoc/au/cases/nsw/NSWCA/2020/102.html>

References

Dent, C. 2018. "The locus of defamation law since the constitution of Oxford." *Monash University Law Review*, *44*(3), 491. www.monash.edu/__data/assets/pdf_file/0010/1980127/01_Dent.pdf

Pearson, M. 2012. *Blogging and tweeting without getting sued: A global guide to the law for anyone writing online*. Sydney: Allen and Unwin.

7 Crisis communication and reporting

Glossary

Crisis: A sudden or unexpected event that causes disruption to an organisation and has a significant financial or reputational impact.

Crisis communication: The collection and delivery of essential information during a crisis event.

Crisis communication theory: Recommended strategies when communicating during a crisis, including how to define and manage a crisis.

Disaster: A sudden or unexpected event, normally unavoidable, such as a natural disaster or pandemic, that causes major disruption to an organisation and/or community.

Issue: A sudden or unexpected event that causes disruption but can be resolved by applying strategies.

Social media crisis: A sudden or unexpected event that develops on social media and causes disruption to an organisation and has a significant financial or reputational impact.

Social media outrage: Outrage that is expressed on social media contributing to the escalation of trending topics, potentially detrimental to the organisation.

Abstract

Social media outrage has changed the approaches to crisis communication. It has sped up the expected response timeframes and provides a platform for organisations to be open and transparent in times of crisis. This chapter discusses some overarching crisis communication theories and how they are now interpreted when engaging with the audience during a crisis. This has strong alignment to journalism and media reporting, particularly when social media activists set the agenda that media engage with. Many of the examples presented in the chapters of this book would in fact be defined as crisis events, and this puts into perspective the severity of risks associated with social media use. However, as this chapter outlines, crisis communication theory can provide strategies for managing the reputation of an organisation throughout such episodes.

DOI: 10.4324/9781003180111-10

In this chapter

- Defining a crisis
- Crisis management theories
- Social media and crisis management
- Crisis communication planning
- Case study 7.1 – Southwest Airlines mid-flight emergency
- Social media crises
- Case study 7.2 – American Red Cross rogue tweet – #gettingslizzerd
- Case study 7.3 – United Airlines passenger removal
- Stakeholder theory and crisis management
- Discussion questions and project topics
- Practice tips
- References

Defining a crisis

Before defining the term 'crisis', let's first explore the difference between an issue and a crisis. Leading crisis communication scholar Tony Jaques uses a simple but effective metaphor to define the difference:

> *Issue management is about steering the ship out of troubled water, while crisis management is about saving the ship after it has struck an iceberg.*

(Jaques 2014, 7)

A basic definition of a crisis event is any sudden situation that causes disruption to an organisation and has a legal, financial or reputational impact. Something to consider when defining a crisis is to revisit the impact/probability risk matrix explored in Chapter 3. Crisis planning should involve mapping the potential scenarios that could occur based on the probability of them occurring and the impact they might have. By first mapping the possible risks, you can then determine which of these will become issues and further which could become a crisis. Any scenario mapped on the risk matrix as high impact can be defined as either an issue or a crisis. Using Jaques' (2014) metaphor for issue versus crisis, it becomes apparent that high probability and high impact scenarios are the matters that should be classified as issues in advance because it is important to help steer the organisation away from these incidents occurring and becoming crises. This can be done using mitigation strategies that help limit the high probability of them occurring. For instance, a large manufacturer might have a scenario mapped against high impact and high probability involving electrical equipment causing fire. If a fire broke out in a manufacturing warehouse, it could have devastating effect, but the company can implement electrical safety and training recommendations to reduce the probability of such a fire occurring, thus averting a crisis.

However, scenarios mapped in the high impact, but low probability quadrant are considered potential crises. They are often sudden and unexpected scenarios resulting in disruption that can lead to financial loss and reputation harm. Because of the low probability of them occurring, it is difficult to implement strategies to prevent them. For instance, a large fire breaking out at the manufacturer's warehouse due to a severe electrical storm is an example of a low probability but high impact scenario. Although the organisation may have safety and training strategies in place to prevent electrical fires, when there is little likelihood and an unexpected nature to the scenario not much can be done to prevent it. The mapping process can help to develop a definition of a crisis tailored to the specific organisation. Keep in mind that every organisation is different and while the basis to defining a crisis will remain similar – any unexpected incident that has financial or reputational impact – the specific scenarios that could develop into a crisis will vary across most organisations.

Bear in mind that communication on social media can play a role in managing the issue or crisis, but it can also trigger or exacerbate the issue or crisis. This chapter deals with both kinds of situations. We first look at how social media can be used to help manage an issue or a crisis.

Crisis communication theory

Some crisis communication scholars suggest organisations should listen and engage actively in social media discussion during times of crisis (Bratu 2016; Sandman 2015; Coombs & Holladay 2014). When in a crisis, negative commentary is expected and can contribute to the harm being felt, but actively engaging in social media discussions and acknowledging the reaction of an audience has proven to help consolidate or even enhance reputation in some circumstances. Social media has added complexity and although its use pre-dates social media, Situational Crisis Communication Theory (SCCT) can help organisations safeguard reputation by linking crisis response strategies to crisis types (Coombs 2017, 2018). The crisis types are known as *victim clusters* when the organisation is also a victim of the crisis; *accidental clusters* where the organisation's actions are unintentional leading into the crisis; or *intentional clusters* where an organisation's actions have created risks that have led to the crisis (Coombs 2017).

The impact of the crisis can be intensified both positively or negatively, and this can be linked to the theory of outrage factors as discussed in Chapter 3. Outrage factors can contribute to the intensity of a crisis because of the emotional aspects that contribute to the overall perception. The outrage factors discussed in Chapter 3 are:

- *Voluntariness* – Stakeholders are more likely to accept risks they take voluntarily.
- *Trust* – Trust in an organisation or a brand can have a lasting impact on perceptions both during and after a crisis.
- *Control* – Stakeholders can become outraged when control is removed, either from them or from an organisation.
- *Familiarity* – Familiarity with a situation can impact the overall perception.
- *Effect on the vulnerable* – Where the vulnerable are at risk, outrage is usually assured.

A crisis can be intensified if stakeholders feel or perceive any of these outrage factors. This forms an 'expectation gap', which refers to the gap between how an organisation behaves and how audiences, stakeholders or public believe it should have behaved. The expectation gap, if not properly managed, can lead to social media outrage and the development of issues and crises. The link to stakeholder theory is discussed again later in this chapter, but it is important to note here that stakeholder expectations play a key role in the expectation gap, and if the gap is significant, then unanticipated publics may form on social media platforms, mobilise and lobby against the organisation. There is a link back to stakeholder theory here because it is imperative to know who the stakeholders are and what stake they have in the crisis situation to understand how they might react and what potential social media impacts they could generate.

This helps us understand the power held by stakeholders. In crisis communication theory there is reference to the role of activists. One such group of activists is titled 'not in my backyard' (NIMBY) activists – people who are objecting to some proposal or action in their geographical area. NIMBY activists can hold great power. They are normally local parents, families (including children) and other citizens, all who have strong connections to the locality and potentially strong power over the outcomes. It is often these NIMBY activist groups who facilitate the creation of unanticipated publics because they use social media to create commentary that goes viral. The raw emotions and subsequent outrage factors that are often connected to these activist groups feed into the virality of social media. Of course, all activists can wield considerable power because of the message that comes with their activism. It is important to know what contributions these groups might make to a crisis situation to assist in managing the response.

Attribution theory, which is the parent theory of SCCT, is also of particular relevance to social media crisis management despite pre-dating social media developments. It involves the tendency of an audience to attribute blame and accuse an organisation of acting irresponsibly (Coombs 2007). According to Weiner (1995), by attributing blame a public can insist upon action, and often these demands further exacerbate the negative emotions already being felt through the crisis for both the organisation and its audience, stakeholders and the public. Organisations are expected to respond to such demands and engage in the conversation. Expressing genuine sympathy is one way to reduce the attribution of blame placed on an organisation. Expressing sympathy or taking responsibility for the situation does not mean admitting fault. It is important to accept that a crisis has occurred regardless of who or what is at fault. Even when the crisis being experienced sits within the victim cluster, it is crucial to take responsibility for the ways the audience, public and stakeholders are affected. It is even more important to take responsibility when the organisation or one of its staff is at fault. Social media provides a level of immediacy for this type of announcement. But a word of warning: any expression of sympathy must be genuine and heartfelt because audiences are sophisticated and can see through disingenuous expressions of compassion. Further, any such social media posts should be legalled to avoid misguided admissions or potential loss of defences.

Ethical and moral decision making is another important aspect to crisis communication. Even prior to social media, the role of ethical decisions was central to crisis communication management. Take for instance the Tylenol case from the 1980s. In 1982 the United States paracetamol/acetaminophen brand, Tylenol, was at the centre of a crisis when seven people in Chicago died after taking the medication. At the time the brand was blamed for the deaths and Tylenol took full responsibility for the situation using crisis communication approaches, despite not fully understanding what had occurred. To ensure the prevention of any further deaths they removed all of their products from the shelves across the country, costing the company millions. Later it was found the deaths were actually caused by one person lacing the product with potassium cyanide in stores. However, despite having had no way of preventing it, they took responsibility for the situation, making a morally sound but financially damaging decision to ensure no further deaths. As a result, Tylenol survived the crisis, remaining one of the top paracetamol/acetaminophen brands in the United States.

Just as SCCT provides ways to identify the type of crisis, it also suggests four response strategies (Coombs 2018). The first is the *rebuilding strategy*, where the aim is to rebuild the relationships with stakeholders. It is often achieved by expressing sympathy and taking on a level of responsibility regardless of where the blame lies. The second strategy is the *diminishment strategy*, which aims to minimise the amount of responsibility by justifying any involvement. For instance, if a single employee was responsible for the situation, the diminishment strategy would highlight that it was an isolated incident and should not reflect upon the organisation. Next is *denial strategy*, which is when an organisation denies any involvement. This strategy is only successful when the crisis is based on invalid accusations or false rumours. An organisation that uses the denial strategy when it is actually involved can cause irreparable damage to its reputation. Lastly there is the *bolstering strategy*, which is achieved by highlighting past good deeds or reminding stakeholders of the positive approach the organisation takes to corporate social responsibility and ethical and moral decision making. The case studies presented in this chapter explore the application of some of these strategies.

In the realm of social media law, co-author Pearson has mapped the link between morals, ethics and media law via a range of situations and emotions the professional communicator might face, using a strategy of 'mindful reflection' (Pearson & Polden 2019, chap 2). This involves developing the ability to pause and reflect before acting when an emotional response or the cognitive recollection of media law learning raises a red flag. For example, a communicator might pause to research and reflect on appropriate courses of action whenever a social media post has something to do with crime or the courts because that area has so many potential legal risks as explained in Chapter 9.

Social media and crisis management

Social media plays an important role in managing crisis situations. The key approach to managing a crisis is open communication, and one way to ensure open communication is by incorporating social media engagement and two-way discussion into the response. The specific channels you choose during crisis communication should take into account your audience. Consider Chapter 4 and the need to understand the audience to then determine the appropriate platform. This detail is essential in using social media as part of a crisis management approach because the only way the message will be delivered is if it is sent through the right channels to target the appropriate audience. Although social media is becoming a core channel used in crisis communication, you should still remember the need for other communication channels because in some circumstances social media may not be the best choice. Again, this comes back to audience. If the audience is not using social media regularly, it is not the appropriate channel. Instead, you might incorporate some social media into a traditional communication plan. As discussed more throughout this chapter it is important to 'fight fire with fire', and if the issue is on social media, and the discussion or outrage that is causing financial or reputational harm is occurring on social media, then the organisation should respond within that environment.

Crisis communication planning

It takes a long time to build a reputation but might take only seconds for it to be destroyed, so it is crucial to have a strong crisis plan that includes the use of social media and outlines the risks that social media can create. Although the plan must be strong, it must also be flexible. Every crisis is different and must be managed in a nuanced way. Because of the fluidity of these circumstances, the response must also be fluid if an organisation is to continue to react appropriately. It is not a set of instructions but instead a guideline on options and strategies available to manage a crisis. The document should be brief and contain processes and decision-making channels; contact details for all relevant internal personnel including the crisis team members; a list of stakeholders and their contacts; recommended strategies and communication channels; plus templates or factsheets that may be required quickly. Because crises are time-critical events, everything that might be required for the response should be accessible either within the plan or as a link in a digital copy of the plan. Although a number of scholars make suggestions for what a crisis plan should contain, the following is adapted from Coombs (2018).

Crisis teams – These are essential. It is important for a crisis plan to have a crisis team identified. A crisis team must have a team leader who is the person who will take responsibility for final decisions. This person should be senior but does not need to be the face of the organisation. In fact, it is sometimes best if the person fronting public communications as the spokesperson is free to conduct those important tasks exclusively and therefore should not be the crisis team leader. The team should also involve a senior communications staff member who has full access to and training in social media management, and the heads of department for any other relevant area. It should be a cross-functional team whose members have been specifically selected for the types of crises that can occur.

Spokespeople selection – Most large organisations have a specific person who is the face of the organisation. Often this person will take on the role of main spokesperson during a crisis. Keep in mind that during a crisis consistency is key, so it may be appropriate to use this trusted face, particularly if they are well equipped to conduct media interviews and appear in relevant social media videos and posts. However, as some crises extend over many days, it is not always realistic to have just a single spokesperson. Therefore, it is extremely important to have a pool of potential spokespeople who are media trained and confident to take on that role if necessary. The spokesperson should be a member of the crisis team because they need to familiarise themselves with potentially technical responses that may be required to ensure transparency. The actions of the spokesperson are vital to the outcome of the crisis. An appropriate spokesperson must be chosen because any mishap in formal communication can be damaging, particularly when damaging clips or quotes go viral on social media in the form of social media outrage.

Practice makes perfect – There are a number of ways an organisation can practice its crisis plan. Organisations where crises can be anticipated may wish to run simulation exercises to allow everyone involved an opportunity to practise their roles. For instance, military and police exercises require specific and fast action, so practising in a simulated environment adds confidence to those involved. However, not all organisations need full-scale exercises. It may be appropriate to do a smaller version such as an interactive exercise that still allows for real-time practice but does not require a full-scale approach. It may also be appropriate to do a facilitated exercise where those involved are stepped through a potential scenario and can practice their role in a non-timed environment. There is no right or wrong approach. It is important that an organisation determines what is right for them based on the types of crises that could occur. If a competitor has experienced a crisis, it can be worth running a simulation on the same scenario in your own organisation so you learn from their mistakes.

Stakeholder map – Although every crisis is different, the main stakeholders for an organisation often remain similar. The priority placed on the stakeholder groups will change. Because a crisis is a time-critical event, it is essential to have a list, along with key contacts for the main stakeholder groups. This will allow members of the crisis team to communicate easily with those identified as having both high stakes and high power in the crisis.

Response – The crisis plan should have a guideline on how to respond in the event of the crisis. It will not dictate a word-for-word response to be lifted and used but instead will detail a range of available options, including media and social media templates and factsheets or relevant webpages that can be linked in social media posts. The plan should highlight approaches that must be avoided. For instance, 'scapegoating' – the act of blaming another for the crisis – is generally ineffective and often morally questionable and should usually be avoided. If this is an approach the organisation does not want to take, it must be highlighted in the plan. This section is also an opportunity to highlight terminologies or jargon that should be avoided, particularly from a technical perspective.

Learning from experience – While not an essential section of a crisis plan, it is advised that evaluation take place soon after the crisis is resolved. Not only can an organisation learn from their own mistakes and successes, but so can others. Sometimes this process is a roundtable discussion resulting in a short report while other crises have prompted full-scale case study analyses.

Case study 7.1 – Southwest Airlines mid-flight emergency

On 17 April 2018 a Southwest Airlines flight from New York to Dallas experienced engine failure caused by a broken fan blade 20 minutes into the flight. Shrapnel from the rupturing engine broke a window, created an air vacuum and partially sucked out a female passenger who later died in hospital. Despite the devastating facts related to this event Southwest Airlines have since been praised for their management of the incident. It was clear that they had a crisis management plan which was actioned immediately once they were advised of the situation. They used social media successfully to communicate with the audience and to investigate the incident as it unfolded, in clear and concise language. A number of passengers on the flight were posting to social media or sharing content with friends and family, and Southwest Airlines examined these photos, videos and tweets to get a better understanding of what was happening to help inform their response. They issued a short apology video from the CEO on their social media channels within 24 hours of the incident occurring and continued to use social media to issue multiple updates with what they knew at the time. These are all considered successful crisis management approaches, and the use of social media meant they were seen by a wider audience to be acting appropriately. However, not only the outputs contributed to this success. It was also apparent behind-the-scenes actions were beneficial, such as ensuring that appropriate resources were available in Philadelphia where the flight made its emergency landing, assigning passengers to employees to assist with further travel arrangements to get those passengers to where they needed to be despite the tragic disruption. A number of their actions were praised, particularly the CEO's apology, but also within 24 hours they issued compensation to all passengers on board in the form of $5,000 cheques – with no strings attached. Passengers who accepted the compensation were still able to sue the company without prejudice to their cases. All promotions that were scheduled were stopped out of respect for those involved. It was the accumulation of these outputs that resulted in success. They closed the expectation gap between customers and themselves, clearly understanding what it was that the audience wanted to know and also what they wanted to see them do. Social media management played a significant role in their successful navigation of a major crisis.

Social media crises

As highlighted throughout this textbook, social media can sometimes be the cause of a crisis. Although we present a number of ways to understand the risks associated with social media use, in some circumstances these risks will mutate into crises. For example, in Chapter 6 we explained that in many jurisdictions social media hosts might be held responsible for the comments made by third parties on their sites. Establishing appropriate terms of use for commenters and routine and thorough moderation strategies can help prevent an issue such as a defamatory comment becoming a crisis. In most places, effective moderation and speedy removal of defamatory material within a reasonable time, or immediately when notified, will avert the crisis. Defamatory comments by third parties on your sites can have high impact but remain a low probability when provocative posts are not published and routine and efficient moderation is in place.

In Chapter 4 the need for a social media strategy was discussed. One aspect of a social media strategy involves having an appropriate process to be followed. It is essential that this is outlined to all staff who could have access to the social media accounts to prevent accidental posts being sent from official accounts. Case study 7.2 analyses one such case that resulted in the American Red Cross official Twitter account briefly hosting a personal tweet. The nature of social media presents further risk as it allows audiences, stakeholders and the public the opportunity to voice opinions in a public sphere. This means that all representatives of an organisation must be aware that everything has the potential to go public. Chapter 10 talks more about employment law and policies that can be implemented to help educate employees and representatives. Case study 7.3 discusses an example of members of the public filming an incident which was then uploaded to social media where it went viral and prompted a crisis.

Case study 7.2 – American Red Cross rogue tweet – #gettingslizzerd

At 11:24 PM on 15 February 2011 the American Red Cross official account tweeted:

> *Ryan found two more 4 bottle packs of Dogfish Head's Midas Touch beer. . . . [W]hen we drink we do it right #gettingslizzerd.*

The tweet was visible to more than 250,000 followers of the account and was retweeted hundreds of times while it remained online. However, the error was picked up, and at 12:40 AM Monday 16 February a further tweet was sent stating:

> *We've deleted the rogue tweet but rest assured the Red Cross is sober and we've confiscated the keys.*

The American Red Cross took full responsibility for the mistake. This aligns with the SCCT rebuilding strategy. Further it is clear they understood their Twitter audience and used humour in the approach to taking control of the situation. The use of humour appealed to the beer community online and sparked a number of light-hearted jokes and suggestions for donations – of both blood and money. The brewery mentioned in the original tweet also got onboard and further encouraged its followers to support the American Red Cross by retweeting many of the suggestions encouraging the community to donate such as:

> *After I drop off a pint of blood to the @RedCross, I'm replacing it with a pint of @dogfishbeer #gettingslizzerd*

I think we should all donate $5 to @RedCross anytime we're #gettingslizzerd. What a difference we would make. Ha!

A key lesson from this example is that not all crisis incidents automatically morph into major problems. Managing the situation promptly and taking responsibility for what has occurred can sometimes help convert a crisis into a positive. The American Red Cross has blogged about their experience (Harman 2011) and highlighted that although they are a humanitarian organisation, they are still human beings and therefore can make mistakes. Even in their analysis of the incident they continued to use humour with two words of caution at the bottom of the post:

1   *You'll want to space out giving a pint of blood and drinking a pint of beer for health reasons.*
2   *Be careful of Hootsuite!*

(Harman 2011, URL)

Case study 7.3 – United Airlines passenger removal

In April 2017 a video of airport security forcibly removing a passenger from a plane went viral on social media. The video showed the man, who was later identified as 69-year-old doctor David Dao, being ripped out of his seat by security – causing physical injury to his body and his face left visibly bloody. In the coming days it was revealed that Dr. Dao's injuries included a concussion, a broken nose, damage to his sinuses and the loss of teeth. It is understood that United Airlines had randomly selected Dr. Dao and three other passengers to give up their seats for maintenance employees because the flight was overbooked. Dr. Dao refused to leave the plane on the basis that he was a paying customer with a need to fly that day but was subsequently removed by force. The CEO of United Airlines issued an apology on Twitter which stated:

> *This is an upsetting event to all of us here at United. I apologize for having to re-accommodate these customers. Our team is moving with a sense of urgency to work with the authorities and conduct our own detailed review of what happened. We are also reaching out to this passenger to talk directly to him and further address and resolve this situation.*
>
> *– Oscar Munoz, CEO, United Airlines*

The choice of words in this apology was the focus of a lot of social media commentary. Using the word 're-accommodate' to describe what was witnessed as a violent and forceful removal was viewed as insensitive – both by passengers on the plane and viewers around the world in the viral video. The ability for video to spread to many on social media meant that his words were out of sync with the footage people had seen. Social media requires an organisation to be transparent in all responses to crises – and avoid understatement and euphemisms – as the audience can often access evidence of the actual event. The CEO further sent an internal letter to employees, which was leaked to the public, that described Dr. Dao as 'disruptive' and 'belligerent' and showed little sympathy for the victim, again in direct contrast to the video that the world was watching. This approach sparked further outcry, exacerbating the negativity already being felt, with some accusing the organisation of victim blaming or 'scapegoating'. Three days after the incident the CEO issued another apology via an ABC News interview, during which he disclosed his shame about the incident and promised it would never happen again. He indicated the apology had not been made sooner because the company had been investigating. One of the main points from this example is the need to maintain consistency in all messaging throughout a crisis. Social media allows no room for error. This means that both internal and external communications should express the same or similar messages. It is important to remember that nothing is truly internal and might be made public and go viral, triggering social media outrage. Therefore, although crisis communication theory places employees as essential components to a successful response, you must ensure that anything released internally or externally is appropriate for public consumption and in line with the existing responses. The decision to release internal correspondence that contradicted any apology and placed further blame on a victim who was seriously injured was a downfall of the response, exposing the original apology as insincere. Social media moves fast, and in this environment an organisation must move at the same pace to counteract the negativity being voiced.

Stakeholder theory and crisis management

Identifying stakeholders and being able to see their perspectives is a key component of good crisis management. In a crisis there are often many stakeholders involved. As explained in Chapter 2, it is important to get a feel for who to deal with first, who is the main priority and who can be dealt with last. You must prioritize stakeholders, identify those most affected and manage stakeholder relationships. During a crisis – and remember that most crisis events are situations where an organisation has minimal time, information and resources – stakeholder groups might only give you 48 hours to decide whether they are going to support you, remain neutral or oppose you. If an event goes viral on social media, the timeline can be much shorter. If you lose your stakeholders, you lose the crisis. It is critical that stakeholder mapping is done prior to any crisis event and that it exists within the crisis plan so it can be accessed, adjusted and used as the crisis unfolds.

Organisations must be able to see the situation from the perspective of their stakeholders to assess whether a crisis has occurred according to the crisis plan definition. This is why identifying stakeholders and developing appropriate relationships to enable effective channels of communication with them is so important. When there is an expectation gap between how stakeholders expect a company to behave and how that company actually behaves, the risk of a crisis developing increases (Coombs 2018). This can be influenced by how an organisation exhibits transparency or accountability in response to the crisis. If stakeholder expectations are being met, then there is generally no issue that can escalate. However, a crisis can occur when the gap increases between stakeholder expectations and an organisation's behaviour. Essentially, the application of stakeholder theory is to monitor the expectation gap and anticipate the behaviour of these different stakeholders. Remember that stakeholders can transform from being 'passive' to 'active' and engaged publics and may fit into many social identities that can influence their actions – both in real life and on social media.

Discussion questions and project topics

1   Return to the risk matrix you created at the end of Chapter 3 or create a new one for your organisation or university and start developing a crisis plan for that organisation.

2   Research the 1982 Tylenol case further and take note of the response of the organisation. How might the response need to change in the current technology and social media environment? What are some of the further risks that Tylenol could face if the same incident were to occur now?

3   Choose one of the case studies presented in this chapter and create a stakeholder map for the organisation. Then rank the stakeholders according to their stake and power in the crisis experienced. Explain your reasoning.

Practice tips

- All organisations should have a crisis management plan. This does not need to be a large document but should be thorough and clearly outline a recommended approach when responding to a crisis.
- Fight fire with fire. If an incident occurs on social media, then use social media in the response. Follow the audience to where the conversation is happening and contribute to the discussion with transparent and honest information, consulting with your legal team throughout the process.
- Avoid using specific names of personnel in a crisis plan. Instead allocate roles to positions to avoid confusion if someone is away or unavailable when a crisis unfolds.

References

Bratu, S. 2016. "The critical role of social media in crisis communication." *Linguistic and Philosophical Investigations*, *15*, 232–238.

Coombs, W.T. 2007. "Attribution theory as a guide for post-crisis communication research." *Public Relations Review*, *33*(2), 135–139.

Coombs, W.T. 2017. "Revising situational crisis communication theory: The influences of social media on crisis communication theory and practice." In L.L. Austin & Y. Jin (eds.), *Social media and crisis communication*. New York: Routledge. pp. 21–39.

Coombs, W.T. 2018. *Ongoing crisis communication: Planning, managing, and responding* (5th ed.). Thousand Oaks, CA: Sage Publications.

Coombs, W.T. & S.J. Holladay. 2014. "How publics react to crisis communication efforts: Comparing crisis response reactions across sub-arenas." *Journal of Communication Management*, *18*(1), 40–57.

Harman, W. 2011. "Twitter faux pas." *American Red Cross*. https://redcrosschat.org/2011/02/16/twitter-faux-pas/

Jaques, T. 2014. *Issue and crisis management: Exploring issues, crises, risk and reputation*. South Melbourne: Oxford University Press.

Pearson, M. & M. Polden. 2019. *The journalist's guide to media law: A handbook for communicators in a digital world*. London: Routledge.

Sandman, P. 2015. *10 things you need to know about outrage management and social media*. Accessed 12 January 2021. www.psandman.com/col/social-media.htm

Weiner, B. 1995. *Judgement of responsibility: A foundation of theory for social conduct*. New York: Guilford Press.

Part 4

Risks at the intersection of human rights, law and ethics

8 Privacy in social media

Glossary

Breach of confidence: The legal action allowing someone to sue over the release – or threatened release – of information that has been conveyed in confidence.

Data protection: Laws controlling the collection, storage, management and use of private identifying information.

Privacy breach: The act of releasing information or observing conduct which most people would find to be a highly offensive disclosure or intrusion.

Abstract

There are both ethical and legal dimensions to privacy in social media. There are key elements of privacy, confidentiality and data protection that all professional users of social media should understand. Legislation and legal actions protect both personal data and citizens' rights against serious invasion of their personal privacy, but these vary across countries. Human rights play a part here but understanding how it all fits together is essential to effective social media use in a global context. This chapter establishes the discussion about privacy and anonymity both within professional work and with regard to audiences. At an organisational level there is significant risk of misinformation and disinformation when using social media professionally, particularly when dealing with anonymous commenters and posters.

DOI: 10.4324/9781003180111-12

In this chapter

- Defining privacy, confidentiality and data protection on social media
- Privacy: historical and global perspectives
- Legal, ethical and regulatory dimensions
- Data protection issues
- Elements of breach of privacy and confidentiality actions
- Defences
- Strategies for minimising privacy risk
- Case study 8.1 – Facebook and the 'This Is Your Digital Life' app
- Case study 8.2 – Using consumer law to combat revenge porn
- Stakeholder theory and privacy
- Discussion questions and project topics
- Practice tips
- Cases cited
- References

Defining privacy, confidentiality and data protection on social media

Privacy, confidentiality and data protection have overlapping meanings and laws at both a personal and professional level. This is equally true on social media. Privacy settings, anonymous handles, terms and conditions agreements and data breaches are just some of the situations where such issues arise in the social media context. The terms have so much in common that even judges and legislators have had difficulty defining and distinguishing them internationally, as we will learn shortly. Put simply, a breach of privacy usually refers to the release of information or the intrusion into someone's private domain that most people would consider an offensive disclosure or intrusion. In some circumstances, it shares some meaning with breach of confidence, which refers to a betrayal of someone's confidence, usually by sharing some confidential information that the person expected you to keep secret, often to their hurt or disadvantage. This might occur at a personal or organisational level, given there are also trade secrets and material that is deemed 'commercial in confidence'. Data protection might well be covered by privacy or confidentiality laws, but also by special legislation controlling the collection, storage, management and use of identifying private information such as names, ages, addresses, contact details, health records and so on. Social media – being a highly personalised and sharing medium – is an ethical and legal minefield for the potential breach of privacy, confidentiality and data protection.

Privacy: historical and global perspectives

The United Nations views privacy as a fundamental human right. Article 17 of the International Covenant on Civil and Political Rights (ICCPR 1976) prohibits unlawful or arbitrary interferences with someone's privacy, family, home and correspondence (as well as reputational protections). It proclaims that people should have legal protection against such intrusions.

Privacy is viewed as a foundational right because most cultures have endowed some aspects of our personal lives as private. There are examples from indigenous societies.

Australian Aboriginal culture features 'women's business' – including the private matters of menstruation, pregnancy, childbirth, contraception and abortion – where 'shaming' would occur if they were intruded upon, particularly by men (Maher 2002). European societies shared some of these privacy considerations and excluded men from their partners' childbirth until well into the 20th century. Traditional Hawai'ians' liberal attitudes to nudity and sex in public shocked the English explorer Captain James Cook in 1773 because both activities were considered particularly private matters in his society (Diamond 2004). Such contrasts between the public and the private continue within, and between, cultures today, with most Muslim countries requiring minimal exposure of the body in public in contrast to beach culture in many Western nations, where nudity and semi-nudity are the norm (almost the reverse of the situation to Captain Cook's England in 1773).

While there were indeed cultural taboos and criminal penalties for offensive behaviour, a formal notion of a 'right' to privacy in Western legal systems did not emerge until the 19th century. The celebrity French writer Alexandre Dumas (author of *The Three Musketeers*) famously won a court action in 1867 after a photographer attempted to sell intimate images from a private studio shoot of Dumas and his girlfriend, 32-year-old celebrity stage actress Adah Isaacs Menken. The judge ruled against Dumas' attempt to claim copyright in the images he had commissioned, but instead found the photographer had breached the author's 'right to privacy' in a landmark legal decision. Near the end of that century two leading United States lawyers – Samuel Warren and Louis Brandeis – mapped out that country's new right to privacy in an article in the prestigious *Harvard Law Review* (Warren & Brandeis 1890). Their interest in the topic followed Warren's anger at the publication in a newspaper of a list of all the guests he had hosted at a high society function at his Boston mansion. Warren and Brandeis wrote: 'The press is overstepping in every direction the obvious bounds of propriety and of decency. Gossip is no longer the resource of the idle and of the vicious, but has become a trade, which is pursued with industry as well as effrontery'. Such concern continues to this day. In more than a century since those cases, celebrities have been at the centre of many cases forging an actionable right to privacy. However, in the United States privacy rights are often trumped by the constitutional First Amendment protections of a free press and associated free expression, particularly when it concerns public figures.

Jurisdictions have varied in their approaches to privacy protections, with some focussing more on such legal actions (torts) empowering people to sue over serious invasions of their privacy, while others have focussed more strongly on protecting their citizens from the misuse of their data by governments and organisations. Several have a combination of both approaches. In the United Kingdom, a series of celebrity actions from 2001 persuaded the courts to bend and stretch the civil action of breach of confidence into an invasion of privacy tort. In New Zealand, another celebrity case involving the photography of television personalities' twin babies outside their home led that country's High Court to spell out its own elements of a privacy action (*Twins case* 2004). At the time of printing, Australia had not yet developed an actionable right to privacy either in a legislative or judge-made form but featured strong data protections in its *Privacy Act 1988*.

Legal, ethical and regulatory dimensions

Privacy, like many areas covered in this book, can be viewed on a moral and cultural spectrum, with the law stepping in to protect actions that a reasonable person in that society would find intrusive or offensive. At a personal level there are many words and actions we use or resist using related to someone's privacy. It might be a simple matter of averting our eyes when someone is getting undressed nearby, refraining from opening someone's mail or viewing their messages on their screen when they have stepped away, avoiding discussing with others sensitive relationship issues a friend might be experiencing, or asking a friend's permission before posting photos of them to social media. There is a strong cultural foundation to both privacy and confidentiality.

Some words or actions related to privacy or confidentiality go beyond this moral level to have ethical, regulatory and legal implications. Posting private and embarrassing images of someone in communications directly to them or to their friends or public over social media would likely break the criminal law (cyberbullying, stalking, harassment, extortion) and prompt other legal actions like invasion of privacy or trespass. Opening someone's mail or hacking their emails or social media accounts would trigger postal and communications tampering laws and would breach most professional ethical codes. Betraying other people's secrets on social media or in the press might well prompt a breach of privacy or breach of confidence action and would also contravene the privacy provisions of ethical charters of occupations like journalists and public relations professionals.

Beyond the moral, ethical and legal dimensions there is a range of regulatory and self-regulatory frameworks that feature behavioural controls over privacy invasion, sometimes with serious consequences. In the social media context, the terms and conditions of use/service of all platforms include privacy provisions. The consequence of their breach can be the suspension or termination of your account and the reporting of your behaviour to law enforcement agencies. For example, Instagram lists a host of privacy related rules and advice at its Privacy and Safety Center (Instagram 2020) including community guidelines, tips for controlling a user's visibility, addressing abuse, blocking people, parental advice, sharing images safely, law enforcement information, data retention and use and avenues for reporting inappropriate behaviour.

Of course, one of the key privacy regulatory environments for a social media user within a work situation is that organisation's corporate policy framework – particularly social media and privacy policies. These usually feature obligations for both the organisation and its staff under employment law, with the employer required to ensure such policies are fair, that they comply with the broader legal requirements, to communicate them effectively to staff with associated training, and to keep them up to date. Employees are usually bound contractually to be aware of reasonable and lawful policies and to comply with them, with adverse consequences typically including a scale of penalties from warnings through to dismissal. Quasi-government tribunals and courts often deal with disputes over such dismissals that some employees appeal, claiming they were treated unfairly.

Data protection issues

Considerable privacy law internationally – and associated risk for social media managers – sits in the domain of 'data protection'. These are the laws that control the way we obtain, store, manage and share the personal information of our organisations' various stakeholders, particularly consumers. The laws vary across jurisdictions in both their letter and enforcement, but basic default requirements have been set within the Organisation for Economic Co-operation and Development (OECD) Guidelines on the Protection of Privacy and Transborder Flows of Personal Data, updated in 2013 (OECD 2020). They aimed to harmonise international privacy legislation by ensuring those who control data in the public and private sectors are consistent in the way they handle information relating to identifiable individuals. They covered such concerns as the need for limits on the amount of personal data organisations could collect lawfully and required that collection should be lawful and fair and with the consent of the individual concerned. The collection should be relevant to the purpose (which should be stated) and should be accurate, comprehensive and updated. Any data should not be disclosed or used for other purposes without the consent of the individual unless that was permitted by law. Individuals should have rights to obtain information about the data held on them and avenues of appeal should be available to them.

An example of data protection legislation is the Australian *Privacy Act 1988*, which embodies all of those requirements after important updates in 2014. It includes Australian Privacy Principles which apply to Australian government agencies, businesses and not-for-profit organisations with turnovers of more than $3 million per year.

'Personal information' was defined broadly to include:

> *information or an opinion about an identified individual, or an individual who is reasonably identifiable:*
> (a) *whether the information or opinion is true or not; and*
> (b) *whether the information or opinion is recorded in a material form or not.*

The Australian Information Commissioner and Privacy Commissioner was empowered to conduct investigations into potential privacy breaches, handle complaints, review decisions, direct an agency to provide a privacy impact assessment and facilitate dispute resolution. (Links to privacy authorities in several other countries and internationally are listed in the Appendix.) Despite these kinds of national regimes, major data breaches continue to occur, with international tech companies and social media platforms sometimes the offenders.

For example, in 2018 the United States Federal Trade Commission (FTC) reached a settlement with the ride-sharing company Uber Technologies over allegations it had deceived customers over the access its employees had to customers' personal information and over its cloud-storage policies for customer data. This followed two breaches including a large breach of both driver and rider data which it had failed to disclose. That was a leak of 600,000 names and drivers' license numbers, 22 million names and phone numbers, and more than 25 million names and email addresses. The settlement placed numerous demands on Uber to revise and file with the FTC updated privacy policies and evidence of record keeping and compliance monitoring for the ensuing 20 years (FTC 2018).

Elements of breach of privacy and confidentiality actions

Nations and jurisdictions vary widely in the extent to which they allow people to sue others over an invasion of their privacy or a breach of their confidentiality. While most Western democracies have data protection laws to discourage governments and organisations from releasing private information about citizens, the law of privacy and confidentiality has been widely divergent and sometimes underdeveloped.

In Australia for example, as we saw earlier, the *Privacy Act 1988* protects against government and corporate misuse of private data and there is a well-established civil action for breach of confidence. However, legislators have not acted upon law reform commissions' recommendations that a new tort be introduced allowing actions over serious invasions of privacy, and the higher courts have been hesitant to introduce a judge-made (common) law in this area (although the High Court has flagged its potential willingness to do so).

By contrast, in New Zealand and the United States such privacy invasion actions have been developed in the courts. The New Zealand law emerging from the High Court in the *Twins case* (2004) required a plaintiff to establish two key platforms to win a claim over the invasion of their privacy:

1   that it involves facts that would carry a reasonable expectation of privacy; and
2   publicity be given to those private facts that a reasonable person would find highly offensive.

The United States Supreme Court developed four categories of actions for privacy invasion, borrowing heavily from the *Harvard Law Review* article written by Warren and Brandeis in 1890.

They include:

*   *Intrusion*: including trespass, covert surveillance and misrepresentation;
*   *Appropriation*: misappropriating the names or likeness of someone else;
*   *False light*: highly offensive portrayal of someone in a false or reckless way (like defamation); and
*   *Public disclosure of embarrassing facts*: by revealing private material about someone that is not of public concern and the revelation would be offensive to the ordinary person (similar to the New Zealand law).

Each is tempered to varying degrees by First Amendment protections of free expression and a free press.

The United Kingdom introduced the law of breach of confidence in 1948 via the common law throughout the former empire. To establish there has been a breach of confidence worthy of damages (or an injunction to prevent the breach), a plaintiff must prove:

*   Confidential information has been conveyed;
*   It was communicated in confidence;
*   The person who received the confidential information misused it (or planned to); and
*   That use or proposed use was damaging to the plaintiff.

In a series of celebrity cases in the first decade of this century (involving the likes of actors Michael Douglas and Catherine Zeta-Jones, model Naomi Campbell, Princess Caroline of Monaco and members of the British royal family) the UK courts allowed this breach of confidence action to morph into an action for serious invasion of privacy. The Douglas and Zeta-Jones case was the trailblazer in 2001, when they won damages from *Hello!* magazine for breach of confidence after the celebrity gossip publication snuck a photographer into their wedding by posing as a guest and published unauthorised photos of the ceremony (*Douglas wedding case* 2001). Soon after, supermodel Naomi Campbell won a breach of confidence action because the *Mirror* newspaper published a photo of her leaving a drug rehabilitation clinic (*Supermodel case* 2004). The court held that even though the image had been taken in a public place it revealed a private fact about her health to her disadvantage. In many cases, celebrities sought and won injunctions preventing the media from publishing the private revelations about them and in some instances even won court-ordered 'super injunctions' – which banned publication of even the fact that an injunction had been issued.

The United Kingdom courts also pioneered the use of the 'Norwich order' (*Norwich order case* 1974) where courts were given the power to order major Internet and social media platforms to reveal the identities of their users who were breaching the confidence of others or using their platform to infringe on other rights. Such an order was issued against Twitter in 2017 to disclose the identity of account holders who had created false 'handles' (accounts) in the names of two senior corporate executives of an Australian company and had used them to post confidential financial information. Other orders demanded Twitter reveal the identities of those who had established the damaging accounts (*Financial Tweets case* 2017). This demonstrates that anonymity in social media is not always guaranteed, particularly if it is being used as a cloak for illegal activities.

Defences

Once the elements of a privacy or confidentiality action have been established, there are only a few defences that can be used by a defendant against them. Of course, in the United States there are strong First Amendment arguments that can be made on the grounds of 'newsworthiness' or the 'public interest'. These apply much more readily to the traditional media – television, radio, newspapers and their online versions – than they do to blogging or social media communications that betray confidences or invade privacy. That is because the mainstream media are more likely to be pursuing stories that hold genuine public concern and substance than many social media users who might be tempted to share material to advance their own interests or for gossip mongering and entertainment. There are exceptions on both sides of course, but the bar is set high when revealing private secrets about people who might not be public figures and, even for such individuals, if the confidential material has nothing to do with their public role.

In the United Kingdom and other Commonwealth jurisdictions there are just a few defences available. The strongest defence is that a court has ordered you to reveal the confidential information – a requirement that sometimes brings journalists unstuck (and sometimes even jailed for contempt of court) when they refuse such an order on ethical grounds because it might identify a confidential source. But of course, the court order to breach a confidence would not likely take the form of a social media post, so this defence does not hold much promise for a social media user or editor.

The United Kingdom and related jurisdictions also feature a 'just cause or excuse' or 'exposure of iniquity' defence. In other words, if the defendant can show there were important reasons why they had to reveal this private or confidential information – particularly if it exposed some serious wrongdoing by the plaintiff – then a defence might apply as a 'justified disclosure'. The 'just cause' defence might also arise if others have revealed the secret or private information while addressing parliament or while giving evidence in court. Short of any order suppressing the revelation of the secret, it could then be published as part of a fair and accurate report of the court proceedings. Again, this is less likely to apply to a social media context, unless perhaps extended court or parliamentary reports are being posted to a Facebook page or as a series of tweets to a designated hashtag covering the court or legislative session.

The primary consideration would be that some overriding matter of public concern must be involved. Various news groups tried unsuccessfully to argue that line in a breach of confidence action in Australia when they were ordered not to publish the fact that some Australian Football League (AFL) players had two infringements against them under the AFL's 'three strikes and you're out' drug use policy. The identities of players with just one or two disciplinary proceedings for drug use were meant to be kept confidential. The court held there was no overriding public interest in revealing them before the third offence, and the purpose of the publication was not to 'disclose an iniquity' but to satisfy public curiosity and build an audience (*AFL players case* 2006).

Strategies for minimising privacy risk

Professional communicators need to develop a mindful awareness of privacy, data protection and confidentiality issues arising in their social media communications and in the posts of others whose material they host. It is wise to follow the specific legal risk assessment steps identified in Chapter 5, applied to these concerns.

1   Identifying the potential (or existing) legal problem

Key to this first step is understanding the basic concepts covered in this chapter to suspect there might be a potential legal problem related to a stakeholder's privacy or confidentiality or that data protection protocols might be compromised. Questions driving this identification are:

- Is information being shared in a post that relates to the private domain of someone's life, such as their health, sexuality, living arrangements, or finances, to a level that a reasonable person might find offensive?
- Is there any indication of a secret or confidentiality being revealed that might operate against the interest of the person it concerns?
- Does the social media post, material or campaign involve the collection, storage, management or dissemination of data about individuals such as their names, ages, addresses, contact details or other private information?
- Is someone's social media anonymity being betrayed?

If so, the alarm bells should be ringing, and you should be delving deeper into the law of the area as it applies in your jurisdiction.

2   Reviewing the areas of the law involved

This book can only outline some of the key basic principles of the laws of privacy, confidentiality and data protection. Once those alarm bells have sounded, you will need information on the specific laws in these areas applying to the jurisdiction where you are based – and also perhaps to the main jurisdictions where you are publishing and do business. This means accessing the key legislation and recent cases in the area to determine your level of exposure to legal action over any invasion of privacy, breach of confidentiality or data breach. Of course, a defence might also apply in the relevant jurisdiction, so you also need to assess the likelihood of it being available in your circumstance. Relevant organisational privacy policies and social media platform terms and conditions also need to be researched and assessed for compliance.

3   Projecting the possible consequences for stakeholders

People resent intrusions into their privacy and the betrayal of their secrets and information about them. These feelings can arise among any of your stakeholder groups, but flagrant disregard of this basic human right and expectation can lead to considerable stakeholder outrage in society, mainstream media and on social media. Customers, clients and staff are among the stakeholders most likely to be at the wrong end of your privacy or confidentiality breach. Of course, a damages judgment can be extremely costly for breach of privacy or confidentiality or a class action by those affected by a data breach (or a fine by a government authority). This can impact the balance sheet and share price of your business or those of your clients, at considerable cost and potential impact on your own employment tenure and professional reputation.

4 Seeking advice/referring upward

Any hint of a breach in these key areas should trigger your upward referral/legal escalation policy in your organisation. This will vary according to its nature and size, but there should always be someone assigned responsibility for deciding whether or not to seek legal advice on such an issue. In other words, someone has to carry the burden of making the important decision about whether the situation warrants the cost of engaging lawyers to advise on the matter. There will also be reporting requirements of statutory and industry authorities in the area of data breaches. Some industry and regulatory bodies will offer advisory support in deciding what needs to be done in such a situation, and several are listed in the Appendix.

5 Publishing/amending/deleting/correcting/apologising

Once all advice has been taken, you will decide whether to go ahead and publish the material or perhaps amend or delete it. Apologies for any privacy, confidentiality or data-related breach should be cleared with lawyers unless the situation warrants the use of a standard pro forma notice suited only to the most minor infringements.

Case study 8.1 – Facebook and the 'This Is Your Digital Life' app

The Australian Information Commissioner pursued Facebook in the Australian Federal Court in 2020 (*Facebook privacy case* 2020) over the social network's provision of personal information (some sensitive) about more than 300,000 Australians to a third party application called 'This Is Your Digital Life' – a personality survey or quiz.

At the time of the alleged disclosure (2014–2015) Facebook allowed app developers to 'self-assess' whether requests for sensitive information were complying with the platform's rules when they used a tool called the Graph Application Programming Interface (Graph API) to harvest a host of personal information from users who had installed the app – and any of their friends who might not have installed it. The app developers sold the personal information to the political consulting firm Cambridge Analytica, which in turn was able to disclose it, earn revenue from it and develop political profiles from it. (An online search for 'Cambridge Analytica' will reveal details on the global extent of the broader scandal.) The Information Commissioner alleged Facebook breached two of its key privacy principles under the *Privacy Act 1988* by disclosing the information for a purpose different from the purpose for which it was collected; and that it failed to take reasonable steps to protect the personal information from unauthorized disclosure, which constituted serious interferences with the privacy of the Australian citizens.

The case was still being contested in the courts when this book was being written, but regardless of the outcome, there are key lessons to be learned:

- Multinational social media platforms need to be aware of the privacy and data protection laws and regulations wherever they operate and take measures to comply with them, because in this case Facebook was found to be 'carrying on business' in Australia.

- Personal data collected by companies for a particular purpose should not be used for a different purpose.
- Organisations should take reasonable steps to prevent the disclosure of personal and sensitive information to third parties.

Case study 8.2 – Using consumer law to combat revenge porn

This case showed that consumer laws could be used to pursue serious invasions of privacy in the United States. Most jurisdictions in that country have laws prohibiting the dissemination of intimate images, and at federal level a law criminalises the use of a computer to harass or intimidate in a way that would cause someone substantial emotional distress. However, First Amendment publishing rights sometimes present a barrier to litigation. It was predominantly consumer and trade law that underpinned this action by the FTC and the State of Nevada against the revenge pornography site 'myex.com'. The site openly solicited intimate images of ex-partners from disgruntled former spouses, boyfriends and girlfriends as material for their porn site. It advertised with the slogan 'Get the dirt before you get hurt or submit your ex gf and bf and get revenge!' (*Revenge porn case* 2018). Part of their revenue model involved charging victims hundreds – and sometimes thousands – of dollars to have their images and data removed from the site. The FTC and Nevada argued successfully the company had engaged in deceptive and unfair acts or practices in violation of federal trade laws and had participated in deceptive trade practices prohibited under state law. They won the case and the myex.com site was shut down, with EMP Media Inc. and its owners ordered to pay more than $2 million in compensation and abide by strict conditions into the future. The key lesson here is that revenue streams based on immoral actions are often in breach of the law – and sometimes a range of different laws can be used to prosecute a particular type of transgression, in this case privacy breaches litigated under trade laws.

Stakeholder theory and privacy

The first step in applying stakeholder theory to privacy laws is to recognise when stakeholders need to be identified. Stakeholders are particularly pertinent when it comes to privacy matters because often the privacy breach has a personal element; therefore the stake in the matter is high, as is the power the group will have. Outrage can also be exaggerated because of the emotions attached to privacy breaches. As mentioned earlier in this chapter, customers, clients and staff are among the stakeholders most likely to be at the wrong end of your privacy or confidentiality breach. The corporate social responsibility strategies of the organisation should also be considered here. Given stakeholder theory is about how a company sits in an ethical way within society, it becomes obvious why privacy and confidentiality concerns would create significant harm for an organisation.

While both case study examples can be used to grasp why it is important to identify stakeholders and the impact they can have on these legal risks, of particular note is Case Study 8.1. When considering this case, it is clear that a core stakeholder group is Facebook users. Although many citizens do not fully understand the laws surrounding privacy, in this particular case that did not matter because the outrage that came from hearing about private personal information being inappropriately shared was enough for this to turn into a significant event. The stake this group had in the situation was significantly high, even for those who were not directly affected, because of the level of consequence that it carried. Where there is consequence people will also have opinions that are strengthened through echo chambers, and the potential to form an unanticipated public. The power they have to implement action is also high because social media has built a public sphere where differing opinions can be viewed, but those with similar opinions can connect to create a stronger voice. Although defences exist for a legal breach of privacy and confidentiality, there is no defence for damaging relationships with stakeholders. A damaged stakeholder relationship carries significant consequence and has the potential to be ongoing.

Discussion questions and project topics

1 Search for an example in the news of a major international data breach related to social media. Explain the key aspects of the breach, how it contravened data protection or privacy laws and how a similar organisation might adjust their data management to minimise the risk of such breaches in the future.

2 You are the CEO of a boutique public relations consultancy. Develop a ten-point social media privacy protection tip-sheet for your staff, setting out your organisation's key rules and expectations for privacy and data protection on social media. Use the Appendix to find relevant privacy bodies and laws in your jurisdiction.

3 Your marketing department wants to run a social media branding contest to promote your company's newest line of cosmetic products on Facebook. Prizes would include gift packs of the products, restaurant vouchers and accommodation. Research and explain the privacy and data protection limitations and requirements for such a contest. (See the Appendix for some links to privacy sites globally and in selected regions.)

4 A strong critic of your government department has been operating via an anonymized Twitter handle. A colleague tells you they have good evidence the critic is actually a colleague in your department. What privacy, confidentiality or data protection barriers might stand in the way of you identifying them and exposing them a. to your boss, and b. via social media? Can you find and report upon a legal case with a similar fact scenario? (See the Appendix for guidance on legal databases.)

Practice tips

- Print out copies of the relevant data protection/privacy legislation in your jurisdiction, along with any handy compliance sheets or brochures produced by relevant government agencies for ready reference if a data protection or privacy issue arises. See the Appendix for links.
- Make a calendar note to access annually the latest privacy/data protection cases and examples in your jurisdiction related to social media breaches. Trawl both the superior court reports and the privacy regulator's website for the examples and circulate them to your colleagues. The Appendix suggests case law databases.
- Research and review the best practice for managing your privacy settings on your main devices and social media platforms. Implement them for the benefit of both yourself and your organisation, realising the settings required will likely be different for each context.
- Compare and contrast the privacy guidelines in the terms and conditions of use for the social media platforms your organisation uses with those of your organisation and discuss with your colleagues how inconsistencies should be managed.

Cases cited

AFL players case. 2006. *Australian Football League & Anor v the Age Company Ltd & Ors* [2006] VSC 308. 30 August. <www.austlii.edu.au/cgi-bin/viewdoc/au/cases/vic/VSC/2006/308.html>

Douglas wedding case. 2001. *Douglas v Hello! Ltd* [2001] 2 WLR 992; [2001] 2 All ER 289. <www.5rb.com/case/douglas-v-hello-ltd/>

Facebook privacy case. 2020. *Australian Information Commissioner v Facebook Inc (No 2)* [2020] FCA 1307. File number: NSD 246 of 2020. <www.judgments.fedcourt.gov.au/judgments/Judgments/fca/single/2020/2020fca1307>

Financial Tweets case. 2017. *X v Twitter Inc.* [2017] NSWSC 1300. <www.caselaw.nsw.gov.au/decision/59cadc2be4b074a7c6e18fa3>

Norwich order case. 1974. *Norwich Pharmacal Co. & Others v Customs and Excise Commissioners* [1974] AC 133.

Revenge porn case. 2018. *Federal Trade Commission and State of Nevada v. EMP Media, Inc et al.* US District Court, District of Nevada Case No. 2: 18-cv-00035-APG-NJK. <www.ftc.gov/system/files/documents/cases/emp_order_granting_default_judgment_6-22-18.pdf> and <www.ftc.gov/news-events/press-releases/2018/06/ftc-nevada-obtain-order-permanently-shutting-down-revenge-porn>

Supermodel case. 2004. *Campbell v MGN Ltd* [2004] UKHL 22. <www.bailii.org/uk/cases/UKHL/2004/22.html>

Twins case. 2004. *Hosking & Hosking v Simon Runting & Anor* [2004] NZCA 34. 25 March. <www.nzlii.org/cgi-bin/sinodisp/nz/cases/NZCA/2004/34.html>

References

Diamond, M. 2004. "Sexual behavior in pre contact Hawai'i: A sexological ethnography." *Revista Española del Pacífico*, *16*, 37–58. www.hawaii.edu/PCSS/biblio/articles/2000to2004/2004-sexual-behavior-in-pre-contact-hawaii.html

FTC. 2018. *Federal Trade Commission gives final approval to settlement with Uber.* Accessed 10 December 2020. www.ftc.gov/news-events/press-releases/2018/10/federal-trade-commission-gives-final-approval-settlement-uber

ICCPR. 1976. *International covenant on civil and political rights.* Accessed 1 December 2020. www.ohchr.org/en/professionalinterest/pages/ccpr.aspx

Instagram. 2020. *Help centre: Privacy and safety center.* Accessed 7 December 2020. https://help.instagram.com/

Maher, P. 2002. "A review of 'traditional' aboriginal health beliefs." *The Australian Journal of Rural Health*, *7*, 229–236. https://doi.org/10.1046/j.1440-1584.1999.00264.x

OECD. 2020. *OECD guidelines on the protection of privacy and transborder flows of personal data.* Accessed 15 December 2020. oecd.org/sti/ieconomy/oecdguidelinesontheprotectionofprivacyandtransborderflowsofpersonaldata.htm

Warren, S. & L. Brandeis. 1890. "The right to privacy." *Harvard Law Review*, 4(5), 193–220. https://jjllplaw.com/The-Right-to-Privacy-Warren-Brandeis-Harvard-Law-Review-1890.html

9 See you in court

Fair coverage versus a fair trial

Glossary

Contempt of court: Acts or communications that tend to interfere with the administration of justice or show disregard for the authority of the court.

National security laws: Anti-terror laws that sometimes restrict publications, inquiries and activities that could impact public safety, intelligence operations or upcoming trials.

Open justice: The principle that the public should be generally free to attend court proceedings and that the media should be free to report upon them.

Scandalising the court: Publications that tend to undermine public confidence in the administration of justice, perhaps by implying judicial officers have an improper motive.

Sub judice contempt: Publication of material that has a real risk of prejudicing an upcoming trial or interfering with the administration of justice. (From the Latin meaning 'under a judge').

Super injunction: A higher level suppression order that even prohibits publication of the fact that a suppression order has been issued.

Suppression order: An order issued by a court to prevent publication of all or part of a matter it is hearing.

Abstract

Society has an expectation that judicial matters are dealt with fairly and appropriately. Yet some cases trigger substantial public curiosity in traditional and social media. Most citizens – including many communication professionals – do not understand fully the risks that can arise when discussing matters before a court. There have been examples of social media commentary causing cases to be dismissed, reinforcing the need to assess legal and organisational risks in posting and hosting material about court matters. This chapter considers the implications for journalists and citizen journalists who write and blog; communication managers (particularly those who work in not-for-profit industries where they feel they should contribute to public discussion about matters and sentences); social media influencers and activists who engage and shape online discussion.

DOI: 10.4324/9781003180111-13

In this chapter

- Contested space: the intersection between the courts and social media
- Fundamental rights at issue
- Open justice and social media
- Varieties of contempt of court
- Prejudicial publicity on social media – *sub judice* contempt
- Scandalising the court
- Breaching suppression orders
- Social media in the courtroom – tweeting, blogging and court communication
- National security laws and secret trials
- Social media as evidence
- Strategies for minimising risk with crime, contempt and the courts
- Case study 9.1 – The Yahoo! 7 contempt case
- Case study 9.2 – The Facebook streaming case
- Stakeholder theory and court-oriented social media
- Discussion questions and project topics
- Practice tips
- Cases cited
- References

Contested space: the intersection between the courts and social media

Everyone loves a classic 'whodunnit' – one of those sensational crimes where there is an element of mystery about finding a suspect and then speculation about whether an accused did the dreaded deed. Social media posts about such crimes, lawsuits and the court process can be among the most popular, particularly if a celebrity or a person in a position of power is involved. At one extreme such discussion represents the workings of an important principle called 'open justice', which requires that the public gets to see and hear what happens in the courtroom (with notable exceptions). At the other extreme they can pose serious risks to some of the key stakeholders in the judicial process – particularly for victims whose privacy and mental health might be at stake and for the accused whose fair trial might be compromised by adverse publicity.

Some social media managers in organisations might never encounter posts about crime or court proceedings. Others routinely engage with the court system because of the nature of their business – such as non-government organisations (NGOs) representing asylum seekers, indigenous prisoners, consumer action groups and environmental lobbies. Corporations might also have the need to manage public communications about civil litigation such as mining leases, trademark breaches and vexatious actions from competitors. A few social media roles actually deal with crime and the courts on a daily or hourly basis, including police communication officers, court information personnel and news media outlets.

In many ways, those with the less frequent interactions with crime and courts face the greatest risks when this kind of material is posted to their sites or as a comment to a discussion. That is because the social media managers dealing with it regularly will likely have the legal knowledge along with risk management processes and policies in place to navigate most scenarios. This chapter is designed to give others the basics of such a toolkit.

Fundamental rights at issue

Several key human rights are at play in the criminal and judicial process. These include the most obvious, with Article 10 of the Universal Declaration of Human Rights stating:

> *Everyone is entitled in full equality to a fair and public hearing by an independent and impartial tribunal, in the determination of his rights and obligations and of any criminal charge against him.*

(United Nations 1948)

Article 11 reinforces this:

> *Everyone charged with a penal offence has the right to be presumed innocent until proved guilty according to law in a public trial at which he has had all the guarantees necessary for his defence.*

(United Nations 1948)

Important here is that social media discussion of cases needs to strike a balance between the presumption of the innocence of the accused and the public nature of a trial. Other important human rights might also be at stake depending on the type of court case and the material that is being posted to social media, including the rights to privacy, honour, reputation, security and protection against discrimination.

Open justice and social media

This notion of a right to a public trial is acknowledgement of the principle of 'open justice' which stems back many centuries in the British legal system. It operates on the basic assumption that, except in specified circumstances, the courts should be open to the public to attend proceedings and the media should be free to report upon them – as if they were the 'eyes and ears' of the citizenry in court (as one judge put it). The extent to which this principle applies to social media communications is still a work in progress with judicial systems throughout the world handling it in different ways.

The limits the courts in various countries place upon media and social media commentary on cases sits on a spectrum of approaches. In the United States, for example, the phenomenon of 'trial by media' exists where there are few limits on public commentary about criminal matters before the courts, although states do vary somewhat in their approaches. This is partly due to the free expression rights inherent in the First Amendment to that nation's Constitution. In celebrity trials like those of Michael Jackson and O.J. Simpson in recent decades, this can include televised proceedings, media and social media speculation about the guilt or innocence of an accused person and even interviews with jurors about their deliberations. In other Western democracies a much more conservative approach has been taken, with the courts issuing so-called super injunctions to prevent publicity in matters involving the footballer Ryan Giggs in the United Kingdom and Cardinal George Pell in Australia and contempt charges laid against some who used the traditional media or social media to breach the orders. The aim of policy makers and judges in this space is to strike a balance between open justice/free expression and an accused's right to a fair trial, privacy and confidentiality.

Varieties of contempt of court

The courts and prosecutors can charge anyone who interferes with the administration of justice with contempt of court – and that includes people posting material to the

Internet or commenting on social media. There are many types of contempt situations and charges, but the main ones that might arise in the social media space are contempt in the face of the court, prejudicial publicity ('*sub judice*' contempt), scandalising the court, disobedience contempt, and revealing the deliberations of jurors. In the more liberal United States judicial system, contempt is largely limited to misbehavior in the courtroom and disobeying a court order.

Contempt 'in the face of the court' relates to inappropriate behavior in the actual courtroom, which could involve a host of actions, but social media users should be most concerned about the possibility of facing these charges if they misuse their devices in court. Obviously the most alarming potential is for a device to ring and interrupt proceedings during a trial (particularly if the ring tone is a sound grab from an obscene song). Devices ringing in court have prompted contempt charges in recent years in many places including India, the United States and the United Kingdom. Depending on the jurisdiction, the posting of social media messages from the courtroom or taking images in the court might also trigger this type of contempt, which we consider in the details that follow.

Publishing material about jurors and their deliberations can be in contempt in many places, and social media misbehavior by jurors can also qualify. A British juror in a drug trial, Joanne Fraill, received an eight-month jail sentence for 'friending' the accused on Facebook in an early instance of this kind of misconduct (*Juror's case* 2011). The United States is another exception to juror confidentiality, offering much more licence to identify and interview jurors. The Pennsylvania Supreme Court even ruled that the revelation of the names of jurors improved the prospect of a fair trial for an accused and contributed to open justice and transparency, although it made exceptions in a 2018 case following a mistrial because it believed revealing the names of the jurors would prevent a further fair trial (TribLive 2020).

Prejudicial publicity on social media – *sub judice* contempt

Trial by media has become all too common in modern times – particularly in the social media era when anybody can publish prejudicial information about an accused person that could prompt a wrongful conviction, a mistrial or even an acquittal on appeal. Such prejudicial publicity about a court case is called '*sub judice*' contempt – coming from the Latin term meaning 'under a judge'. In Commonwealth countries (including the United Kingdom, Australia, New Zealand and so on) the *sub judice* period or criminal time zone starts from the moment an accused has been arrested or charged with a crime, and ends after they have been convicted, acquitted or the appeal period has expired. This is the sensitive period during which publications – including those on social media – can contribute to an injustice occurring, particularly if it is material that could affect the recollection of witnesses or sway the opinion of jurors hearing the case.

Particularly sensitive material during this time zone that can trigger contempt charges includes any assumption of guilt (or even innocence), evidence that has not been presented to the jury (including material from earlier proceedings), visual identification of key participants (particularly the accused) and damning evidence about the accused such as alleged confessions, criminal behavior or social media posts. For example, a journalist who published Facebook communications from a murder victim predicting her partner would kill her was found in contempt because the jury was not meant to know about those posts (*Yahoo! 7 contempt case* 2016 & 2017 – see Case Study 9.1).

The courts are most concerned with material published into the jurisdiction of the trial which jurors or witnesses might be likely to see – material which might cause a 'real and substantial' risk of prejudice to the trial as a matter of practical reality. While many comments on social media fall within this category – particularly when there is an upcoming or in-progress high profile trial of a renowned suspect or celebrity defendant – many commenters are not charged with contempt despite posting highly prejudicial information or comments. This can be because they are beyond the reach of the particular judicial system, perhaps in another country, or because their following on social media is so small that it would be unlikely a juror or witness would view that particular offensive post. Those more likely to be charged with *sub judice* contempt are individuals or organisations with much larger followings on their social media accounts who also have some legal or corporate presence in the jurisdiction where the trial is scheduled. These might include celebrities, social media influencers, media commentators, online media outlets and other organisations with substantial social media followings.

One former journalist was acquitted on a charge of contempt for his prejudicial publicity about a prominent sex murder case where he had tweeted and blogged that the accused was on parole for a related sexual conviction when the trial was pending and that he had an extensive criminal record. The court held it was not convinced beyond reasonable doubt that it stood to prejudice the case because of the small readership, the time remaining before the trial, and the fact the material had been widely published elsewhere on social media. He was, however, convicted of disobedience contempt because he had breached a suppression order banning publication of the prior convictions and served 100 days in jail (*Rape Priors cases* 2013).

There are two defences to *sub judice* contempt. The first, and most common, is the simple strategy of only publishing fair and accurate reports about cases containing material that has been presented in court while the jury was present. (This is problematic for coverage on social media because the fairness of a single post might be questionable when taken out of the context of the whole coverage, perhaps to a hashtag.) The second, which is very difficult to prove, is that the contemptuous material is so important it is overwhelmingly in the 'public interest' that it be published. It would be a rare situation indeed where a judge would excuse a social media post on this basis.

Also worth considering here is the possibility that third parties might post contemptuous material to your organisation's website or social media comment stream. As pointed out in Chapters 6 and 11, jurisdictions vary on the level of responsibility you might carry for the comments of others on sites you host, but it is likely you will be required (at the very least) to remove any contemptuous material within a 'reasonable time'. That might be as part of your routine review and moderation of comments or immediately after it has been brought to your attention.

Scandalising the court

Some litigants and politically motivated social media users blame the judge when a court decision does not go their way. Occasionally this snowballs into a full conspiracy theory implying judges are biased or corrupt, and these kinds of allegations can erode the public's confidence in the administration of justice. This form of contempt is called 'scandalising the court'. In the United States and Canada it is never used because of free speech protections. In many other countries, particularly those of Commonwealth origin, it usually involves the implication that a judge might reach their decision under some improper influence or motive. Three Australian government ministers and a major newspaper faced the threat of this type of contempt from the Victorian Court of Appeal in 2017 after the newspaper published tweets from the politicians suggesting the court would go easy on some convicted terrorists by reducing their sentences because the judges were left-leaning appointments with an ideological agenda. The court issued a statement that the criticism was designed to undermine public confidence in the administration of justice. No action was taken after the newspaper and then the politicians apologised (*Liberal Ministers case* 2017). Of course, this law should not prevent legitimate criticism of the judiciary based on provable facts, but expert legal advice should be taken before doing so because both contempt and defamation actions could arise.

Breaching suppression orders

Disobeying any order by a court is a contempt. Court orders restricting publication in some way are called 'suppression orders' or 'non-publication orders'. Such orders might ban the publication of just one element of a case – such as the name of a protected witness or the details of the previous convictions of an accused. Or they might prohibit any reporting of the case until a certain time, perhaps until after other related proceedings have finished.

Depending on the jurisdiction, these orders might be well publicised to the traditional media via special court distribution lists and communication with court reporters. However, the onus is on those using social media to approach the courts to see whether such restrictions are in place. That's because it is almost impossible for the courts to circulate such a prohibition so widely that all social media users would be aware of it. If they did, it would defeat the fundamental purpose of the order – which is to prevent the widespread publication of the censored fact or segment of proceedings. In some cases, the order suppresses even the fact that a suppression order has been issued. This is called a 'super injunction', and it has been criticized as an imposition on free expression and open justice.

Eighteen journalists and 12 news outlets faced contempt charges in the Victorian Supreme Court in Australia in 2020 over the breach of suppression orders put in place during the trial of a prominent church figure for historical child sex abuse charges. Some of them had referred their readers to offshore news sites that had carried the suppressed details about the case as a device to avoid publishing the material themselves. Others had not identified the accused. These techniques did not prevent prosecutors bringing the disobedience contempt charges against them (Cooper 2020). The individual's conviction was overturned after an appeal to the High Court but the contempt charges proceeded until several of the charges were dropped and 12 news companies pleaded guilty and fined a total of more than $1 million. Countless social media posts breaching the suppression orders were not prosecuted.

Disobedience contempt charges can apply to many situations beyond the breach of a suppression order. Journalists face this type of contempt charge if they refuse to answer a question in court related to the identity of their confidential source, or if they refuse a court order to hand over devices or notebooks that might reveal their informant.

In addition to suppression orders, a host of reporting restrictions apply to different kinds of individuals and proceedings. These vary markedly between jurisdictions, but in most Western democracies the identities of juvenile accused and witnesses and sexual assault victims are kept anonymous. Other identification restrictions can apply to the accused in sexual criminal cases during the preliminary proceedings, to mental health tribunals and cases, family law matters and national security trials. All this underscores the fact that social media commentary about the criminal and judicial systems requires considerable research and legal advice.

Social media in the courtroom – tweeting, blogging and court communication

Professional communicators who are accustomed to using social media as part of their daily routine will need to pause and check before continuing their normal device use in a court room. There are tough restrictions on the use of any devices – including mobile phones – in the courts of many jurisdictions, and contempt charges can be laid for disobeying them. You will need to check the specific requirements and protocols of your local courthouse before turning on your device in the court precincts. Some courts allow extensive use of new technologies for accredited journalists but ban the use of devices for members of the public. Others allow devices to be used if in silent mode on the condition that images are not taken within the courtroom. Courts began to allow journalists to tweet from the courtroom with special permission from as early as 2010, but it took some years before they developed protocols around it. In some places the media are allowed to live blog and live tweet from the courtroom about a case that is in progress, while others require a delay before tweeting (such as 30 minutes) to allow time for material to be suppressed if the court sees fit.

From time to time, courts have to remind people of the rules around technology. That happened in 2021 in the midst of COVID-19 when court hearings were being conducted remotely online and a witness to a case circulated a screen capture taken in the middle of proceedings. The British court ruled the action was in breach of Section 85C of the *Courts Act 2003* (as inserted by the *Coronavirus Act 2020*) which provides that it is 'an offence for a person to make or attempt to make an unauthorised recording or transmission of court proceedings, which includes images' (*Screen capture case* 2021).

Some social media contempt cases relate to a breach of several areas of contempt, including the use of a device. For example, as discussed in Case Study 9.2, the live Facebook streaming outside a United Kingdom court when a sexual offence criminal jury was considering its verdict led to convictions for filming within the court precincts, breaching a reporting restriction order, posing a substantial risk to the course of justice in the case, and interfering directly with the course of justice by aggressively filming defendants (*Facebook streaming case* 2019).

National security laws and secret trials

Cyber attacks by foreign agents upon a nation state have become a major security issue and can take a variety of forms including hacking, denial of service, trolling and the insidious insertion of propaganda into social media streams. Communication professionals – particularly those working for government and defence agencies, large corporations and their strategic partners – need to be on the alert for these kinds of activities.

At the same time, a host of national security and anti-terrorism laws introduced in most countries this century can have dire consequences for social media managers. The new laws cover a litany of social media communication situations, typically including:

- The powers of governments to monitor communications and access historical metadata.
- Search and seizure powers to investigate suspicious online activities.
- Direct channels of communication with social media platforms demanding account details of users.

- Limitations on what might be posted about national intelligence networks and personnel, with jail penalties applying.
- Imprisonment for leaking classified information and for sharing it with others.
- Powers to close courts during national security trials and suppress information about their findings.

Sometimes the simple act of sharing elements of your job description on platforms like LinkedIn can represent an unacceptable risk. In 2020 the spy agency ASIO (Australian Security Intelligence Organisation) launched an advertising campaign to discourage people from announcing on social media that they had been given special security clearances in their workplaces. The fear was that foreign agents might use such information to target them or to simply learn more about Australian government security and processes (ASIO 2021).

Social media as evidence

The digital trail we leave on social media can come back to haunt us in future litigation. A key part of the mindful use of social media by communication professionals is in acknowledging this and behaving as though every social media post is on the public record and will have the potential to be used as evidence against us in the courts. Investigating authorities have the powers to subpoena our communications from Internet service providers and telcos and even to de-encrypt information we thought had been sent securely. Depending on the rules of evidence in the particular jurisdiction, much of this might be admissible in a criminal trial, or perhaps in a civil dispute between an organisation and a competitor or claimant.

Strategies for minimising risk with crime, contempt and the courts

All of the above highlights the fact that the criminal, civil and judicial processes can be fraught for communication professionals wanting to post or host material about the court system or cases. Jurisdictional practices, expectations and penalties vary widely so it is wise to engage experts in the field if news and commentary in this space is part of your routine business. If, as is more likely, it is only something that comes onto your radar occasionally, you need to seek legal advice before commenting on a case or posting information about it. If your organization is a party to the action, then any communication about it should be run past your lawyers because an error can impact the outcome of the case and the monetary settlement – and could even land you in jail for contempt of court. The specific legal risk assessment steps foreshadowed in Chapter 5 might apply to this topic as follows:

1 **Identifying the potential (or existing) legal problem**

   Crucial here is to place a red flag on any social media post that concerns a crime, the court system or national security and to reflect immediately on the situation. If it relates to a serious crime, you need to assess the *sub judice* period or criminal time zone that applies at the time of proposed posting. For example, if nobody has yet been arrested or charged with a crime, then the period for *sub judice* contempt has not yet started. However, if an arrest or charge has occurred, it means the judicial process has started and there will be a risk of contempt of court right through until any opportunity for appeal has expired. That restricts material implying the guilt or innocence of an accused, visual identification and material not shown to a jury. Throughout this time period there are also risks of other contempts such as approaching or identifying jurors, scandalising the court and contempt in the face of the court. Of course, other laws such as defamation, breach of privacy/confidentiality and the range of potential national security laws could also apply.

2   Reviewing the areas of the law involved

Because so much of the law of courts, contempt and national security can vary markedly across jurisdictions, your review of the laws needs to be focussed on those applying in your own nation, state, province or territory. If you are doing this sort of publishing often, then a good local media law desktop reference text would be useful for some quick revision of the legislation and recent cases in the area. Links to some of the major courts in several countries appear in the Appendix.

3   Projecting the possible consequences for stakeholders

Stakeholders in a social media post about a court, criminal or national security matter can extend well beyond the walls of the particular organisation hosting or posting the material. Of course, there can be impacts of a miscommunication about these matters upon the usual stakeholders such as shareholders, staff, the board, customers and clients. But a serious legal breach in this area can compromise the right of an accused to a fair trial, reputations of litigants and judges and perhaps even the very safety of members of the public if it is a national security matter. Corporate social responsibility principles require that an organisation act ethically and responsibly in its public communications, and this certainly applies when using social media in the important democratic domain of justice. At a financial level, the organisation's balance sheet can be impacted by abandonment by institutional shareholders, fines and damages payouts for serious breaches, and even the jailing of personnel who have committed a serious contempt.

4   Seeking advice/referring upward

Few areas of social media law are more deserving of expert counsel than those involving the courts, crimes and national security. The stakes are so high and the laws so varied and sometimes technical that legal advice is most likely warranted. Of course, this might first require referral upward to a supervisor designated under your organisation's legal escalation policy. In this domain, it is likely there will also be communication officers assigned to the court systems in your jurisdiction, and they can be useful as a point of consultation about the restrictions that might apply, particularly if there is a chance that a suppression order is in place or if the matter has other restrictions on publication, such as those that usually apply in sexual, juvenile and family law cases. Search the links to key courts in the Appendix to see if a courts communication officer is available in your jurisdiction.

5   Publishing/amending/deleting/correcting/apologising

The adage 'if in doubt, leave out' applies to social media posts about crimes, courts and national security. It is better to hold off publication if there is any doubt about the law or possible consequences. Of course, you would go through the normal processes of trying to amend or delete material to fit within legal defences, and if something has already been published that is in some way in breach of the previously mentioned laws, then you should screen-capture it then delete it before seeking legal advice on the wording of any proposed correction or apology.

Case study 9.1 – The Yahoo! 7 contempt case

One of the most important lessons for the news media to learn about reporting on crimes and courts is that they cannot use many of the approaches they might use with other stories. To avoid problems with *sub judice* contempt (prejudicial publicity) and defamation, they need to stick to fair and accurate reports of what transpires in open court in the presence of the jury. This means none of the interviewing they would normally undertake for a story, and also the need for extreme care when using material sourced from the Internet or from earlier stories about the case as background. The latter was the trap Yahoo! 7 journalist Krystal Johnson encountered when she wrote and published a court report about a murder trial happening in a different Australian city. The jury was already hearing the case at the time Johnson posted her article. She included Facebook posts that had been taken from earlier media coverage where the victim had predicted her accused partner would murder her and detailed episodes of violence by the accused against her. Particularly prejudicial was a Facebook post from the victim three months before she died: 'It won't be long and he will put me six feet under. I love him until the day he kills me. He needs a punching bag, we all do'. This damning evidence had not been presented to the jury. The judge concluded that it 'objectively and as a matter of practical reality, had a real and definite tendency to prejudice the trial of the accused' (*Yahoo! 7 contempt case* 2016). Given her inexperience in the role and the lack of training in her organisation, Johnson escaped with a two-year good behaviour bond after which the contempt charge was dismissed – but her employer, Yahoo! 7, copped a $300,000 fine for the infringement and instituted new training and legal review protocols for its court stories. Key lessons from the case included the need to have others check your work before publication and that social media posts that might be evidence in court proceedings cannot be reproduced during the *sub judice* contempt period.

Case study 9.2 – The Facebook streaming case

Activist and political organisations need to exercise special caution when they decide to use social media to report or comment upon court cases. Far-right and anti-Muslim United Kingdom activist Stephen Christopher Yaxley-Lennon (better known as Tommy Robinson, founder of the English Defence League) was jailed for nine months in 2019 on several counts of contempt of court related to his live-streaming outside a high-profile sex crime trial involving Muslim defendants. The High Court judgment cited here tracked the complicated series of cases leading up to his imprisonment for having live-streamed within the courthouse and surrounds, publishing material online in breach of a reporting restriction order, creating a substantial risk to justice by live-streaming while a jury was considering its verdict and for interfering directly in the course of justice by live-stream filming the accused in an aggressive way. This amounted basically to what we have described in this chapter as contempt in the face of the court, disobedience contempt and *sub judice* contempt. More than 10,000 viewers watched his videos live, while millions downloaded them later. The appeals court distinguished between Robinson's live-streaming and 'professional journalists reporting on legal proceedings (who) are generally well informed, careful, and well-advised'. The court highlighted the impact of inflammatory language:

> *The dangers of using the un-moderated platforms of social media with the unparalleled speed and reach of such communications, are obvious. . . . His words had a clear tendency to encourage unlawful physical or verbal aggression towards identifiable targets. . . . . [T]here was plainly a real risk that the defendants awaiting jury verdicts would see themselves as at risk, feel intimidated, and that this would have a significant adverse impact on their ability to participate in the closing stages of the trial. That in itself would represent a serious impediment to the course of justice.*
>
> (*Facebook streaming case* 2019, para 76)

There are key lessons in this case for social media professionals. Risks escalate if you are reporting upon crimes or cases where your organisation is involved or has strong stance or a vested interest. Live streaming has dangers at the best of times, and they are amplified in this kind of highly charged situation. As the judgment said, it calls for communications by professionals who are 'well informed, careful, and well-advised'.

Stakeholder theory and court-oriented social media

As mentioned earlier, there are many stakeholders in the court process – particularly when attention is centred upon a high-profile civil case or a criminal pursuit or trial. The most obvious ones are the suspect or the accused (who deserves to be considered innocent until proven guilty in court), witnesses and jurors whose testimony and judgement might be tainted by adverse publicity, police and lawyers whose efforts might be stymied by prejudicial publicity and judicial officers whose proceedings might be compromised. Beyond these key individuals, many other stakeholders can be impacted by inappropriate social media commentary, including the families and social groups of the parties to an action through to society as a whole where the 'rule of law' in a democracy requires that nothing should interfere with justice being seen to be done – and actually being done. Thus, this area of law requires a much broader consideration of potential stakeholders and the impacts of communications in line with the complexities of social identity theory. The five-step process from Chapter 5 provides a basis to analysing the legal risk related to communicating on matters before the court and the impact this might have on stakeholders.

Discussion questions and project topics

1   If someone posts to your organisational social media site something highly prejudicial to a current case (such as the criminal record of the accused), should your organization be held responsible for hosting it? Check the local law on this and explain your answer.
2   The chief financial officer in your organisation has been charged with fraud. Your CEO wants you to post to all your social media channels a statement

saying the accused has been stood down pending the trial and expressing her confidence in the CFO's integrity and innocence. Apply a legal risk analysis to this situation and explain your likely course of action.

3   Court reporting restrictions vary markedly across jurisdictions. List three arguments for allowing more discussion about criminal matters in your jurisdiction, and three arguments for limiting such discussion.

4   Look up the key laws limiting the identification of certain personnel in court cases in your jurisdiction and list them in a one-page summary. Use the Appendix to help find legislation databases in your region. Without limiting your search, at least include the restrictions on identifying sexual assault victims, sexual crime accused, juveniles, mental health patients and people involved in family law proceedings.

Practice tips

- Brush up on the laws of contempt, criminal procedure, reporting restrictions and national security laws in your jurisdiction so you are well versed in the topic to identify when the alarm bells should be ringing. Use the Appendix as a starting point.
- Instigate a routine social media moderation regime so you can identify and act upon any comments about crimes, the judicial system or national security as soon as they are posted to your sites.
- Remember the adage 'If in doubt, leave out' and use this as the default position when posting or hosting material about crimes, court cases, national security or the legal system.
- If litigation is likely involving your organisation or personnel, develop a risk management action plan mapping out the potential social media consequences of the matter throughout the court process.

Cases cited

Facebook streaming case. 2019. *AG v Yaxley-Lennon* [2019] EWHC 1791 (Admin). <www.judiciary. uk/wp-content/uploads/2019/07/ag-v-yaxley-lennon-jmt-190709.pdf>

Juror's case. 2011. *Attorney General v Fraill and Another* [2011] EWCh 1629. <www.casemine.com/ judgement/uk/5a8ff71160d03e7f57ea70d1>

Liberal Ministers case. 2017. Supreme Court of Victoria, 16 June, 'Statement of the Court of Appeal in terrorism cases'. <www.supremecourt.vic.gov.au/contact-us/news/statement-of-the-court-of-appeal-in-terrorism-cases>; Supreme Court of Victoria. 23 June. 'Statement of the Court of Appeal in *DPP v MHK and DPP v Besim*'. 23 June. <www.supremecourt.vic.gov.au/law-and-practice/ judgments-and-sentences/judgment-summaries/statement-of-the-court-of-appeal-in-dpp>

Rape Priors cases. 2013. *R v Hinch* [2013] VSC 520. 2 October. <www.austlii.edu.au/au/cases/vic/VSC/ 2013/520.html>; *R v Hinch (No. 2)* [2013] VSC 554. 18 October. <www.austlii.edu.au/cgi-bin/sinodisp/ au/cases/vic/VSC/2013/554.html>

Screen capture case. 2021. *SLF Associates Inc v (1) HSBC (UK) Bank Plc & Ors* [2021] EWHC 5 (Ch). 6 January. <www.bailii.org/ew/cases/EWHC/Ch/2021/5.html>

Yahoo! 7 contempt case. 2016 & 2017. *DPP v Johnson & Yahoo!7* [2016] VSC 699. 28 November. <www. austlii.edu.au/cgi-bin/viewdoc/au/cases/vic/VSC/2016/699.html>; *DPP v Johnson & Yahoo!7* (No 2) [2017] VSC 45. 17 February. <www.austlii.edu.au/cgi-bin/viewdoc/au/cases/vic/VSC/2017/45.html>

References

ASIO. 2021. "Think before you link." *Australian Security Intelligence Organisation*. Canberra. Accessed 10 January 2021. www.asio.gov.au/TBYL.html

Cooper, A. 2020. "Pell contempt charges against media whittled down, but most remain." *The Age*. 4 December. www.theage.com.au/national/pell-contempt-charges-against-media-whittled-down-but-most-remain-20201204-p56kpt.html

TribLive. 2020. "Editorial: Names of jurors in held trial should be released." *TribLive Tribune Review*. 18 July. https://triblive.com/opinion/editorial-names-of-jurors-in-held-trial-should-be-released/

United Nations. 1948. *Universal declaration of human rights*. UN, New York. www.un.org/en/universal-declaration-human-rights/index.html

Part 5

Legal risks of social media in business

10 Employment law – private versus professional social media risk

Glossary

Code of conduct: A policy that sets out the rules and responsibilities regarding behaviour for employees and representatives of an organisation.

Corporate governance: A set of rules or regulations that define an organisation's approach, behaviour and operation, with a strong focus on corporate social responsibility.

Employee advocacy: Employees, either specifically chosen or granted permission through organisational policies, advocating for their organisation.

Employment law: A set of laws that apply to the rights and responsibilities of both employees and employers.

Private messaging: Social media platforms that do not have a public-facing approach to sharing information and instead facilitate private conversations between members.

Private social media use: The use of social media platforms as a private citizen expressing personal views or sharing personal content.

Professional social media use: The use of social media in an official capacity on behalf of an organisation.

Social media policy: A corporate policy that outlines expectations of employees who post to social media either in an official or unofficial capacity.

Abstract

Employees are considered important stakeholders, but managing internal stakeholders can carry significant risks. Internal policies and codes of conduct must be in place to help mitigate risks and encourage employees to work in partnership with their employers. While it must be established that most organisations have some form of code of conduct or social media policy, this chapter discusses some unique cases that show that such codes and policies cannot cover all potential risks. Professional communications are a space where social media promotion is essential to growth and prosperity, and the rise of employee advocates or ambassadors is contributing to this success. For employees to be prepared to advocate for their employer, they must understand the impact that their personal social media use can have. This chapter also establishes the need for all publishers to understand the difference between private messaging and professional social media use and where the boundaries blur. It looks at cases that have led to careers being destroyed by ill-conceived social media posts.

DOI: 10.4324/9781003180111-15

Employment law – what is it and why is it important?

Employment law is an important area of commercial law and a key consideration for any business. It covers workplace relations and human resources, along with relevant internally developed contracts and policies. Employees are at the core of an organisation and employers must ensure fair work conditions and rights to maintain a healthy, happy and safe employee stakeholder group. In most jurisdictions fair work regulations exist through government agencies or regulators relying on legislation specific to the jurisdiction. It is essential that all organisations are run in accordance with these laws, but it is equally important for employees to be familiar with expectations about their social media behaviour to ensure a breach of either legislation or specific policies does not occur. Employment law exists to protect everyone involved including internal stakeholders, external stakeholders and an organisation's reputation.

Does private communication on social media really exist?

This question has been asked many times since social media's inception. In an ideal world, individuals should be able to post to social media in a private capacity about things they want to share with friends, relatives and acquaintances. There are also a number of social media platforms that do not have public-facing aspects, such as Facebook Messenger, WhatsApp and WeChat, which feature private messaging interfaces. Although these are considered private and confidential, the truth of the matter is that everything online is published in a way that has capacity to be seen by anyone. Although a number of social media platforms, including public-facing platforms, have rigid privacy settings that can be applied, they do not prevent information from being copied and forwarded, or even subpoenaed as part of the discovery process for a trial. The best approach to private social media is to treat it as a space where you share private information without posting anything that could have ramifications if sent publicly.

Although you can attempt to draw a clear distinction between private and professional social media use, you should still only post content on the assumption that your employer or other important stakeholders might see it. And although admirable levels of self-control are required, you should avoid commenting on social media with your personal opinions, particularly if they differ from the position of your employer or stand to damage your organisation's brand or reputation.

There are a number of examples of people misconceiving the true level of privacy of a social media post, particularly in the realm of job-seeking and new employment. For instance, there have been cases of newly appointed staff posting questions to social media asking how to pass drug tests and other examples where employees have expressed their displeasure about a job they have just started. It is also important to consider past social media posts on private accounts as there are many examples of people losing jobs because of past social media comments. One such situation is explained in the Paris Brown Case Study 10.3 later in this chapter, but all social media can resurface at some point.

In 2013 Lindsay Stone and her friend, who both worked as carers for high-functioning disabled people, were in Washington, DC, on a work trip when they visited Arlington Cemetery with the group they were caring for. The pair had a running joke where they would take pictures of themselves disobeying signs. Stone noticed a sign in the cemetery that said 'silence and respect', and proceeded to take a picture pretending to shout while holding up her middle finger. The image was posted to Facebook and although the women discussed its appropriateness, they both decided it was harmless and kept it posted because their small social media following knew about their joke images. Four weeks later, the image surfaced publicly, and online outrage resulted in both Stone and her friend losing their jobs (Ronson 2015b).

We discuss codes of conduct and social media policies in the next section, and it is important to know what these documents say about personal social media use. Often they will include wording that suggests the code or policy applies at any time that you can be identified as an employee. Sometimes, as will be discussed in Case Study 10.2, a code can apply even if your social media posts are anonymous. Government departments can use data retention laws and demands to platforms to discover the identities of users. The major platforms issue 'transparency reports' where they reveal government requests for user identification information. For example, in the first six months of 2020, Google reported it handed over user information to governments more than 103,000 times globally for 'civil, administrative, criminal, and national security purposes' (Google 2021). Even so-called encrypted communications are sometimes penetrable.

Many people state on their private social media sites their place of work. Sometimes identification material on different social media platforms can be cross-referenced to reveal an author of seemingly anonymised posts. It is easy to identify a place of work if the user has added or follows colleagues, has 'checked in' at their workplace or somewhere nearby, has been tagged in or appeared in a video or image used in an official post or has used their social media to promote or advocate for their place of employment.

If you do any of these things, you can be identified. An example of this obvious identification is the *Election Post case* (2020). Danyelle Bennet was a long-term employee who worked for 16 years as an emergency telecommunicator at the Emergency Communications Centre in Nashville. She was dismissed from her position after a lengthy investigation into some comments she made on social media following the 2016 presidential election. The social media posts were considered racially offensive despite Bennet claiming they were in jest as a response to a comment that initiated the use of the language. However, her comments were publicly available, and her profile identified her as being employed by both the Emergency Communications Centre and the Metro Police Department. In 2020 Bennet filed an unfair dismissal claim on the argument that she had a constitutional right to free speech under the First Amendment to the US Constitution. Her case was heard in the US Court of Appeals. The court ruled in favour of the employer on the following grounds:

> *Based on the above analysis and in light of the discretion we must grant leadership at Metro, its interest in maintaining an effective workplace with employee harmony that serves the public efficiently outweighs Bennett's interest in incidentally using racially offensive language in a Facebook comment.*
>
> (*Election post case* 2020)

Another dismissal case where an employee clearly identified her place of work was the United Kingdom *Social media policy case* (2016). In this case the employee identified her place of work on social media and proceeded to write a number of negative comments about her organisation in a public capacity despite a social media policy being implemented at the company only months prior. Her posts were brought to the attention of her employer, and she was dismissed after a disciplinary hearing. She then took the matter to the Employment Tribunal but was found to have been fairly terminated because of the presence of a social media policy that clearly stated she should refrain from posting about certain aspects of her employment. Both of these cases highlight the strength of employment laws and the role they play in maintaining workplace harmony. It is therefore essential that all social media publishers understand the impact of online publication regardless of whether its use is in a personal or professional capacity.

Jurisdictions vary in the application of the law to these dismissal cases, but there is a common thread: an organisation's successful defence of an unfair dismissal claim over social media will often hinge on whether it has a social media policy distinguishing between public and private social media use; whether it keeps the policy updated and trains its staff on its requirements; and whether the policy is reasonable, taking into account the type of industry and what might determine appropriate private use of social media by employees (Pearson & Polden 2019, 510).

Case study 10.1 – Justine Sacco and her viral tweet

In December 2013 Justine Sacco, then aged 30 and a senior director working in public relations, was on her way from New York to South Africa to visit family when she began tweeting little jokes about her travels. For instance, on her layover at Heathrow airport she tweeted:

> *Chilly – cucumber sandwiches – bad teeth. Back in London!*

But before the final flight to Cape Town, she tweeted to her 170 followers:

> *Going to Africa. Hope I don't get AIDS. Just kidding. I'm white!*

Despite sitting in the terminal for 30 minutes awaiting her flight and occasionally checking her phone to see no replies, by the time she completed the 11-hour journey she had become the number one worldwide trend on Twitter, prompting the hashtag

#HasJustineLandedYet. The world watched and discussed the topic while Sacco was in the air. It was like a live soap opera unfolding on Twitter. A Cape Town Twitter user went so far as to go to the airport and document her arrival. When her plane landed, she was inundated with replies, comments, calls and text messages. Her friend worked fast to delete her Twitter account, but the damage was done. Arriving in a foreign country as a despised person, Sacco found that hotel staff were threatening to strike if she arrived at the places she had booked and was told that there was no guarantee for her safety. The family she was visiting were angry because they were racial equality activists and felt tarnished by her comments.

This is an early example of an unanticipated public forming on social media and contributing to a trending topic but ultimately publicly shaming Sacco. It speaks directly to the outrage factor of 'Effect on vulnerable' because her comment was directed at two key vulnerable populations – people of colour and those living with AIDS. The tweet was interpreted as her flaunting her privilege and it was this that enraged the online community. In an interview, Sacco indicated that the tweet wasn't meant to be racist but instead a 'reflective critique of white privilege' (Ronson 2015a). The word count restrictions on Twitter and the interpretive nature of the written word meant that it was not what might have been intended – but it was what was interpreted that stuck.

Corporate governance – social media policy or code of conduct

Employment contracts play an essential role in binding social media use. As we establish in the next section, an employment contract does not have to silence employees but instead sets boundaries regarding what is expected. What is corporate governance and how does it apply to social media? Corporate governance has played a key role in business for some time and can be defined as a set of rules or policies that define an organisation's approach, behaviour and how it operates. It works alongside jurisdictional legislation related to fair work and other employment laws and case law precedents and is a set of instructions specific for the organisation that keeps them in line with employment law. It has a strong association with the organisation's corporate social responsibility as it assists with the representation of the organisation in the view of its stakeholders, audiences and publics. An organisation with strong corporate governance is often trusted because it appears well managed, in control and in line with societal expectations. With burgeoning employee access to social media, governance around social media use, both official and unofficial, has become a crucial inclusion in any corporate governance portfolio.

In some communication professions such as journalism, employees are encouraged to use social media to spark debate. Although many news organisation policies ask employees to identify themselves with full disclosure, they also ask that staff highlight the distinction between private and organisational opinions. However, it is still a key point that journalists can be identified as working for a news organisation, and their posts will be seen to reflect an organisation's opinion. In January 2021, the *New York Times* was at the centre of debate around a freelance editor with the claim being that she was fired for partiality after posting a tweet before the presidential inauguration of Joe Biden. In her tweet she had exclaimed that she had 'chills' watching him arrive. This caused right-wing activists to lobby the media organisation and her. The *New York Times* would not confirm for privacy reasons whether they had parted ways with the freelance editor but stated nobody had been fired over a single tweet. Yet they did state the organisation's policy was clear that employees are prohibited from publishing 'anything that damages *The Times's* reputation for strict neutrality in reporting on politics and government' (Gabbatt 2021). This is a common theme in social media policies.

Some scholars have conducted research into similarities across social media policies. For instance, Johnston (2015) analysed a sample of 20 international social media policies – including government, corporate and news media – and found that the common themes across these policies were:

* Identification with organisation and disclosure
* Private versus public distinction
* Transparency and fake promotions
* Leading debate and expressing commentary
* Staff as ambassadors and creating conversations
* Prohibitions and confidentiality
* Legal guidelines
* Non-compliance
* Moderation of comments
* Impact and global message
* Purpose or aim
* 'Help you' clause
* Links or reference to other policies.

(Johnston 2015, 180)

Duffy and Knight (2018) considered the social media policies of 17 news organisations in the United States, United Kingdom, Canada and Australia and found that some of the key concerns related to private versus professional use and the blurring of lines between the two, along with apprehension over potential bias or impartiality that may occur, as was seen in the *New York Times* example given previously.

Further, Stohl et al. (2017) conducted a study of social media policies for 112 top global companies and found that close to 60% of these policies addressed social media risk as one of the key rationales for having the policy. They further found that social media policies were overrepresented in particular industries, such as pharmaceuticals, where communication is often strictly regulated, reinforcing the link to risk. The research also found 59% of these policies were actually embedded in the company code of conduct rather than as stand-alone policies. This is a common occurrence in many government departments as will be discussed in Case Study 10.2. The role of codes of conduct is to set boundaries for employees on all forms of conduct when they work for their employers, particularly within government agencies. A code of conduct should highlight the rules and values of the organisation along with its ethical principles and overarching vision. A code of conduct provides staff with clear expectations on how they should do their jobs, and how they should behave and represent their workplace. The code should be written in simple language, avoiding technical or legal jargon. It should include important details that impact employees and be accessible for employees and key stakeholders to view. It is important for staff to understand and agree to the code of conduct as their compliance helps to build reputation and support corporate social responsibility. It must also be supported by the leadership team.

Further, there are codes of ethics that govern the ethical publication of content across many professional communication industries, particularly in journalism. While this chapter doesn't go into depth here, it is important to consider the professional codes of ethics that apply to your occupation within your jurisdiction.

Case study 10.2 – Michaela Banerji and her anonymous tweets

Michaela Banerji was an Australian Commonwealth public servant and had been working for the then–Department of Immigration and Border Protection since 2006. In 2011 she joined Twitter under the pseudonym @LaLegale and began posting anonymous tweets that criticised her own department's policies related to immigration. Most of her tweets were sent in her own time and from her own device and did not disclose confidential information. However, she had posted more than 9,000 tweets when an internal investigation confirmed her identity. She was disciplined, and dismissal processes commenced in 2012 because it was alleged she had breached the Australian Public Service Code of Conduct by not acting in an apolitical way. Banerji initially attempted to stop her termination before the Federal Circuit Court, claiming that her posts were her own opinion and posted outside of work hours anonymously from a personal device, and therefore a termination would be a breach of her constitutional freedom to communicate on political matters. In *Banerji v Bowles* (2013) Justice Neville dismissed the application, noting that Banerji's political comments as an employee of the department were a breach of the code of conduct as she had no unfettered constitutional right to freedom of political communication. She was dismissed from her role in September 2013. By the following month she had lodged a claim for workers' compensation which was refused in 2014. The outcome was appealed and taken to the Administrative Appeals Tribunal (*Banerji and Comcare [Compensation] [2018]*), which found that her dismissal based on the code of conduct was unjust as it had inhibited her freedom of political communication. The matter was further appealed to the High Court of Australia, where Banerji's main argument was that the code should not extend to employees' anonymous communications and that her termination was thus unjustified (*Comcare v Banerji [2019]*). However, in 2019 the High Court unanimously ruled that the code of conduct was fair in its purpose of preserving an apolitical public service and ruled again against Banerji. This case followed a lengthy trajectory, but the outcome confirmed the strength of internal policies and as such is an important example for all organisations and employees on the role of social media policies and codes of conduct (*Anonymous tweets case* 2013, 2018, 2019).

Employees as ambassadors or advocates

There is a trend towards employers encouraging employees to be ambassadors or advocates on their personal social media accounts, allowing more freedoms for staff to comment about their organisations. Put simply, an ambassador or brand advocate is someone who speaks positively about a brand. The role they play on social media involves posting to their own audiences positive insights into the organisation or brand. This is why employees are suitable candidates for this role. Most employees already have their own social media audiences who might not form part of the organisation's audience, thus helping widen the reach of the organisation's messages to new audiences. By allowing employees the freedom to speak on behalf of the organisation, an impressive marketing impact that complements traditional marketing approaches can be achieved. If an audience recognises that those who work for the organisation love their job and its products and services, then they are more likely to trust the brand. Although it can be beneficial to have this type of further promotion available for your organisation or business, there are of course a number of risks that go along with allowing employees the freedom to speak on behalf of the enterprise.

Some organisations have turned this type of advocacy into an official program within the employee group. One example is Reebok, which started its employee advocacy program in 2015 because it recognised that many of its employees were actually within its target audience. They encouraged employees to post messages and images of themselves wearing the company's products using a custom hashtag – #FitAssCompany. Another example of a successful advocacy program is Electronic Arts (EA), a global gaming company, which set up its advocacy program in 2014 called 'EA Insiders'. Employees globally are involved and generate social media content reaching a network of more than one million.

Developing an official program allows for guidelines and policies to be created to help standardise the ways employees can advocate for their employers. It is essential to conduct a risk analysis that considers the types of scenarios that could occur. Using the risk matrix from Chapter 3 is a good starting point. Only by identifying what could occur can you mitigate some element of risk appropriately. Once the overarching risks are identified this information can be used to create training programs that highlight to staff what is and isn't suitable in their advocacy. Of course, this training would need to point to relevant policies and codes of conduct that employees must follow at all times while advocating for the employer.

Case study 10.3 – Paris Brown – how past social media posts can destroy a job offer

In 2013 Paris Brown, then aged 17, was appointed as the first Kent youth police crime commissioner (PCC) from a pool of 164 applications. She was to earn £15,000 annually in this role. However, before she started in the position, she resigned from her appointment because her historical tweets had been found and republished, casting doubt upon her suitability for the position. Brown had posted the tweets when she was aged between 14 and 16 and they included derogatory terms for homosexuals and people of certain races, along with comments about drinking, violence and drug use. Initially the Kent Police Commissioner backed Brown, indicating that she should remain in the role because the purpose of the position was to create a connection between the youth of the area and the police through someone relatable to that group. However, as complaints continued to pour in, Brown resigned stating:

> *I strongly reiterate that I am not racist or homophobic. I have fallen into the trap of behaving with bravado on social networking sites. I hope this may stand as a learning experience for many other young people. I now feel that in the interests of everyone concerned – in particular the young people of Kent who I feel will benefit enormously from the role of a youth commissioner – that I should stand down as I feel that the recent media furor will continue and hamper my ability to perform the job to the level required.*
>
> (Dodd 2013)

Within a few days Brown became subject to a police investigation over whether any criminal activity was connected to her tweets after the police received complaints from members of the public. The police investigation found that no further action was required, but she was at the centre of media reporting across the United Kingdom for some time, ultimately affecting her reputation and future employability. This was a big hit for someone so young but holds lessons for us all that our digital identities can stalk us throughout our lives.

Stakeholder theory and employment law

As we have discussed in the previous sections, there is a strong connection between employment law and employees as stakeholders. Stakeholder theory places employees as central stakeholders in most circumstances, and therefore an organisation must consider its employees and the impact their social media use may have on the corporate brand and reputation – for better or worse. Although the main stakeholders involved in employment law are employees, the impact of the risks associated with staff social media use can further affect external stakeholders. Some of the main stakeholders could include the organisation's shareholders and suppliers who may choose to sever ties depending on the severity of the situation. There can also be additional influence on other employees, resulting in distrust in their employer or disfavour for their role. Social identity theory should also be considered here because employees can take on various identities. Their social identities might include views, memberships, hobbies, religions or interests spanning well beyond the organisation, and action against them for their posts can trigger outrage among such publics. Depending on how the organisation handles employment law and the use of social media within its employee groups, staff can mobilise and become unanticipated publics contributing to trending topics that then affect the organisation and may turn into a crisis.

Discussion questions and project topics

1   Find two publicly available social media policies and conduct a comparison. In what ways are they similar and in what ways are they different? Consider why. Are the differences because of the type of organisation/industry, or because of the stakeholders, audience or public that may be affected? Or both? Explain.
2   Research further an example of an employee advocacy program and conduct a risk analysis on that program. Write a paragraph identifying risks with the program and whether the organisation has attempted to mitigate any of them.
3   Undertake a stakeholder mapping exercise on the three case studies presented in this chapter. Compare the sets of stakeholders and identify the relevant elements that could appear in a social media policy related to the organisations they work for.

Practice tips

•   Download the key recent cases in your jurisdiction where dismissal for misuse of social media has been appealed. Summarise their findings and circulate them to staff as part of your routine social media workplace training. Turn to the Appendix for case search resources in your region.

- All induction packages for new employees should include a copy of the code of conduct/social media policy. It is advised that formal training sessions be held and that a record be taken of those who attend. When starting a new role, if a social media policy has not been provided to you, seek it out and get familiar with it and the consequences of breaching it. Think of the policy as a way you can work with employees to achieve the organisation's communication goals.
- Consider commencing an employee advocacy program. Ensure that it is run with rigid governance but allow employees to be involved and participate in promoting the organisation they work for and hopefully love.
- Search for relevant professional codes of ethics that apply to your jurisdiction and be familiar with what they set out, along with any consequences for a breach of the code via social media. In some jurisdictions the code of ethics is related to the relevant regulator and does result in serious implications if breached. See the Appendix for regulators in your region.

Cases cited

Anonymous tweets case. 2013, 2018, 2019. *Banerji v Bowles* [2013] FCCA 1052. <www6.austlii.edu. au/cgi-bin/viewdoc/au/cases/cth/FCCA/2013/1052.html> and *Banerji and Comcare (Compensation)* [2018] AATA 892. <www6.austlii.edu.au/cgi-bin/viewdoc/au/cases/cth/AATA/2018/892.html> and *Comcare v Banerji* [2019] HCA 23 7 August. C12/2018. <www6.austlii.edu.au/cgi-bin/viewdoc/ au/cases/cth/HCA/2019/23.html>

Election post case. 2020. *Bennett v. Metropolitan Government of Nashville and Davidson County, No. 19–5818.* 6 Cir. <www.opn.ca6.uscourts.gov/opinions.pdf/20a0324p-06.pdf>

Social media policy case. 2016. *Plant v API Microelectronics Ltd.* ET/3401454/16. <https://assets.publishing. service.gov.uk/media/5909db43e5274a06b30002d3/Mrs_E_Plant_v_API_Microelectronics_Limited_ 3401454.2016.pdf>

References

Dodd, V. 2013. "Youth crime commissioner Paris Brown stands down over Twitter row." *The Guardian.* www.theguardian.com/uk/2013/apr/09/paris-brown-stands-down-twitter

Duffy, A. & M. Knight. 2018. "Don't be stupid." *Journalism Studies, 20*(7), 932–951. https://doi.org/1 0.1080/1461670X.2018.1467782

Gabbatt, A. 2021. "New York Times fires editor targeted by rightwing critics over Biden tweet." *The Guardian.* 25 January 2021. www.theguardian.com/media/2021/jan/25/lauren-wolfe-new-york-times-editor-fired-biden-tweet

Google. 2021. *Google transparency report: Global requests for user information.* https://transparencyreport. google.com/user-data/overview

Johnston, J. 2015. "'Loose tweets sink fleets' and other sage advice: Social media governance, policies and guidelines." *Journal of Public Affairs, 15*(2), 175–187. https://doi.org/10.1002/pa.1538

New York Times. N.D. Ethical journalism (policy). Accessed 1 March 2021. www.nytimes.com/editorial-standards/ethical-journalism.html#

Pearson, M. & M. Polden. 2019. *The journalist's guide to media law: A handbook for communicators in a digital world.* New York: Routledge.

Ronson, J. 2015a. "How one stupid tweet ruined Justine Sacco's life." *New York Times*. 15 February. www.nytimes.com/2015/02/15/magazine/how-one-stupid-tweet-ruined-justine-saccos-life.html

Ronson, J. 2015b. "'Overnight everything I loved was gone': The internet shaming of Lindsey Stone." *The Guardian*. 21 February. www.theguardian.com/technology/2015/feb/21/internet-shaming-lindsey-stone-jon-ronson

Stohl, C., M. Etter, S. Banghart & D. Woo. 2017. "Social media policies: Implications for contemporary notions of corporate social responsibility." *Journal of Business Ethics*, *142*(3), 413–436. www.jstor.org/stable/44253079

11 Business, corporate and consumer law and social media

Glossary

Business law: The umbrella term for laws and regulations targeted at business operations generally or essential to risk management in any business (company, partnership, non-profit organisation or sole trader), such as the laws of professional negligence and breach of contract.

Consumer law: The suite of laws designed to protect consumers from false, misleading or deceptive behaviour in business or advertising.

Corporate law: An array of laws impinging upon the corporate relations of a company. These can include laws related to securities, trade practices and directors' powers and duties.

Publisher liability: The extent to which the owner of a social media site (or other media) is liable for material appearing there, varying across jurisdictions according to where the material has been published and whether it has been published by themselves or by third parties.

Securities law: The suite of financial laws controlling investment in public companies and their interactions with investors and the share market.

Abstract

A host of business laws arise in the social media context, varying between countries and legal systems. With social media defying jurisdictional borders, communication professionals need to be aware of risks particularly in the areas of consumer, securities and trade practices law. Using social media to promote products or services in a false, misleading or deceptive way can have legal ramifications and can also trigger consequences from social media platforms under their terms and conditions of use. Posts which might impact stock market performance, manipulate markets or influence the floats of new companies also carry risk. So too do regulatory infringements such as the promotion of therapeutic goods and services, tobacco, alcohol, gambling and posts targeting children. In some jurisdictions, the organisation's responsibility for comments by third parties on their social media sites becomes a critical issue.

DOI: 10.4324/9781003180111-16

In this chapter

- Mapping the terrain of risk with business laws on social media
- Misleading and deceptive conduct
- Securities laws and social media
- Special industry-based restrictions: health, drugs, alcohol and gambling
- Organisational responsibility for the comments of others on its social media sites
- Case study 11.1 – Allergy Pathway, consumer law and liability for third party comments
- Case study 11.2 – Urthbox and the misleading reviews
- Stakeholder theory and business laws
- Strategies for minimising risks with business laws
- Discussion questions and project topics
- Practice tips
- Cases cited
- References

Mapping the terrain of risk with business laws on social media

Numerous laws and regulations are targeted at business operations in particular jurisdictions, and many of these have implications for social media use and site management. Full courses at law school are devoted to particular topics in business law, while Master of Business Administration (MBA) students typically address the main ones in a single course with a compendium textbook. Examples are Gibson and Fraser (2011) and Griggs, Clark and Iredale (2009). Professional social media managers working in a corporate environment should purchase such a specialist text from their own jurisdiction to have available for ready reference because a single chapter in this book can only offer an introduction to the key hazards in business law in the social media space. The risks also underscore the importance of having a suitable professional indemnity insurance policy covering the key business law areas, as emphasised in Chapter 5.

Two key areas of business law that could be impacted by social media are actions for negligence and breach of contract. An action for negligence could arise over a social media post that exposed a client to financial losses because a communication professional had not taken reasonable care to prevent foreseeable damage, particularly if a reasonable person in that position would have known to take precautions to prevent such damage (Gibson & Fraser 2011, 165). Sometimes a professional body's standards or regulatory requirements will indicate a special duty of care obligation on the communicator or their industry, enhancing the risk potential (Griggs, Clark & Iredale 2009, 127). Such extra duties are considered more closely later in the chapter in the realm of special industries including tobacco, alcohol, health and gambling. A professional communication consultant might seek to limit their exposure to possible breaches of their duty of care via conditions in their contracts with clients.

This underscores the importance of contract law to social media managers. Contracts are legally enforceable promises, and they arise in multiple situations in a business context. Professional communicators can encounter them as contracts of employment which – as explained in Chapter 10 – can be crucial to a staff member's livelihood if he or she faces dismissal for misuse of social media. Contracts also apply commonly to agreements to perform services or purchase goods. Key to each are the terms and conditions attached, allocating responsibilities and limiting liability. According to Gibson and Fraser (2011, 305–306) the three key elements required for a contract are:

- The parties' intention to enter the contract;
- An agreement between the parties including an offer and an acceptance; and
- 'Consideration' – which they define as 'something of value passing from one party to another in return for a promise to do something'.

(Gibson & Fraser 2011, 305–306)

Modern communication methods now mean that these elements of a contract can be met digitally and include the possibility that the intention to contract, along with the offer and acceptance, could be conducted over social media by a party to the contract (or by their legally empowered agent), while the 'consideration' could take the form of an electronic funds transfer. Traditionally, many contracts were entered into via a verbal agreement and a so-called handshake, but they were often difficult to prove in court for lack of evidence of the agreement. The 'social' dimension of social media now creates a permanent retrievable record of these kinds of agreements entered via online conversations.

A South African case in 2019 highlighted how the elements of a contract could operate via social media. A man who had won almost 21 million rand in the national lotto six months prior sent a WhatsApp message to the mother of one of his children stating 'If I get 20m I can give all my children 1m and remain with 13m. I will just stay at home and not driving up and down looking for tenders' (*WhatsApp case* 2019). When the woman discovered he had actually won lotto she sued him, claiming it constituted an enforceable agreement to pay her child the 1 million rand. The trial judge agreed with her, but the appeals court overturned the decision on the basis that the man's intention to enter a contract was absent. While the intention was missing in this case, it was clear that in different circumstances the correspondence via the social media application could well have initiated a valid contract (*WhatsApp case* 2019).

In addition to allowing people to enter contracts, social media communications can also contribute to so-called breaches of contract, where the posted material breaks the terms of a previously formed contract. A clause in an employment contract might require the staff member to desist from harming the organisation via social media, as Rugby Australia contended in its dispute with international star Israel Folau, as explained in Case Study 1.3 in Chapter 1.

Confidentiality agreements can also be broken via social media. A headmaster reached a settlement agreement with the Gulliver Preparatory School in Florida over his claims of age discrimination and retaliation when his employment contract was not renewed. The settlement stipulated he and his wife should tell nobody else about the negotiated agreement. Just four days later his college-aged daughter bragged to her 1,200 Facebook friends: 'Mama and Papa Snay won the case against Gulliver. Gulliver is now officially paying for my vacation to Europe this summer. SUCK IT.' The appeals court ruled this was evidence the headmaster had revealed the terms of the agreement to his daughter in breach of the confidentiality clause, rendering the settlement void (*Facebook bragging case* 2014). Of course, such a breach of a clause can also operate the other way, with an organisation's representative potentially responsible for a contract-breaching post.

Clearly social media communications can hold significant risks for individuals and organisations in the areas of negligence and contract law. Many other business laws can come into play via social media posts, and we examine some of the key ones here.

Misleading and deceptive conduct

Organisations use advertising, marketing and public relations campaigns and sponsorships to promote their goods and services and to enhance their brands, with social media playing a key function in the modern era. However, laws and regulations operate internationally and in most national and state/provincial jurisdictions to prohibit the use of false, misleading or deceptive conduct in the course of business – and that includes overt or covert information or claims on social media. The United Nations introduced its 'Guidelines on Consumer Protection' in 1985, and they were updated in 1999 and 2015 to keep pace with globalised commerce and communication. The guidelines cover key principles and minimum standards of fair and equitable treatment of consumers, legal and ethical commercial behaviour, disclosure and transparency, education and awareness-raising, privacy protections and complaints-handling processes. They call on all nation-states to develop laws encouraging this, including a framework for combating fraudulent and deceptive commercial practices (UN Conference on Trade and Development 2016, 9–10). Supporting this, more than 65 countries are members of the International Consumer Protection and Enforcement Network (ICPEN), collaborating globally to combat fraudulent, deceptive and unfair trading practices.

Relevant to social media are the laws in most countries requiring the distinction between paid advertising, sponsorships and promotion material from independent analysis, reviews and news content. For example, the Australian Consumer Law (and mirror legislation at state level) makes it illegal for a business to engage in conduct that misleads or deceives consumers or other businesses. It applies regardless of whether there was an intention to deceive or whether someone has suffered loss or damage as a result. Social media traps in this space are numerous, and professional communicators need to be on guard against messaging that makes promises or enticements without making clear the terms and conditions upon which they are based. Special offers, competitions and prizes promoted via social media all carry such a risk, as do posts making unsubstantiated claims in the course of business.

Authorities internationally have been clamping down on social media influencers who purport to be giving endorsements to products and services without revealing they are being paid for their glowing reviews or references – another version of misleading and deceptive conduct. For example, in the United Kingdom in 2019 the Competition and Markets Authority (CMA) issued guidelines for influencers on disclosing when they have been paid, or otherwise rewarded, to endorse goods or services – under threat of consumer law action if they neglect to do so (CMA 2019). The Federal Trade Commission (FTC) in the United States followed soon after, with its Disclosures 101 for Social Media Influencers (FTC 2019a). It claimed to answer these common questions so influencers could minimise their risk of consumer law prosecution:

- How does the disclosure requirement apply in pictures, videos, and live streams?
- What about tags, likes and pins?
- What kind of wording effectively discloses a material connection?
- What about influencers who post from outside the United States?
- What if a person doesn't have a relationship with a brand but is just telling others about a product they bought and happen to like?
- Is it OK to assume a platform's disclosure tool is good enough? (Spoiler alert: No, that's not OK.)

(FTC 2019a)

Despite the education campaign, the undisclosed sponsorships continued. Skincare and tea marketer Teami and its owners paid Instagram influencers to claim their product – Teami 30 Day Detox Pack – would help users lose weight, treat cancer, blocked arteries, migraines, influenza and colds – with inadequate disclosure. (Disclosures could only be read if followers clicked a 'more' link.) The company had to pay a $1 million fine, and ten influencers were sent warning letters, including Cardi B, Katya Elise Henry, Brittany Renner and Adrienne Bailon (*Teami influencer case* 2020).

In another example, highlighted in Case Study 11.2, a snack box company was fined $100,000 for providing customers with free products to post positive reviews on its website and on social media and representing those reviews to be unbiased and independent (*Urthbox reviews case* 2019).

The field of influence has other dimensions. There are also numerous examples of consumer authorities acting against companies deceiving customers as to their level of influence. The Netherlands Authority for Consumers and Markets (ACM) acted against online store Bicep Papa B.V. in 2021 to stop it using fabricated likes and fake followers when using social media promotions of its nutritional supplements and products, backed by a threatened penalty of 100,000 euro periodic payments (ACM 2021). In another case, the FTC in the United States and state authorities reached a settlement with Devumi, LLC, over the sale to customers of fabricated indicators of social media influence. These included thousands of LinkedIn, Twitter and YouTube followers and subscribers. The company's CEO also had a $2.5 million judgment awarded against him (FTC 2019b).

Self-regulatory bodies have stepped in to encourage the disclosure of payments and enticements to influencers. For example, in 2021 the Australian Association of National Advertisers (AANA) introduced a revised Code of Ethics imposing a 'positive obligation on influencers to disclose commercial relationships in a clear, upfront manner that can be easily understood' (AANA 2021a). The practice note to the new Code stated:

> *Influencer and affiliate marketing often appears alongside organic/genuine user generated content and is often less obvious to the audience. Where an influencer or affiliate accepts payment of money or free products or services from a brand in exchange for them to promote that brand's products or services, the relationship must be clear, obvious and upfront to the audience and expressed in a way that is easily understood (e.g. #ad, Advert, Advertising, Branded Content, Paid Partnership, Paid Promotion). Less clear labels such as #sp, Spon, gifted, Affiliate, Collab, thanks to . . . or merely mentioning the brand name may not be sufficient to clearly distinguish the post as advertising.*

> (AANA 2021b, 13)

Yet decisions do not always go in favour of the consumer regulatory bodies. Australia's High Court upheld an appeal by Google against the Australian Competition and Consumer Commission (ACCC), which had claimed the global search engine company should be held liable under the misleading and deceptive conduct laws for claims made by advertisers in the sponsored links featured at the top of search results. The court ruled Google had not created the links and that consumers would have been able to recognise that any claims in the links came from the advertisers and not from Google (*Sponsored links case* 2013).

Running a contest on social media might seem a simple and effective marketing device for launching a new product, but national regulators (data protection, lotteries etc.) and social media platform rules present a series of hurdles that must be studied and followed to avoid prosecutions or account suspension. Pitfalls can include errors with offer terms and eligibility such as age and residency, local registration and approvals, inaccurate tagging, and indemnities for the relevant social media platform. They are too numerous and diverse to cover in detail here, yet are particularly important to the social media manager and marketer. For a simple example, see Facebook's rules for running contests on Instagram (2021), but note it does not specify the many jurisdictional requirements that might apply.

Securities laws and social media

Social media risks also attach to the suite of financial laws controlling the investment in public companies and their interaction with investors and the share market – known generally as 'securities laws'. Communications from directors or representatives about a new public float of a company and important information to do with a company's investment or performance are subject to strict control by the financial regulators in each country. Examples are the United States Securities and Exchange Commission, the Australian Securities and Investments Commission, the Financial Conduct Authority (United Kingdom), the Financial Markets Authority (New Zealand) and various provincial regulators in Canada. (More are listed in the Appendix.) Much of the regulation centres on ensuring there is enough disclosure to allow investors to make informed decisions.

Social media managers in the financial sector need special training in all of the possible pitfalls in posting or hosting material in this domain. Common traps include:

* hosting rumours on social media about major events like potential company takeovers ('rumourtrage')
* misleading advertisements of financial products
* false or misleading claims related to company floats in their prospectuses and initial public offering (IPO) announcements
* posts by or on behalf of a senior executive containing information that should have been notified to the stock exchange or suggesting a potential conflict of interest.

Examples abound. An Australian financial services provider – Financial Choice Pty Ltd – was fined $21,600 over misleading marketing emails and website material implying it was seeking customers' opinions on the request of superannuation funds (ASIC 2017).

In a much more high-profile case, Tesla founder Elon Musk had to stand down as company chairman, and he and Tesla each had to pay $20 million in fines in 2018. Musk had tweeted in 2018 that he had secured funding to take Tesla private at the inflated price of $420 per share, subject to a shareholder vote. The company's share price jumped by 6% as a result. The Securities and Exchange Commission (SEC) argued that much of the information was uncertain and lacked a factual basis (SEC 2018). Unlike some jurisdictions including Canada, the SEC allowed company announcements via social media including Twitter and Facebook from 2013 as long as investors had been alerted which social media would be used to convey the information.

In Australia in 2016, ASIC reviewed corporate practices in communicating initial public offerings (IPOs). They found social media posts sometimes contained misinformation about the IPO and ASIC's role. They also found compliance staff at the companies were sometimes unaware their employees had made the social media posts. They recommended firms control their social media posts as they do with other marketing by educating employees about their legislative obligations and by ensuring social media posts are reviewed before being published (ASIC 2016).

Special industry-based restrictions: health, drugs, alcohol, tobacco and gambling

Many businesses operate within the realm of special regulatory environments because legislators have decided that community standards require them to exercise special caution in their messaging, including on social media. This means there are additional restrictions, and designated bodies can act to prosecute organisations over their miscommunication on topics where citizens' vulnerability or safety might be at issue. Those operating in the areas of health, drugs and complementary medicine, tobacco, alcohol and gaming face special regulations in most jurisdictions. Sometimes self-regulatory bodies also demand special caution with messaging on these types of topics. For example, in Australia the Advertising Standards Bureau (Ad Standards) handles consumer complaints about breaches of industry ethical codes at a self-regulatory level, in addition to the consumer regulator (the Australian Competition and Consumer Commission). Social media complaints come under their purview. In an early example in 2012, comments posted to the Facebook page of the Australian beer brand Victoria Bitter attracted a complaint from two academics that the continued hosting of the posts breached the advertising code. The comments included offensive language, sexual innuendos and both misogynistic and homophobic comments. The page moderation was managed by an agency and supervised by the brewer's marketing department, which agreed to the requirement that it improve its moderation policies (Ad Standards 2012). The decision links to our next topic in this chapter, considering when social media hosts might be responsible for the comments of third parties.

Health and drug regulators have confronted similar problems related to both false or misleading advertising and the claims by third party commenters on social media about their drugs, products and services. In 2020 the United States Food and Drug Administration (FDA) joined with the FTC to issue a warning letter to Honey Colony – a complementary health provider making claims on its website and Twitter and Instagram accounts that its products could help prevent COVID-19 transmission (FDA 2020). The FDA called them unapproved and misbranded drugs and demanded removal of the social media and website material making such claims within 48 hours. This was just one of 145 COVID-19 products to receive such warning letters by early 2021 and listed on the FDA website as 'fraudulent'.

Similar restrictions on claims exist in other jurisdictions. In Australia, the Therapeutic Goods Administration (TGA) operates at Commonwealth level to regulate medicines, medical devices and blood products – and claims made in advertising about them. Its definition of 'advertisement' is broad, taking in social media as it covers: 'any statement, pictorial representation or design, however made, that is intended, whether directly or indirectly, to promote the use or supply of the goods'. In Europe, the European Medicines Agency (EMA) works in a similar way as a decentralised agency for the European Union (EU).

Social media promotion of tobacco and gambling also face regulatory restrictions across major jurisdictions, although promotion of both can be surreptitious and come via third parties on a range of channels and media. Despite World Health Organisation bans on tobacco advertising since 2005, recent research has shown cigarette companies using social media to influence potential smokers, particularly the young. One major study across ten countries found so-called ambassadors and microinfluencers were being used by Big Tobacco to promote smoking and vaping via posted images of the celebrities lighting up, targeted hashtags and links to events where smoking would be promoted (Kaplan 2018).

A comprehensive study of the use of social media in gambling in Australia in 2015 found gambling operators generally complied with advertising codes but used social media to promote their brands and encourage customer engagement. Online casino games, particularly those that attracted young people, were viewed as a potential problem. They found regulations lagged behind technology and industry uptake (Gainsbury et al. 2015, 286–288).

Organisational responsibility for the comments of others on its social media sites

As if it is not enough to face legal risks from our own posts and those of our staff on social media, in some jurisdictions organisations can also be held responsible for the posts of other people – so-called third parties – on their social media sites. We deal with this briefly here in a consumer law context because it was already covered in our discussion of defamation law in Case Study 6.1 in Chapter 6.

There are three potential levels of legal responsibility internationally when we host other people's comments and other material on our sites. In the United States, a combination of First Amendment rights and legislation in the form of Section 230 of the *Communications Decency Act*, has served to protect hosts from litigation over material posted by third parties. This is the highest level of protection an online publisher might have.

The second – and most common – level of protection among Western democracies is the 'reasonableness' test. In most jurisdictions this means that the host of a social media site – and the larger multi-national platforms themselves – will only be held liable for the comments of others if they have not removed them within a 'reasonable' time – as pioneered in the *Golf Club case* (1937) explained in Chapter 6 (where management failed to remove a defamatory note from the club notice board after they had been told about it). For most organisations, this means they must remove defamatory, contemptuous or otherwise illegal material posted by third parties as soon as it has been brought to their attention, or within a 'reasonable' time depending on their organisational size and moderation practices.

Large search engine platforms such as Google and Yahoo! attracted a similar defence to defamation called 'innocent publication', whereby they were protected from liability for the websites and posts they hosted until the point at which it was brought to their attention, at which time they must act to remove it. That happened in Australia in the *Search engine cases* (2012–2018) where the High Court ruled in favour of Melbourne man Michael Trkulja, whose image and name had appeared when users searched for 'Melbourne underworld figures' even though he had no such criminal connections. The judgment cost Google $200,000 and Yahoo! $225,000 because they had failed to address the problem. The court ruled in his favour again in 2018, when autocomplete returns from searches for Trkulja's name in Google again returned Melbourne criminal associations. As the *Allergy Pathway case* (2011) illustrates (see Case Study 11.1), the liability for third party comments is not limited to defamation law. In that case, it was extended to consumer law – a key topic of this chapter.

It also highlighted a distinction between platforms that allow some moderation of individual comments before they are posted and those that do not. Moderated comments on websites would not normally earn the reprieve that a host of a Facebook page might get, because the fact that the comments had been moderated and approved conveyed upon the publisher responsibility for the third party's comments, in a similar way to the selection and publication of a letter to the editor in a newspaper.

The third and riskiest interpretation of liability for third party comments developed in Canada and Australia in recent years. This line of authority holds that publishers will be held responsible for the third-party social media comments of others on their sites if they post material they could reasonably expect would generate infringing comments. This was illustrated in two cases mentioned in Chapter 6 – the *Neighbours case* (2016) in Canada and the *Voller case* (2020) in Australia (subject to appeal). In 2021 Facebook introduced a new feature allowing better control over who can comment on individual posts.

Case study 11.1 – Allergy Pathway, consumer law and liability for third party comments

This is an illustrative case because it links with three of the key areas we have considered in this chapter – consumer law, claims about health products and liability for the comments of third parties on your social media sites. It also harks back to the area of disobedience contempt from Chapter 9. Allergy Pathway was an alternative health company promoting a treatment for allergies (*Allergy Pathway case* 2011). The Australian Competition and Consumer Commission (ACCC) brought an action against it, alleging it had breached the law by misleading and deceiving customers to believe its goods or services could diagnose and treat allergies when its claims lacked medical evidence. The company entered into undertakings that it would desist from making any false and misleading statements on any Internet website or in its advertisements or promotional materials. Yet Allergy Pathway then did nothing to stop clients posting such misleading claims to its website, Facebook page and Twitter account. The Federal Court decided the company was responsible for the comments of these third parties on its accounts and fined both Allergy Pathway and its director for contempt of court, for disobeying the original order. Once it had become aware of the testimonials posted by others and had not removed them, it became responsible for hosting the misleading representations as a publisher. The judge found the company should have conducted routine reviews of its website and social media accounts and should have removed the false claims within a 'reasonable time'. This has been the law followed in most jurisdictions other than the United States (which offers publishers immunity from the comments of others via its *Communications Decency Act*) and more recently in Australia and Canada where some decisions have laden the host publisher with responsibility for the defamatory comments of others from the instant they published material which was reasonably foreseeable would provoke such comments. The lessons here for professional communicators are:

- check your level of responsibility for third party comments for sites and pages you host in your own jurisdiction and in those where your business operates
- ensure you review and moderate material posted to your sites and pages on a reasonably routine basis, which might depend on your type of operation and its resources
- never allow automatic posting of comments to your sites if they allow for pre-moderation
- avoid posting provocative material to the sites where you have no control over the posting of comments by others that might expose your organisation to legal risks.

Case study 11.2 – Urthbox and the misleading reviews

Customer reviews can be vital to a business in an online environment. But consumer laws in all jurisdictions require that such reviews be genuine – and not false, misleading or deceptive. United States snack box company Urthbox suggested the reviews on its website and social media were independent when they had actually given the customers free merchandise in return for them posting positive reviews on two websites and on their personal social media accounts. In its decision the FTC fined the company $100,000 and required detailed procedures be put in place to educate the customers about the endorsement disclosure requirements and to monitor them across social media and third party websites for breaches. Important here is that Urthbox's obligations extended beyond their own websites and social media pages to sponsored endorsements on third party websites and social media sites. The lesson for professional communicators is that transparency and disclosure are key components when soliciting endorsements and that any resulting claims about products or services should not be misleading or deceptive in other ways either (*Urthbox reviews case* 2019).

Strategies for minimising risks with consumer and business laws

Any successful commercial organisation must engage with consumers via social media, but this chapter demonstrates that such engagement in the corporate world comes with a range of risks in business laws. While differences exist across jurisdictions, the global operator can adopt a range of strategies that will minimise the risk of encountering legal action over key business and corporate laws such as breach of contract, negligence, consumer deception and other regulatory infringements. Precautions and routine moderation practices when hosting the comments of third parties within key jurisdictions are also a key factor. Lawyers will advise on specific measures appropriate to the jurisdictions where your organisation operates, but a simple social media risk assessment in the area of consumer and business law might include:

1   **Identifying the potential (or existing) legal problem**

    The number of laws and situations that can arise in the business and corporate context necessitates an initial thorough audit of social media risk exposure across each of the topic areas covered in this chapter. Ideally such a review would be conducted with a legal team with corporate law expertise. Once this baseline study has been conducted, you can follow each of the following steps in relation to the particular risk area, because each will prompt different social media policy and practice adjustments.

2   **Reviewing the areas of the law involved**

    Acquiring a desktop business law reference book for your jurisdiction should be your first step so that you are equipped to swat up on a particular consumer or corporate topic area as it arises. Advisable too is to get hard copies of the key statutes and regulations controlling your specialised area of operation if you work in an industry with specific requirements, as is the case with health, securities, gambling and so on. See the Appendix for useful searchable databases. Your basic knowledge of the law is crucial to the red-flagging process that comes with the ensuing stages. For example, only by understanding the law of contract, negligence, consumer law and specialised industry regulations would you engage social media influencers to post endorsements for your new alternative health remedy. The agreements with the influencers would be contractual, while adverse health advice might breach a duty of care to those with a particular illness sparking a negligence action, false or misleading claims might be pursued by the consumer regulator and the actions or wording might fall foul of the national health and drug agency's regulations. Clearly, legal advice would be essential in navigating such a minefield of laws and regulations.

3   Projecting the possible consequences for stakeholders

Stakeholder analysis needs to drive the decisions in advance of social media actions and as a key part of the response to issues and crises that emerge. For example, who are the various stakeholders in the seemingly simple act of running a contest on social media as part of a marketing strategy for a new product? Stakeholders here would include the usual commercial players of board, staff, shareholders, customers, suppliers and competitors – but such a contest engages a broad cross-section of the community who become new stakeholders as contestants. It also involves the regulatory body which undoubtedly has rules controlling the running of contests and the offering of prizes. So too does the particular social media platform under its terms of use with consequences for your account if they are breached. Contests can go wrong in a range of ways. They can give the perception of being rigged, winners or losers can boast or vent on social media and satirists can poke fun at the brand by hijacking the hashtag with damaging memes and remarks. We should not forget laws and risks covered in earlier chapters either, including the possibility of defamation and brand reputational damage (and share price implications) for directors, shareholders and staff from contestant outrage at losing, and perhaps privacy issues for contestants via breaches of data protection laws. And that is just the example of the contest. A similar analysis of stakeholder implications can be conducted with the other topics in this chapter such as the lack of comment moderation of third-party comments, enticements for reviews, endorsements from influencers, along with the numerous actions regulated by specialist industry authorities in the realms of health, securities, tobacco and gambling.

4   Seeking advice/referring upward

A well-worn joke featured the client asking a lawyer how much it would cost for legal advice. The lawyer replied: 'I charge $200 per question. What's your second question?' (Boom boom! Ba dum tish!). Getting legal advice can be expensive, but preliminary advice costing just a few hundred can save thousands or millions (and potential bankruptcy) after a court judgment or settlement over a decision taken without consulting lawyers. That said, there is sometimes someone in the organisation who knows the law of the area so well that they need only take counsel on the most complex issues. For example, a larger company might have a marketing staff member who has run so many social media promotional contests that they know the platform rules and the jurisdictional laws inside out. However, a boutique public relations agency running their first contest would be wise to seek specialist legal advice on the topic. Similarly, some organisations might pay for a legally drafted contract with a social media influencer and then use that as the model for subsequent contracts with other influencers. The cost of legal advice also means someone in the organisation has to be designated with the authority to retain a lawyer and to be able to justify that in the budget. This 'referring upward'/'legal escalation' policy needs to be clear.

5 Publishing/amending/deleting/correcting/apologising

In most areas of social media law, it is much better to be withholding publication, or even amending or deleting material pre-posting, than having to correct or apologise after the damage has been done or the law has been broken. This is certainly the case in consumer and corporate law because the speed and reach of social media posts can raise the stakes of damage and infringements occurring instantly and widely. Social media policies need to build in the necessary pre-publication review policies working systematically through the steps above. If mistakes have happened warranting corrections or apologies, legal advice is strongly recommended (perhaps after screen capturing then deleting the material) because errors in either can exacerbate a legal problem and stymie some defences.

Stakeholder theory and business laws

Clearly, there are a host of potential stakeholders in the legal and regulatory space of consumer and corporate social media use. Of course, consumers/customers are front and centre as primary stakeholders in the consumer law domain, along with the consumer regulation bodies and the normal corporate stakeholders of directors, staff, suppliers and competitors. In the broader area of other business laws, social media oversights or miscommunication can impact on many others, including other parties to contracts, citizens, clients and competitors who might be harmed by a breach of duty of care, and vulnerable individuals such as children, gambling addicts, the seriously ill and those experiencing addictions to drugs, tobacco or alcohol. This fits closely with outrage factors which contribute to stakeholder reactions and most commonly the development of unanticipated publics.

Discussion questions and project topics

1   An international computer game retailer wants to promote a new space warfare game – AsteroidAssassin+ – rated in your country as suitable for players aged 15 and over. They want to engage five prominent social media influencers to post images of themselves enjoying playing the game and to run a contest giving away games to the best 50 marketing slogans submitted by entrants. List the key stakeholders in this scenario, and research and list the main laws or regulations in your jurisdiction and social media platform rules that arise as risks. The Appendix will offer some starting points for searches. Think of other risks that might arise.
2   Your organisation has invested heavily in a private cryptocurrency start-up that is about to list publicly on your national stock exchange. Your company directors have a large stake in the operation and have started sprouting the float on social media. What legal and regulatory risks arise?

3   An alternative health company has developed a quartz crystal, blessed with a spell by a professed witch and transformational healer, that will protect purchasers against any future pandemics. They propose a marketing campaign on social media with the hashtag #wiccanhealing. Undertake a legal risk assessment of the situation using the framework detailed in the section above.
4   List three situations where the laws of contract or negligence might be triggered via social media communications.

Practice tips

* Undertake a full legal risk audit of consumer and corporate risks in your organisation's social media activities.
* Review your social media and upward referral/legal escalation policies to determine which consumer and corporate social media posts and campaigns might require legal advice.
* Purchase a good text on business and consumer law and keep it handy for staff reference.
* Take special precautions with social media contests and 'lotteries' and check your local jurisdictional regulations along with the specific rules of the social media platforms you plan to use.
* Disclose all rewards or incentives issued to social media influencers and ensure they agree contractually to abide by disclosure and regulatory requirements.
* Identify any special rules or regulations applying to social media communications in your industry (for example health, drugs, children, gaming), train your staff in this area and keep copies in your office for ready reference.

Cases cited

Allergy Pathway case. 2011. *Australian Competition and Consumer Commission v Allergy Pathway Pty Ltd (No. 2)* [2011] FCA 74. <www.austlii.edu.au/cgi-bin/sinodisp/au/cases/cth/FCA/2011/74.html>

Facebook bragging case. 2014. *Gulliver Schools, Inc. v. Snay, No. 3D13–1952* (Fla. 3d DCA). 26 February. <https://caselaw.findlaw.com/fl-district-court-of-appeal/1658875.html>

Golf Club case. 1937. *Byrne v. Deane* [1937] 1 KB 818. <https://swarb.co.uk/byrne-v-deane-ca-1937/>

Neighbours case. 2016. *Pritchard v. Van Nes*, 2016 BCSC 686 (CanLII). <https://canlii.ca/t/gplvp>

Sponsored links case. 2013. *Google Inc. v Australian Competition and Consumer Commission* [2013] HCA 1. 6 February. <www.austlii.edu.au/cgi-bin/viewdoc/au/cases/cth/HCA/2013/1.html>

Teami influencers case. 2020. *FTC v. Teami and others*. Case 8:20-cv-00518, US District Court, Middle District of Florida. 5 March. <www.ftc.gov/system/files/documents/cases/complaint_4.pdf> and <www.ftc.gov/system/files/documents/cases/stipulated_order.pdf>

Urthbox reviews case. 2019. *In the matter of Urthbox Inc., et al.*, File No. 172 3028, before the Federal Trade Commission. Decision No. C-4676 (F.T.C.). 14 May. <www.ftc.gov/system/files/documents/cases/c-4676_172_3028_urthbox_decision_and_order_5-17-19_0.pdf>

Voller case. 2020. *Voller v Nationwide News Pty Ltd: Voller v Fairfax Media Publications Pty Ltd: Voller v Australian News Channel Pty Ltd* [2019] NSWSC 766. <www.caselaw.nsw.gov.au/decision/5d0c5f4be4b08c5b85d8a60d> *Fairfax Media Publications: Nationwide News Pty Ltd: Australian News Channel Pty Ltd v Voller* [2020] NSWCA 102. <www.caselaw.nsw.gov.au/decision/1725e1ead406ec197776976c>

WhatsApp case. 2019. *Kgopana v Matlala* (1081/2018) [2019] ZASCA 174. 2 December. <www.saflii.org/za/cases/ZASCA/2019/174.html>

References

AANA. 2021a. *AANA launches new Code of Ethics.* Accessed 17 February 2021. https://aana.com. au/2020/09/23/aana-launches-new-code-of-ethics/

AANA. 2021b. *Code of Ethics: Practice note.* Accessed 17 February 2021. https://f.hubspotusercontent00. net/hubfs/5093205/AANA_Code_of_Ethics_PracticeNote_Effective_February_2021.pdf?utm_ campaign=Self-Reg-Codes&utm_source=AANA&utm_medium=web&utm_term=self-reg&utm_ content=ethics-notes

ACM. 2021. *ACM forces online store to stop using fake likes and fake followers.* Accessed 15 November 2020. www.acm.nl/en/publications/acm-forces-online-store-stop-using-fake-likes-and-fake-followers

Ad Standards. 2012. *Case report: Case 0271/12: Foster's Australia, Asia and Pacific.* 11 July. http:// ms.adstandards.com.au/cases/0271-12.pdf

ASIC. 2016. *ASIC reviews marketing practices in IPOs.* https://asic.gov.au/regulatory-resources/markets/ resources/markets-articles-by-asic/asic-reviews-marketing-practices-in-ipos/

ASIC. 2017. "17-248MR Financial Choice pays $21,600 in penalties for false and misleading representations." *Media Release.* 25 July. Accessed 22 December 2020. http://asic.gov.au/about-asic/ media-centre/find-a-media-release/2017-releases/17-248mr-financial-choice-pays-21–600-in- penalties-for-false-and-misleading-representations

CMA. 2019. "Guidance: Social media endorsements: Being transparent with your followers." *Competition and Markets Authority.* Accessed 30 October 2020. www.gov.uk/government/publications/social- media-endorsements-guide-for-influencers/social-media-endorsements-being-transparent-with- your-followers

FDA. 2020. *Warning letter: Honey Colony LLC MARCS-CMS 607346.* 4 May. www.fda.gov/inspections- compliance-enforcement-and-criminal-investigations/warning-letters/honey-colony-llc-607346- 05042020

FTC. 2019a. *Disclosures 101 for social media influencers.* www.ftc.gov/system/files/documents/plain- language/1001a-influencer-guide-508_1.pdf

FTC. 2019b. *Devumi, owner and CEO settle FTC charges they sold fake indicators of social media influence: Cosmetics firm Sunday Riley, CEO settle FTC charges that employees posted fake online reviews at CEO's direction.* 21 October. www.ftc.gov/news-events/press-releases/2019/10/devumi-owner-ceo-settle- ftc-charges-they-sold-fake-indicators?utm_source=govdelivery

Gainsbury, S., D. King, P. Delfabbro, N. Hing, A. Russell, A. Blaszczynski & J. Derevensky. 2015. *The use of social media in gambling.* www.responsiblegambling.nsw.gov.au/__data/assets/pdf_file/0004/878314/ The-use-of-social-media-in-gambling.pdf

Gibson, A. & I. Fraser. 2011. *Business law.* Sydney: Pearson Education.

Griggs, L., E. Clark & I. Iredale. 2009. *Managers and the law: A guide for business decision makers.* Sydney: Thomson Reuters.

Instagram. 2021. *Promotion guidelines.* www.facebook.com/help/instagram/179379842258600

Kaplan, S. 2018. "Big tobacco's global reach on social media." *New York Times.* <www.nytimes. com/2018/08/24/health/tobacco-social-media-smoking.html>

SEC. 2018. *Elon Musk settles SEC fraud charges: Tesla charged with and resolves securities law charge.* www.sec. gov/news/press-release/2018-226

United Nations Conference on Trade and Development. 2016. *United Nations guidelines for consumer protection.* https://unctad.org/system/files/official-document/ditccplpmisc2016d1_en.pdf

12 Intellectual property law and plagiarism

Glossary

Copyright: The law protecting the form of expression of a work including an artwork, written work, script, image, film or soundtrack.

Free use/fair use/fair dealing: Legal defences and exceptions to infringing the copyright of others in limited circumstances, such as for educational use or for news and commentary. Each has criteria that must be met to be effective, including attribution to the creator.

Intellectual property: Creations of the mind protected by law. IP can include several areas including copyright, patents and trademarks. Protected works might be inventions, designs, artistic works and images, written works, music, films, names and symbols.

Plagiarism: The ethical breach of appropriating someone else's work without proper attribution to them and passing it off as your own. A broader concept than the legal area of copyright, but with potentially serious consequences such as loss of reputation and professional membership.

Trademark: A sign, symbol or word distinguishing one organisation's products or services from those produced or provided by others.

Abstract

There are ethical and legal aspects to the cutting and pasting of other people's creative work or the appropriation of the ideas of others. Student and professional ethical codes counsel against plagiarism, while the law of intellectual property – most notably copyright – is essential knowledge for social media communicators who want to copy, share or link to the work of others. Basic principles of copyright law are covered here, including the fact that copyright rests with the person who creates the material – and that is not necessarily the person posting it online. Crucial here is the *Naruto Monkey case* involving the wildlife 'selfie' photograph where a United States court was asked to decide whether the human photographer or the animal who pressed the shutter held copyright in the image. The formula 'Freely viewed ≠ freely used' is explored in a social media context. The chapter also considers trademarks, the law of passing off, the moral and personality rights of creators and the phenomenon of cybersquatting.

DOI: 10.4324/9781003180111-17

In this chapter

- Intellectual property and plagiarism – where law and ethics meet on social media
- Ethical dimensions via plagiarism – borrowing and stealing the work of others
- A quick introduction to intellectual property law
- Breach of copyright – elements and pitfalls
- Free use, fair use and fair dealing exceptions
- Moral rights, personality rights and passing off
- Beware the cybersquatters
- Case study 12.1 – Naruto Monkey case: monkey see, monkey do!
- Case study 12.2 – #WTForever21 case
- Stakeholder theory and intellectual property
- Strategies for minimising risks with intellectual property
- Discussion questions and project topics
- Practice tips
- Cases cited
- References

Intellectual property and plagiarism – where law and ethics meet on social media

Social media is based on the notion of sharing, but sometimes there are ethical or legal barriers to sharing original work that others have created. Risks attach to the speedy and straightforward tasks of cutting, pasting and embedding material owned by others. At an ethical level, such appropriation ('borrowing') or misuse can amount to plagiarism, which can involve insufficient attribution. It is forbidden in many professional and student ethical codes where it is considered a form of cheating. To plagiarise in professional communication can risk substantial brand and reputational damage.

The legal protections applying to creations of the mind fall within a body of law called 'intellectual property'. It has several branches, with the most prominent being copyright, trademarks and patent law. People or organisations can sue for the infringement of their intellectual property under each of them with costly outcomes for litigants including court and lawyer expenses, awards of damages, orders to withdraw marketing materials and payouts to account for profits earned from the breach. Resulting adverse publicity and social media outrage can also injure reputations and brands.

It is important to understand that professional communicators using social media can find themselves in the role of the offender or the victim in intellectual property disputes. In other words, it could be your organisation's trademark and materials being parodied in a viral social media protest or perhaps the very words of your own CEO being circulated in a speech delivered by a competitor. On the flip side, someone in your marketing department might be posting copyright images from major news organisations as part of a social media campaign. Such scenarios can position you as the plaintiff or defendant in an intellectual property legal stoush.

Ethical dimensions via plagiarism – borrowing and stealing the work of others

The ethical breach of plagiarism overlaps in some ways with intellectual property law but also has important differences. For example, a student might have plagiarised an author's work in an assignment by using large slabs of material without attribution – but likely will not have published the essay beyond the submission to a digital assignment box. Realistically, no intellectual property action would result because the author would likely never discover the breach had occurred. However, if it is discovered and progressed to a disciplinary committee, there can be dire consequences for the student's academic and professional career including the costs of failing the course, possible suspension of their candidature and the ethical stain of plagiarism on their record which might bar their entry to certain occupations. Plagiarism in the workplace can have other serious outcomes including deregistration from professional bodies and public shaming by competitors, the media and the broader public. So-called moral outrage is one of the most inflammatory types and is best avoided with appropriate risk minimisation strategies.

While plagiarism is an ethical issue, the basic morality of the act of copying, sharing or embedding the creative work of others might not even be questioned in the modern era. We are so used to cutting and pasting words, images, memes, gifs and clips into our personal social media posts that many do not pause to reflect on the possible consequence of doing so in a professional setting. The copyright law of many countries includes so-called 'moral rights' to do with the stealing or misusing of other people's creative works, which we consider later in this chapter. Such rights have existed internationally for more than a century.

A quick introduction to intellectual property law

Intellectual property – also known as 'IP' – covers 'creations of the mind' which have found actual material expression and has been taken to include literary and artistic works, music, symbols, trade marks, commercial names, inventions and industrial designs as listed in the Convention Establishing the World Intellectual Property Organization (WIPO) in 1967 (WIPO 1979). Social media publishers and managers could encounter any of these in their material or attachments and need to do so within the bounds of intellectual property laws which are designed to protect rights of their creators to control and profit from their use.

IP laws are well established at an international level and have enough common features across jurisdictions to allow professional communicators to work to the lowest common denominator of the law when publishing on social media. A post goes globally instantly and therefore might trigger IP laws in several jurisdictions. International treaties dating back to the 1880s underpin this similarity of laws, but there are noteworthy differences in the ways countries regulate and police IP laws. This means legal advice on the law in a particular jurisdiction is essential if you plan to push the boundaries with a potential infringement. The *Directory of Intellectual Property Offices* (WIPO 2021) is a useful referral point to the websites for IP and copyright laws of most countries, including links to information centres, such as the United States Copyright Office. Other resources appear in the Appendix.

An important area of intellectual property law related directly to marketing and brand management is trademark registration and protection. A trademark – the words, signs and symbols distinguishing an organisation's products or services from those of competitors – is integral to brand and reputation. Organisations want to minimise infringement of their trademarks by others, and some will pull out all legal stops to do so. For example, Facebook sued an educational social networking site Teachbook over trademark infringement in 2010, eventually forcing the smaller operator to change its name to TeachQuest in a settlement of the case in 2012 (Golovchuk 2012). The smaller operation likely had to pay for rebranding and legal costs in the fallout. However, a full risk assessment needs to be conducted because some threats of litigation can backfire and escalate into social media outrage of crisis proportions when they are portrayed and viewed by the media as a David versus Goliath battle between small businesses and powerful multinational corporations. Case Study 12.2 involving the satirical website and social media feed #WTForever21 is one example.

Trademark disputes are most likely to involve competing companies. In the *Malishus trademark case* (2018) an Australian court found an infringement in the uploading to Facebook of a trademarked clothing brand name – 'Malishus' – by a company in New Zealand who had registered it in that country, the United States and the United Kingdom. The same trademarked name had already been registered to a musical artist in Australia who also sold apparel by that name, so the word had pre-existing trademarked protection in Australia even though it had subsequently been registered elsewhere. The infringement came about because the New Zealand–based ecommerce website and Facebook pages for the sale of the branded clothing was targeted partly to Australian consumers, where the competing (earlier) Malishus trademark had been registered by the musician. The lesson is that broad social media targeting of sales might infringe trademarks in other countries, even if the name is registered in the home jurisdiction.

Another risk with trademarks occurs when a particular brand's domination of a process or product becomes so well known that the company name enters the language as a synonym for the generic term. Think Velcro, Xerox, iPhone and so on. This can have positive and negative consequences. For example, if someone asks for a rum and Coke in a bar, then Coca-Cola does its best via regulatory measures to ensure it was actually its product in the mix, while the customer might not have really cared which brand of cola soda was used. On the other hand, the Band-Aid brand would be defending its trademark against being used in a negative context – like an influencer suggesting it was a mere temporary fix in a non-medical context by calling something a 'Band-Aid treatment'. The International Trademark Association (INTA) warns against this kind of misuse of trademarked names and offers resources to help avoid errors (INTA 2015).

Breach of copyright – elements and pitfalls

Copyright is the law protecting the form of expression of a work including an artwork, written work, script, image, film or soundtrack. The word 'copyright' sums up the concept – it relates to who has the 'right' to 'copy' or reproduce a work. The fact that copyright protects only the *form of expression* – and not an idea itself – is a foundational principle internationally. It is a key difference from the ethical principle of plagiarism – where the ideas of others should be attributed, even if they are expressed in your own words. The lesson for social media users is that it can be dangerous floating ideas in posts because if someone else adopts and uses them there is no copyright protection unless they have used your actual form of expression or phrasing. Further, some people think copyright only covers higher-level literary or artistic works – but the form of expression protected might be quite plain and technical like a computer program or a database.

Social media contains countless copyright breaches on a daily basis – particularly with the cutting and pasting of images taken by other creators. The key principle here is that copyright is owned by whoever has created the image – in this case the photographer – and any reproduction of the work without that original creator's permission constitutes a breach unless copyright has been assigned or licensed to the user, or unless the copyright owner has explicitly made it freely available on the public domain, in which case appropriate attribution to the creator should be made. Remember, though, that just because the owner of a social media site grants permission to use a photograph does not mean they have the authority to do so. Unless the image is their own selfie, then the permission must be sought from the creator of the work who needs appropriate attribution. Shorthand acknowledgements like 'Photo: Facebook' will not suffice. In short, just because something can be freely viewed does not mean it can be freely used and appropriated, best remembered by the formula:

Freely viewed ≠ freely used

In most countries copyright applies instantly from the moment a work is created, with no need for the use of the copyright symbol ©. The United States is an exception, where copyright in a work needs to be registered before a breach can be litigated. Creators internationally are usually advised to use the symbol anyway – as a means of warning others that their copyright will be pursued if infringed.

Another difference between countries is the duration of copyright after the death of the creator. In most jurisdictions copyright rests with the creator's estate for 50 years after they have died, while in the United States, Australia and the European Union that period extends to 70 years. It becomes important if you want to start reproducing classic words, sounds and images from popular culture and need to know whether they have yet entered the public domain.

Copyright law usually gives the creator the exclusive right to reproduce the work, publish it, perform it, make adaptations of it such as screenplays, and communicate it to the public in other ways such as via social media. The copyright can also be transferred to others in full or in part – so long as that transfer is in writing. Such a transfer might be called either an 'assignment' (a full transfer of ownership) or a 'licence' (where transfer is limited in some way, such as for a particular purpose or for a specified length of time). Copyright can change hands many times. For example, in 1965 the members of The Beatles assigned their ownership of the copyright in their songs to their recording company Northern Songs (in which they held a stake). In 1969 ATV Music won control of the company and its catalogue. ATV in turn assigned the catalogue and many other songs to Michael Jackson in 1985 for $47.5 million, outbidding the surviving Beatle Paul McCartney. Jackson sold half of ATV to Sony in 1995, forming Sony/ATV. After Jackson died, his estate sold the rights to Sony/ATV in 2016, who in turn reached a settlement with McCartney in 2017 when he threatened to action a clawback right for the earlier songs under United States copyright legislation (Rys 2017).

An example of a more limited transfer in the form of a licence appears in Facebook's terms and conditions, stating:

> *You own the intellectual property rights (things like copyright or trademarks) in any such content that you create and share on Facebook and the other Facebook Company Products you use. . . .*
>
> *However, to provide our services we need you to give us some legal permissions (known as a 'license') to use this content. . . .*
>
> *Specifically, when you share, post, or upload content that is covered by intellectual property rights on or in connection with our Products, you grant us a non-exclusive, transferable, sub-licensable, royalty-free, and worldwide license to host, use, distribute, modify, run, copy, publicly perform or display, translate, and create derivative works of your content. . . . This means, for*

example, *that if you share a photo on Facebook, you give us permission to store, copy, and share it with others (again, consistent with your settings) such as service providers that support our service or other Facebook Products you use. This license will end when your content is deleted from our systems.*

(Facebook 2021)

People often claim that the publication of copyright material to the Internet or social media renders it in the 'public domain' and that any copyright is then forfeited. This is wrong. As stated above, works only enter the public domain 50–70 years after the creator's death (depending on the jurisdiction) or when creators dedicate their work to the public domain on a 'some rights reserved' basis, such as by offering it to Creative Commons or Wikimedia Commons or similar platforms. Even there, the terms of the licence are specified (such as whether the licence is for private, educational or commercial use) and they typically require full attribution to the creator. Social media platforms can make such attribution requirements time-consuming and technically difficult, but they are necessary to reduce the risk of intellectual property infringement.

Neglecting to seek permission for material posted to social media can have costly consequences. For example, in 2014 a United States District appeals court upheld an award of more than $1.2 million to a professional photographer who had taken spectacular images of the 2010 Haiti earthquake and uploaded them to Twitter via the now defunct Twitpic interface. Another social media user had copied and posted them into his own Twitter account and the images were then picked up by Agence France Presse and sold to Getty Images with attribution to that second poster, not the photographer. They were then used without the creator's permission by thousands of media outlets internationally (*Earthquake case* 2014).

Free use, fair use and fair dealing exceptions

Given the limitations on using copyrighted material, in what circumstances can social media users incorporate the work of others in their posts and linked sites? Clearly, one way is to contact the copyright owner and negotiate payment for the use of a complete work (such as a photograph) or a substantial part of a work (such as an article, piece of music or film clip). Another is to use material in the public domain such as Creative Commons (or works where the creator has been deceased more than 50 or 70 years) with appropriate attribution to the creator. A further way is to draw on material from subscription-based syndicated libraries of work (such as images, drawings and music clips) where the creators have made their work available for a fee or have created the material as part of their employment for the syndication group. Another mechanism is to link to the material at its original location, without breaching the copyright of the owner in the process. Court decisions on this practice have become complex internationally, particularly when whole works might be reproduced on social media in the form of the linking image to an item in breach of copyright. Further, the law has developed to prevent profiteers mining material to populate their own sites by 'deep linking' through to copyright material on others, bypassing homepages and advertising or sponsorships on the pages of the creators or copyright owners.

A further means to be able to use appropriately attributed work is via the exceptions to copyright law under free use, fair use and fair dealing defences available internationally and in various jurisdictions. The World Intellectual Property Organisation gives three examples of *free use* as:

- quoting from a protected work, provided that the source of the quotation and the name of the author are mentioned, and that the extent of the quotation is compatible with fair practice;
- use of works by way of illustration for teaching purposes; and
- use of works for the purpose of news reporting.

(WIPO 2016, 16)

Many countries have extended these exceptions into the realm of special defences to copyright infringement without the creator's permission for legitimate purposes – called either 'fair use' or 'fair dealing' defences. *Fair use* is a broader approach, allowing the courts to examine key factors including the nature and purpose of the use, whether it is of a commercial nature, the type of work, the proportion of the work used, and the implications of the use upon its potential commercial value to the creator (WIPO 2016, 16). The United States is a major jurisdiction using the fair use approach. In some other countries (including Australia) *fair dealing* defences apply – and the specific situations where a work can be used without compensation to the author are specified in the national copyright legislation. These typically include educational use, news and commentary, criticism and review, or parody and satire – each with specific guidelines and conditions depending on the medium of the work, the commercial nature and the proportion being used. Attribution to the creator is required in all cases. Check the Appendix to see which defence applies in your jurisdiction.

The reality with breach of copyright law is that most social media users get away with cutting and pasting the words or images of others into their posts or stream the audio or video of others. The most they might face is a 'cease and desist' letter from a corporation or lawyer. But as soon as someone starts doing it on behalf of an organisation, the risk of legal action for breach of copyright rises exponentially. It is always best to seek out and get the permission of the creator and pay them or a syndication agency rather than to risk costly litigation – or else to operate within the requirements of the commons, free use, fair use or fair dealing exceptions using appropriate attribution.

Moral rights, personality rights and passing off

As well as the economic rights held by creators, many countries legislated so-called 'moral rights' that have long been protected under international conventions. Moral rights give creators the right to have their works attributed to them, the right to not have authorship falsely attributed to others (or others' work falsely attributed to them), and the right of integrity of authorship (not having their works treated in a derogatory way). The creator retains these moral rights even if they have transferred the ownership of the work to someone else.

Various parts of the world including Europe and the United States also have 'personality rights' or a 'right to publicity', which place limits on how you can use the name and image of others – especially if you are profiting in some way from their likeness. These restrictions are closely connected to laws of privacy. Celebrities and influencers are particularly keen to use legal means to limit the use of their faces in the advertising and marketing campaigns for products and services they have not endorsed without a negotiated commercial agreement.

These restrictions link closely to the law of 'passing off' and the 'misleading and deceptive conduct' provisions of consumer laws covered in Chapter 11. The law of 'passing off' is available in common law jurisdictions like the United Kingdom and Australia to those whose name or likeness has been appropriated to imply falsely an endorsement or commercial arrangement.

Beware the cybersquatters

Domain names and social media account names and handles can be hijacked for commercial, satirical or vindictive purposes using the practice known as 'cybersquatting'. It can also apply to trademarks and business names that require registration in different jurisdictions (normally via various government bodies) and routine renewal processes. The international legal and bureaucratic tangles in these areas can be frustrating and punishing for organisations when a competitor has registered their business name or their domain name. Sensible risk management in this space requires the allocation of responsibility for such renewals to personnel in the organisation with routine calendar reminders.

Sometimes disputes over domain names need to go to international dispute resolution bodies. The World Intellectual Property Organisation runs an arbitration and mediation centre dealing in a speedy manner with disputes over domain name registration for a fee of $1,500 to $5,000, depending on the number of domain names disputed. For example, the international underwear and clothing business Fruit of the Loom Inc filed a dispute with WIPO on 5 January 2021 over the registration by a Danish individual of the domain name 'fruitoftheloom.store'. Within two weeks the centre handed down its decision that the domain name be transferred to Fruit of the Loom Inc. when it found the Danish respondent was not actually using that name, the site was inactive and it had been registered 'in bad faith' (*Fruit of the Loom case* 2021).

Social media platforms' terms of use and terms of service also contain rules about creating false accounts and persona and offer avenues of complaint to have such false identities removed. For example, Twitter's policy states:

> *Impersonation is a violation of the Twitter Rules. Twitter accounts that pose as another person, brand, or organization in a confusing or deceptive manner may be permanently suspended under Twitter's impersonation policy.*

(Twitter 2021)

The procedures vary markedly, and so do the timelines for action.

Case study 12.1 – Naruto Monkey case: monkey see, monkey do!

The basic international principle that copyright rests with the creator was highlighted in a fascinating case involving a professional nature photographer and a monkey (*Naruto Monkey case* 2018). Expert wildlife photographer David Slater set up his expensive camera equipment to photograph a crested black macaque – an Indonesian monkey named Naruto.

He left the gear unattended and the monkey proceeded to photograph itself in what was claimed to be the world's first monkey 'selfie'. Slater published the images in a book, claiming copyright. They soon appeared on Wikimedia Commons, and Slater demanded the free use site take them down because of the breach of his copyright. The platform refused, arguing the monkey actually held the copyright because it was the creator by having pressed the shutter on the camera (Wikimedia Foundation 2017). A court ruled against the photographer, but the animal rights group PETA was unsuccessful in winning damages on behalf of the monkey for Slater's alleged breach of its copyright. The judge held monkeys did not have standing in court and the parties proceeded to settle (Toliver 2017). Despite the photographer having invested in all the equipment, time and set-up for the image, he did not hold copyright in the resulting photograph – which we reproduce here with attribution as Image 12.1. This reinforces the fundamental principle in copyright law that the actual creator of the work owns the copyright unless it has been transferred to another.

Image 12.1 Self-portrait by the depicted Macaca nigra female

Source: [Photograph set up by David Slater.] Public Domain, https://commons.wikimedia.org/w/index.php?curid= 36464057

Case study 12.2 – #WTForever21 case

A satirical blogger, Rachel Kane, was one of the first on social media to find herself under legal threat for intellectual property breaches by a major corporate brand when she started poking fun at some of the outfits sold by Forever 21, a leading US-based fashion retailer priding itself on selling cheap versions of the latest style. Her blog and social media platform hashtags in 2011 were called 'WTForever21' – a play on words combining the commonly used crude acronym with the corporation's name. There, she posted images of the most outlandish examples of, in her view, fashion disasters (Pearson 2012, 145–147). Clearly, the fashion company was not impressed with the damage to its brand and reputation – so it quickly lawyered up with this cease-and-desist letter to the blogger alleging infringements of its name, domain name, trademark and copyright:

> *Your website's name refers to an abbreviation for colloquial expression that the general public may find offensive, and such colloquial expression is being used in conjunction with our Company's name, registered trademark, and domain name. . . . Please note we consider such conduct and other use in your website to infringe upon and dilute the Company's trademarks. Also, you utilise images from our Company's website without permission, which infringes on the Company's copyrights in those images.*

> (Sauers 2011)

After taking legal advice and getting media coverage of the David versus Goliath battle, Kane decided to risk escalating the dispute by blogging in her inimitable satirical style about the company's legal threats:

> *Dear Lovers of Gnarly Fashion:*
>
> *After two legally baseless cease-and-desist letters from Forever 21, two painstakingly researched responses, and zero substantive replies from Forever 21's legal team, I have no choice but to interpret the company's non-responsiveness as an admission that my blog, WTForever21.com, does not infringe any of Forever 21's rights.*
>
> *Through my attorneys . . . I recently imposed my own deadline on Forever 21 which the company has failed to meet. My attorneys and I will not permit Forever 21 to use silence as a strategic tool or intimidation tactic, particularly when the company stood idly by for over a year as I blogged about their design disasters.*
>
> *As such, please enjoy today's long-overdue offering of WTFashions. This is a dark defeat for MC Hammer pants, floral jumpsuits and blinged out mini hats, but a joyous triumph for those who like to make fun of them. Which is pretty much anyone with eyes.*
>
> *With love and lulz,*
> *Rachel*
> (Kane 2011)

The corporate giant backed off, perhaps after taking advice on crisis communication in the midst of social media outrage, and Kane continued her blog and a version of her Forever21 satirical writing on the *Huff Post* through until 2017 (HuffPost 2021). She confirmed to the authors in 2021 that she had heard nothing from Forever 21's lawyers in the ensuing decade. Taking on Goliath can be fraught, but the case certainly demonstrates the range of factors an organisation needs to take into account when undertaking a risk assessment of brand damage and trademark infringement versus social media outrage over its perceived intimidation of those criticising it.

Strategies for minimising risks with intellectual property

Breach of copyright and infringement of others' intellectual property rights such as trademarks can have sobering and concrete consequences – in the form of injunctions to cease the infringement, damages awards, monetary payments to account for profits made from the breach, and even criminal sanctions in some jurisdictions including fines and jail terms. At a reputational level, the stakes are high too. Media coverage and social media outrage against an organisation plagiarising or stealing the work of others can be both costly and damaging to the brand.

1   Identifying the potential (or existing) legal problem

An organisation can find itself on either side of an intellectual property dispute – either the victim of copyright or trademark theft (perhaps by a competitor) or the perpetrator of such an infringement (such as when someone in the marketing department appropriates material without paying or getting permission). While the technicalities of intellectual property law can be daunting, the basic principle of not borrowing what is not yours should be straightforward enough to help identify when a potential infringement might arise. Staff training in this area is wise.

2   Reviewing the areas of the law involved

Given the scope of intellectual property laws and their differences across jurisdictions, it is vital that professional communicators have their local legislation and the international agreements close at hand. A basic business law textbook should suffice for the initial review of the key areas of trademark and copyright because if more technical legal texts are needed, it is an indication that legal advice should be taken. The Appendix offers some useful links to resources. In the area of copyright, Pearson and Polden (2019, 419) offer these key questions to work through when deciding whether to use work created by someone else:

- Has the copyright period expired? (Has the creator been dead for more than 70 years?)
- Has the copyright holder 'assigned' copyright to you? (This is a full transfer of ownership of the material and proof of assignment.)
- Has the copyright holder 'licensed' you to use the material? (This might be a restricted permission to use the material, such as for a certain time or for a particular purpose.)
- If none of the above, do you plan to use a 'substantial' or significant or important portion of the work?
- If so, does one of the 'fair dealing' exceptions apply, such as the exception for the purpose of criticism or review, reporting news, or 'parody or satire'?

If the work has not been made available through either assignment or licence, and if you plan to use a substantial part of the work, you have to be willing to pay for the use, or be able to work within one of the fair dealing exceptions (Pearson & Polden 2019, 419).

3   Projecting the possible consequences for stakeholders

Numerous stakeholders have an interest in an intellectual property matter, including the usual organisational stakeholders of management, customers, staff, clients and competitors, along with the content creators such as authors, photographers, designers, programmers, inventors and suppliers like syndication agencies. The needs and legal positions of all of them need to be mapped to a risk analysis for an intellectual property dispute.

4   Seeking advice/referring upward

Some organisations are dealing with intellectual property issues frequently and have IP or copyright experts on their staff. Typically news and publishing organisations, libraries, research and pharmaceutical centres and educational institutions have either lawyers or trained personnel on hand to navigate the IP issues on a daily basis. Clearly, these staff should be the first port of call for those in doubt about an IP matter. Social media policies should state clearly that appropriation of the works or trademarks of others is banned, and communication personnel working in this space should be given training on basic copyright and IP issues. Managers with responsibility for retaining lawyers and paying for copyright licences should be identified in the escalation chain.

5   Publishing/amending/deleting/correcting/apologising

All communication and marketing personnel should be trained in the basics of plagiarism, copyright and intellectual property law so they are adept at checking all material for breaches before publication. Simple amendments such as the paraphrasing of material instead of using direct words without quotations and the insertion of appropriate attribution can minimise risk and all images and video should be checked for copyright clearance in pre-publication processes. Corrections and apologies should only be published on expert legal advice because of their potential impact on liability, defences and/or damages.

Stakeholder theory and intellectual property

There are several stakeholders heavily invested in an organisation's intellectual property because the trademarks, patents and copyright materials it creates inform its brand and reputation. Rampant theft of intellectual property by an organisation (or a competitor's misleading and deceptive passing off of another's name, domain name or processes as their own) deserves speedy legal advice and often strong action. This is because infringement of intellectual property rights stands to impact on profits and send mixed messages to the market, affecting the key stakeholder groups such as shareholders, staff, customers and clients. However, this needs to be balanced against other impacts such as the outrage that can result from heavy-handedness against critics or satirists as occurred in Case Study 12.2 about Forever 21. In democracies valuing free expression (such as the United States, United Kingdom and Australia), there can be a backlash from stakeholders including customers, suppliers and sponsors when a large corporate entity attempts to kill a fly with a sledgehammer. Other primary stakeholders in an IP dispute are the content creators or inventors whose IP is being infringed in a breach, as well as their community of supporters and representative organisations such as copyright councils and arts groups.

Discussion questions and project topics

1   Given the propensity of sharing images and other material over social media, why might an organisation or an influencer be more susceptible to copyright infringement claims than a personal social media user?
2   Explain some scenarios where an organisation's intellectual property might be stolen and balance this with some scenarios where the organisation might be at fault for infringing the intellectual property of others.
3   Research and summarise the copyright allowances in your country under its fair use or fair dealing provisions for educational use. As one example, specify how much of a book can be photocopied by a student in a library. See the Appendix for resources on this topic.
4   You are communication director for a hamburger corporation that wants to launch an aggressive marketing campaign targeting the major multinational competitor by listing key points of difference between your burgers and theirs. To what extent might intellectual property laws in your country limit the mention of their brand and products? Research local cases where similar scenarios have been contested in court. Use the Appendix as a starting point.

Practice tips

• Pause to reflect on potential breaches of copyright and other intellectual property laws before copying, pasting, linking or sharing material on social media. If in doubt, research the matter and seek legal advice.
• Learn your national copyright laws so you can take advantage of the free use, fair use or fair dealing exemptions to maximum benefit.
• Try visiting the links in the Appendix – starting with WIPO's directory of intellectual property offices – and find information about your own country's IP laws.
• Attribute all material fully and seek to get the formal written permission of creators for the reproduction of their work, negotiating a payment where appropriate.
• Set up organisational calendar reminders for domain name renewals to minimize the chance of competitors or troublemakers registering them once expired.
• Ensure your staff receive routine training in intellectual property law and practices.

Cases cited

Earthquake case. 2014. Agence France Presse v. Morel, 2014 BL 224351, S.D.N.Y., 1:10-cv-02730-AJN-MHD. 13 August. <www.bloomberglaw.com/public/desktop/document/AGENCE_FRANCE_PRESSE_Plaintiff_v_DANIEL_MOREL_Defendant_v_GETTY_I?1614649274>

Fruit of the Loom case. 2021. *Fruit of the Loom, Inc. v. Henrik Bach-Jensen, Supr Group.* WIPO Arbitration and Mediation Center Administrative Panel Decision, Case No. D2021–0016. 18 February. <www.wipo.int/amc/en/domains/decisions/text/2021/d2021-0016.html>

Malishus trademark case. 2018. *Lamont v Malishus & Ors* (No.4) [2019] FCCA 3206. <www8.austlii. edu.au/cgi-bin/viewdoc/au/cases/cth/FCCA/2018/423.html>

Naruto Monkey case. 2018. *Naruto Monkey PETA v Slater.* CA9 No. 16–15469 D.C. No. 3:15-cv-04324-WHO Opinion. April 23. <www.documentcloud.org/documents/4444209-Naruto-Monkey-PETA-v-Slater-CA9-Opinion-04-23-18.html>

References

Facebook. 2021. *Terms of service.* Accessed 10 December 2020. www.facebook.com/terms.php

Golovchuk, S. 2012. "TeachQuest settles with Facebook." *Patch.com.* https://patch.com/illinois/northbrook/teachquest-settles-with-facebook

HuffPost. 2021. "Contributor: Rachel Kane." *HuffPost.* www.huffpost.com/author/rachel-kane

INTA. 2015. "Fact sheet: Introduction to trademarks: Trademark use." *INTA.* New York. www.inta.org/fact-sheets/trademark-use/

Kane, R. 2011. "The blog is back." *WTForever21.* Accessed 5 March 2021. https://wtforever21.wordpress.com/2011/06/28/873/

Pearson, M. 2012. *Blogging and tweeting without getting sued: A global guide to the law for anyone writing online.* Sydney: Allen and Unwin.

Pearson, M. & M. Polden. 2019. *The journalist's guide to media law: A handbook for communicators in a digital world.* New York: Routledge.

Rys, D. 2017. "A brief history of the ownership of the Beatles catalogue." *Billboard.* www.billboard.com/articles/columns/rock/7662519/beatles-catalog-paul-mccartney-brief-history-ownership#:~:text=1965%3A%20Northern%20Songs%20became%20ahe%20received%20in%20the%20deal

Sauers, J. 2011. "Forever 21 sues fashion blogger." *Jezebel.* https://jezebel.com/forever-21-sues-fashion-blogger-5809063

Toliver, Z. 2017. "Settlement reached: 'Monkey selfie' case broke new ground for animal rights." *PETA.* www.peta.org/blog/settlement-reached-monkey-selfie-case-broke-new-ground-animal-rights

Twitter. 2021. *Impersonation policy.* https://help.twitter.com/en/rules-and-policies/twitter-impersonation-policy#:~:text=Impersonation%20is%20a%20violation%20ofsuspended%20under%20Twitter's%20impersonation%20policy.

Wikimedia Foundation. 2017. "Mailbag: What is going on with Wikipedia and the monkey selfie? We love monkeys and photographers, let us tell you more . . ." *Wikimedia Foundation News.* https://wikimediafoundation.org/news/2017/12/22/monkey-selfie/

WIPO. 1979. *Convention establishing the world intellectual property organization.* www.wipo.int/treaties/en/text.jsp?file_id=283854#P50_1504

WIPO. 2016. *Understanding copyright and related rights* (2nd ed.). www.wipo.int/edocs/pubdocs/en/wipo_pub_909_2016.pdf

WIPO. 2021. *Directory of intellectual property offices.* www.wipo.int/directory/en/urls.jsp

Appendix
Further social media law resources

This book has provided an introduction to the basic principles of social media risk management and law. However, each of the hundreds of jurisdictions internationally has its own laws and cases particular to that nation, state or province. This appendix offers some starting points for further information about the main social media law topics in some of the key jurisdictions.

International

General, miscellaneous and news

Guardian media law blog – www.theguardian.com/media/medialaw
International Forum for Responsible Media blog – https://inforrm.org/
Shear on Social Media Law – www.shearsocialmedia.com/media_opportunities

Human rights and free expression

Universal Declaration of Human Rights – www.un.org/en/universal-declaration-human-rights/
Article 19 – article19.org
Reporters Without Borders – https://rsf.org/en
IFEX – International Free Expression – https://ifex.org/
Index on Censorship – www.indexoncensorship.org/
Transparency International – www.transparency.org/en
Media Defence – www.mediadefence.org/about/

Cases and news

World Legal Information Institute – www.worldlii.org/countries.html

Business laws and regulators

International Consumer Protection and Enforcement Network (ICPEN) – https://icpen.org/
Consumers International – www.consumersinternational.org/
International consumer protection agencies – www.ftc.gov/policy/international/competition-consumer-protection-authorities-worldwide

List of securities regulators internationally – www.iosco.org/about/?subsection=me
mbership&memid=1

Crime and justice

UN Global Programme on Cybercrime – www.unodc.org/unodc/en/cybercrime/
global-programme-cybercrime.html

Defamation

International Press Institute – International Standards on Criminal and Civil Defamation Laws – http://legaldb.freemedia.at/international-standards/

Intellectual property

World Intellectual Property Organisation – www.wipo.int/portal/en/index.html
Directory of intellectual property offices – www.wipo.int/directory/en/urls.jsp

Privacy and confidentiality

Global Privacy Enforcement Network – www.privacyenforcement.net/
International Association of Privacy Professionals (IAPP) – https://iapp.org/

Africa

General and miscellaneous

Collaboration on International ICT Policy in East and Southern Africa CIPESA –
https://cipesa.org/

Human rights and free expression

African Freedom of Expression Exchange (AFEX) – www.africafex.org/
African Union – Democracy, Law and Human Rights – https://au.int/en/
democracy-law-human-rights
Freedom of Expression Institute – www.fxi.org.za/component/option.com_frontpage/
Itemid,36/

Case law databases

African case law databases – www.worldlii.org/cgi-bin/gen_region.pl?region=250
African Legal Information Institute – https://africanlii.org/
Veritas Zimbabwe – www.veritaszim.net/

Business laws and regulators

National Consumer Commission (South Africa) – www.thencc.gov.za/
Financial Sector Conduct Authority – www.fsca.co.za/

Crime and justice

Institute for Security Studies – https://issafrica.org/
International Justice Resource Centre – Africa – https://ijrcenter.org/regional/african/

Defamation

INFORRM – South Africa – https://inforrm.org/category/south-africa/

Intellectual property

Department of Deeds Companies and Intellectual Property (Zimbabwe) – www.dcip.gov.zw/

Privacy and confidentiality

Data Protection Africa – https://dataprotection.africa/

Asia-Pacific

General and miscellaneous

Asian Media Information and Communication Centre (AMIC) – https://amic.asia/
Pacific Media Watch – https://pmc.aut.ac.nz/profile/pacific-media-watch
Asian Law Network Blog – https://learn.asialawnetwork.com/
Law and Other Things blog (India) – https://lawandotherthings.com/

Human rights and free expression

Free Speech in China – http://blog.feichangdao.com/

Case law databases

Asian case law (WorldLII) – www.worldlii.org/cgi-bin/gen_region.pl?region=2647
Pacific Islands Legal Information Institute – www.paclii.org/index.shtml

Business laws and regulators

The ASEAN Committee on Consumer Protection (ACCP) – https://aseanconsumer.org/
Singapore Competition and Consumer Commission – www.cccs.gov.sg/
Asia Law Network Blog – Consumer Law – https://learn.asialawnetwork.com/cat/personal/consumer-law/

Crime and justice

International Justice Resource Centre – Asia – https://ijrcenter.org/regional/asia/

Asia Law Network Blog – Criminal and Litigation – https://learn.asialawnetwork.
com/cat/personal/criminal-and-litigation/

Netmission.asia – https://netmission.asia/

Defamation

Asia Law Network Blog – Defamation – https://learn.asialawnetwork.com/cat/
personal/defamation/

Slater and Gordon – Destination Defamation, South-East Asia – www.slatergordon.
com.au/blog/business-law/destination-defamation-south-east-asia

Intellectual property

Intellectual Property Office of Singapore – www.ic.gc.ca/eic/site/cipointernet-
internetopic.nsf/eng/home

Privacy and confidentiality

Asia Pacific Data Protection and Cyber Security Guide 2020 – https://iapp.org/
resources/article/311636/

Australia

General and miscellaneous

Communications and Media Law Association – www.camla.org.au/

Gazette of Law and Journalism – https://glj.com.au/

Professor Mark Pearson's blog – journlaw.com

Human rights and free expression

Australian Human Rights Commission – Social Media – https://humanrights.gov.
au/quick-guide/12098

MEAA media freedom reports – www.meaa.org/category/mediaroom/reports/

Case law databases

Australasian Legal Information Institute (AustLII) – www.austlii.edu.au/

Federal Register of Legislation – www.legislation.gov.au/

Business laws and regulators

Australian Competition and Consumer Commission – Social Media – www.accc.
gov.au/business/advertising-promoting-your-business/social-media

Australian Communications and Media Authority – www.acma.gov.au/

Australian Securities and Investments Commission – https://asic.gov.au/

Law Society of NSW – Guidelines on Social Media Policies – www.lawsociety.com.au/
resources/resources/my-practice-area/legal-technology/guidelines-social-media

Fair Work Commission – www.fwc.gov.au/

Crime and justice

High Court of Australia – www.hcourt.gov.au

Australian Attorney-General's Department – Courts – www.ag.gov.au/legal-system/courts

The Australian Constitution – www.aph.gov.au/About_Parliament/Senate/Powers_practice_n_procedures/Constitution/

Defamation

Defamation Watch (Justin Castelan) – http://defamationwatch.com.au/about/

Intellectual property

Copyright Office – www.communications.gov.au/what-we-do/copyright

Copyright Agency – www.copyright.com.au/

Australian Copyright Council – www.copyright.org.au/

IP Australia – www.ipaustralia.gov.au/

Privacy and confidentiality

Office of the Australian Information Commissioner – Social Media Privacy – www.oaic.gov.au/privacy/your-privacy-rights/social-media-and-online-privacy/

Australian Privacy Foundation – https://privacy.org.au/

Canada

General and miscellaneous

Department of Justice – Canada's System of Justice – www.justice.gc.ca/eng/csj-sjc/index.html

Canadian Bar Association – www.cba.org/Home

Legal Line Canada – www.legalline.ca/

Human rights and free expression

Canadian Charter of Rights and Freedoms – www.justice.gc.ca/eng/csj-sjc/rfc-dlc/ccrf-ccdl/index.html

Canadian Journalists for Free Expression – www.cjfe.org/

Case law databases

Canadian case law (WorldLII) – www.worldlii.org/catalog/51528.html

Supreme Court of Canada – www.scc-csc.ca/case-dossier/index-eng.aspx

Canadian Media Lawyers Association – https://canadianmedialawyers.com/

Business laws and regulators

Canadian Advertising and Marketing Law – www.canadianadvertisinglaw.com/

Office of Consumer Affairs – http://consumer.ic.gc.ca/eic/site/oca-bc.nsf/eng/home

Canadian Bar Association – Social Media Policies in the Workplace – www.cba.org/Publications-Resources/CBA-Practice-Link/2015/2014/Social-media-policies-in-the-workplace-What-works

Canadian Securities Administrators – www.securities-administrators.ca/

Crime and justice

Supreme Court of Canada – www.scc-csc.ca/home-accueil/index-eng.aspx

Media Smarts – Online Hate and Canadian Law – https://mediasmarts.ca/digital-media-literacy/digital-issues/online-hate/online-hate-canadian-law

The Court.ca – blog on Canadian Supreme Court – www.thecourt.ca/

Defamation

Mondaq Canada – A Primer on Defamation – www.mondaq.com/canada/libel-defamation/725558/a-primer-on-defamation

Intellectual property

Canadian Intellectual Property Office – www.ic.gc.ca/eic/site/cipointernet-internetopic.nsf/eng/home

Privacy and confidentiality

Office of the Privacy Commissioner of Canada – www.priv.gc.ca/en/

Privacy Canada – https://privacycanada.net/

David T.S. Fraser's Privacy Law Resources – http://privacylawyer.ca/

Europe (see farther down for UK)

General and miscellaneous

Droit de technologies (France) – https://cours-de-droit.net/droit-des-ntic-droit-des-nouvelles-technologies-de-l-information-et-de-a121602690/

Human rights and free expression

ECHR blog – www.echrblog.com/

The Irish for Rights – www.cearta.ie/

Case law databases

Eastern Europe case law (WorldLII) – www.worldlii.org/cgi-bin/gen_region.pl?region=2210

Western Europe case law (WorldLII) – www.worldlii.org/cgi-bin/gen_region.pl?region =251

Business laws and regulators

European Consumer Centre Network (ECC-Net) – https://ec.europa.eu/info/ live-work-travel-eu/consumer-rights-and-complaints/resolve-your-consumer-complaint/european-consumer-centres-network-ecc-net_en
Citizens Advice – www.citizensadvice.org.uk/

Crime and justice

European Justice – Courts – https://e-justice.europa.eu/content_eu_courts-15-en.do
Court of Justice of the European Union – https://europa.eu/european-union/ about-eu/institutions-bodies/court-justice_en

Defamation

Council of Europe – Defamation – www.coe.int/en/web/freedom-expression/ defamation
Czech Defamation Law – https://czechdefamationlaw.wordpress.com/

Intellectual property

European Commission – Intellectual Property Rights – https://ec.europa.eu/info/ business-economy-euro/doing-business-eu/intellectual-property-rights_en
Manual on European Defamation Law – Media Defence – www.mediadefence.org/ resources/manual-on-european-defamation-law/

Privacy and confidentiality

General Data Protection Regulation – EU – https://gdpr.eu/
Europe Data Protection Digest – https://iapp.org/news/europe-data-protection-digest/

New Zealand

General and miscellaneous

Ministry of Justice – Harmful digital communications – www.justice.govt.nz/courts/ civil/harmful-digital-communications/
NZ Law Society – Social media's legal criteria – www.lawsociety.org.nz/news/ lawtalk/issue-812/social-medias-legal-criteria/

Human rights and free expression

NZ Government – Human rights in NZ – www.govt.nz/browse/law-crime-and-justice/human-rights-in-nz/
Human Rights Commission – www.hrc.co.nz/

New Zealand Bill of Rights Act 1990 – www.legislation.govt.nz/act/public/1990/
0109/latest/DLM224792.html

Case law databases

New Zealand Legislation – www.legislation.govt.nz/
New Zealand Legal Information Institute Databases – www.nzlii.org/databases.html
Courts of NZ Judgments – www.courtsofnz.govt.nz/judgments

Business laws and regulators

Commerce Commission – https://comcom.govt.nz/
Consumer Protection – Online safety laws and rules – www.consumerprotection.
govt.nz/general-help/consumer-laws/online-safety-laws-and-rules/

Crime and justice

Ministry of Justice – Courts – www.justice.govt.nz/courts/
Courts of NZ – www.courtsofnz.govt.nz/

Defamation

Defamation Update NZ – https://defamationupdate.co.nz/

Intellectual property

NZ Intellectual Property Office – www.iponz.govt.nz/

Privacy and confidentiality

Office of the Privacy Commissioner – www.privacy.org.nz/
Ministry of Justice – Key Initiatives – Privacy – www.justice.govt.nz/justice-sector-
policy/key-initiatives/privacy/
Privacy Foundation NZ – www.privacyfoundation.nz/

South America

General and miscellaneous

Marco Civil Law of the Internet in Brazil – www.cgi.br/pagina/marco-civil-law-
of-the-internet-in-brazil/180

Human rights and free expression

American Convention on Human Rights – Article 13 – www.oas.org/en/iachr/
expression/showarticle.asp?artID=25&lID=1
Article 19 – Brazil and South America regional office – www.article19.org/regional-
office/brazil-and-south-america/

Case law databases

Legal Information Institute – World legal materials from South America – www.law.cornell.edu/world/samerica

Business laws and regulators

OECD – Corporate Governance in Latin America – www.oecd.org/daf/ca/corporategovernanceinlatinamerica.htm

Crime and justice

Legal Information Institute – World legal materials from South America – www.law.cornell.edu/world/samerica

Wilson Center – The Brazilian Judicial System – www.wilsoncenter.org/publication/the-brazilian-judicial-system

Defamation

Committee to Protect Journalists – Criminal Defamation Laws in South America – https://cpj.org/reports/2016/03/south-america/

Intellectual property

BizLatin Hub – Overview – Intellectual Property Regulations in Latin America – www.bizlatinhub.com/overview-intellectual-property-regulations-latin-america/

Intellectual Property Magazine – South America – www.intellectualpropertymagazine.com/world/south_america/

Privacy and confidentiality

Bloomberg BNA – Privacy Law in Latin America and the Caribbean (Cynthia Rich) – https://iapp.org/media/pdf/resource_center/Privacy_Laws_Latin_America.pdf

United Kingdom

General and miscellaneous

International Forum for Responsible Media blog – https://inforrm.org/

Brett Wilson Media Law blog – www.brettwilson.co.uk/blog/category/media-law/

Information Law and Policy Centre – https://infolawcentre.blogs.sas.ac.uk/

Human rights and free expression

Transparency Project – www.transparencyproject.org.uk/blog/

Case law databases

British and Irish Legal Information Institute (BAILII) – www.bailii.org/

Business laws and regulators

Competition and Markets Authority – www.gov.uk/government/organisations/competition-and-markets-authority

ACAS – Unfair Dismissal – www.acas.org.uk/dismissals/unfair-dismissal

Financial Conduct Authority – www.fca.org.uk/

Crime and justice

Courts and Tribunals Judiciary – Structure of the courts and tribunal system – www.judiciary.uk/about-the-judiciary/the-justice-system/court-structure/

The Supreme Court – www.supremecourt.uk/

Defamation

BBC News – Defamation cases – www.bbc.co.uk/news/topics/cxwke9d43kkt/defamation-cases

Scandalous blog – www.fieldfisher.com/en/services/dispute-resolution/defamation-and-privacy/defamation-blog

Carruthers Law – Defamation definitions – www.carruthers-law.co.uk/our-services/defamation/defamation-definitions/

Intellectual property

UK Intellectual Property Office – www.ipo.gov.uk/

UK Copyright Service – https://copyrightservice.co.uk/

Privacy and confidentiality

Gov.UK – Data Protection – www.gov.uk/data-protection

Information Commissioner's Office – https://ico.org.uk/

United States

General and miscellaneous

Social Media Law Bulletin – www.socialmedialawbulletin.com/

HG.org Law and Social Media – www.hg.org/legal-articles/the-law-and-social-media-31695

Technology and Marketing Law Blog – Eric Goldman – https://blog.ericgoldman.org/

Human rights and free expression

Centre for Internet and Society (Stanford University) – http://cyberlaw.stanford.edu/

Committee to Protect Journalists – cpj.org

US Courts – What does free speech mean? – www.uscourts.gov/about-federal-courts/educational-resources/about-educational-outreach/activity-resources/what-does

Freedom Forum Institute, First Amendment Center – www.freedomforuminstitute. org/first-amendment-center/

Case law databases

US case law (WorldLII) – www.worldlii.org/us/
Justia US law – https://law.justia.com/
Legal Information Institute – Cornell University – www.law.cornell.edu/
Internet cases – Evan Law blog – http://evan.law/blog/

Business laws and regulators

Federal Trade Commission – www.ftc.gov/
US Department of Health and Human Services – Social media policies – www.hhs. gov/web/social-media/policies/index.html
US State Consumer Protection Offices – www.usa.gov/state-consumer

Crime and justice

Supreme Court of the United States – www.supremecourt.gov/
United States Courts – www.uscourts.gov/
Cybersecurity and Infrastructure Security Agency – www.cisa.gov/cybersecurity
Homeland Security – Cybersecurity – www.dhs.gov/topic/cybersecurity

Defamation

Legal Information Institute – Defamation – www.law.cornell.edu/wex/defamation
Freedom Forum Institute – Quick guide to libel law – www.freedomforuminstitute. org/first-amendment-center/primers/libellaw/

Intellectual property

US Copyright Office – www.copyright.gov/
US Patent and Trademark Office – www.uspto.gov/

Privacy and confidentiality

Data protection law – HG.org – www.hg.org/data-protection.html
US Department of State – Privacy Office – www.state.gov/bureaus-offices/under-secretary-for-management/bureau-of-administration/privacy-office/

Index

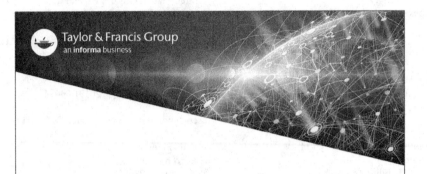

Printed in the United States
by Baker & Taylor Publisher Services